*The Simon and Schuster
Pocket Guide to*

German Wines

Ian Jamieson

Simon and Schuster

KEY TO SYMBOLS

w.	white wine
r.	red wine
(in parentheses)	relatively unimportant
★	everyday wine
★★	above average
★★★	excellent, highly reputed
★★★★	exceptional, prestigious, expensive
★★ → ★★★	for example, indicates above average to excellent

SMALL CAPS indicate a cross-reference within the A-Z section

ABBREVIATIONS

Hess. Berg.	Hessische Bergstrasse
Mrh.	Mittelrhein
M-S-R	Mosel-Saar-Ruwer
Rhg.	Rheingau
Rhh.	Rheinhessen
Rhpf.	Rheinpfalz
Würt.	Württemberg

g	grams	m	meters
g/l	grams per liter	m.	million
ha	hectares	mg/l	milligrams per liter
hl/ha	hectoliters per hectare	pop.	population
km	kilometers	v'yd	vineyard

See pages 6-7 for more information

Copyright© 1984 by Mitchell Beazley Publishers
Published by Simon and Schuster
A Division of Simon & Schuster, Inc.
Simon & Schuster Building
1230 Avenue of the Americas, New York, NY 10020
SIMON AND SCHUSTER and colophon are registered trademarks of Simon & Schuster, Inc.
Typeset by Hourds Typographica Limited, Stafford
Reproduction by Chelmer Litho Reproduction, Maldon
Printed in Italy by New Interlitho, Milan

Library of Congress Cataloging in Publication Data
Jamieson, Ian.
    The Simon and Schuster pocket guide to German wines.
    Includes index.
    1. Wine and wine making – Germany (West) I. Title.
II. Title: Pocket guide to German wines.
TP559.G3J35 1984   641.2'22'0943   84-10508
ISBN 0-671-52743-6

Editor	Dian Taylor	Proofreader	Kathie Gill
Art Editor	Ruth Levy	Production	Jean Rigby
Maps	Eugene Fleury	Executive Editor	Chris Foulkes

Contents

Preface

German wines, and all the sensuous subtleties of pleasure they offer, are rather like a story-book castle whose key is hidden in a tortuous labyrinth guarded by ravaging heraldic beasts. The generality of wine-drinkers take the autobahns labelled Liebfraumilch, Niersteiner or some such safe and familiar name. They skirt the problem, and never find the reward. Our hero, though, steadies his gaze at the menacing Gothic script, braves the barbed entanglements of nomenclature, and carries off the chalice of golden nectar. In other words, if German labels scare you, you will never discover how glorious German wine can be.

This book is the code-cracker. It can put the chalice in your hands. I won't pretend that all obscurities will dissolve as you turn the first page. But Ian Jamieson is a practical man, a wine-merchant whose knowledge of Germany and its wine has been sharpened on the steel of commerce. He knows the ways of grower and merchant. He knows the laws. And he knows and cares where the real treasures lie.

Ian has often been my guide through the more arcane complexities of his favourite subject. To me it has fascinations, and offers rewards, that are a match for any category of wine. Let Jamieson lead you to them.

Hugh Johnson

Introduction

A profile of the wine most consumers look for today shows it to be white and light in alcohol, and balanced in sweetness and acidity. German wine fits this description exactly and is appealing increasingly to the new generation of wine drinkers, especially in the English-speaking world. Much that is seen abroad is of the cheap and cheerful variety, but as soon as we expect more of a German wine than that it should simply be thirst-quenching and refreshing we are faced with the complications of the language of wine and what it tries to tell us.

Communication is the aim of this book. I have not set out to tell the story of wine from vineyard to consumer but to provide answers to direct questions. What does that word on the restaurant list or bottle mean? How much does the label tell about the wine in the bottle? How can one distinguish the varying qualities and styles of wine that are so comprehensively – and incomprehensibly – described on the label? How to spot the difference between a true German wine and a blend of wines from other countries bottled in Germany, when the labels of both are so essentially Germanic in design, down to the last flourish of the Gothic script on the brand name? These are the matters with which the book is concerned. German wine is more than capable of speaking for itself, provided one can understand its language. This book is here to help.

For those who enjoy individuality in wine, the estate bottlers have much to offer. The most famous names among the growers are found mainly in the northern regions, particularly in the Mosel-Saar-Ruwer and in the Rheingau. Here many estates, including some of the less well known, date from the 18th century or earlier. All of them have built their reputation on the Riesling grape, which supplies the fresh, firm, positive wine made unique by the German climate. Other vines tend to play a supporting role, offering the interested wine lover a diversion from Riesling but never a substitute for it.

Although the future of Riesling in the best vineyard sites seems certain, there is a gentle swing to the red Spätburgunder (Pinot Noir) on many Rheinland estates to provide the light, pale-coloured wines the home market enjoys but which the overseas markets find difficult to understand. That there is no such problem with German white wine is a fact clearly recognized by the large and impressive cooperative cellars that handle more than a third of the German wine harvest. Their wines, particularly those of the Mosel-Saar-Ruwer and the Rheinhessen, are widely available, usually under well-known Bereich (district) or Grosslage (collective site) names. Unfortunately, the law allows them to be offered as "estate-bottled", although the members of the cooperatives, who supply the grapes, have no direct control over the wine makers and vice versa.

From the large number of estate bottlers, some 225 have been chosen for a potted but detailed description in this guide. The great and the famous selected themselves and account for about 80 of the estates in the A-Z section. The record of the remainder, particularly their achievements at the DLG (German Agricultural Society) national wine competitions, ensured their selection, but one of the exciting facets of German wine-making is the number of estates that remain to be "discovered". Every visit to the vineyard area can bring with it new and stimulating introductions, and the results of formal viticultural school training are obvious. Twenty years ago the outlook of many growers was parochial to say the least, but that has now changed and most are well aware of the developments in wine-making elsewhere in the world. Many have contributed towards the changes, and the skills of German wine producers are valued as highly in the Napa Valley as they are on the Mosel.

Of all the wine villages, approximately 180 are included in the pages that follow. Inevitably and deliberately, those in the regions best known outside Germany are well represented, for these are the names found in the wine stores of the world. But recognition has also been made of a number of relatively unfamiliar villages whose wines are seldom seen beyond the borders of their Bereich. They, in particular, have earned their inclusion because their wines deserve wider appreciation.

Finally, I should like to thank all those vineyard owners and wine makers who interrupted their day's work to supply the details about themselves that are recorded in this book. The always accurate technical and legal information so efficiently and pleasantly offered over the years by Manfred Völpel of Deinhard & Company has also been of great help to me. *Die Weinwirtschaft*, with its up-to-date reporting of the German wine-trade scene, and the many books produced under the auspices of Dr Hans Ambrosi have provided a valuable source of reference, as has the work of Dr Horst Dohm and also of Dr Karl Ludwig Bieser of the Weinabsatzzentrale Deutscher Winzergenossenschaften. Herr Riquet Hess of H. Sichel & Söhne read this book in proof form and his experienced advice has been most welcome. If order and precision have been maintained, it is thanks to the guidance of Christopher Foulkes and the eye for detail of Dian Taylor of Mitchell Beazley, to both of whom I am very grateful. And last, but certainly not least, I am indebted to my wife Ulla, who has excused my absence from the family while I enjoyed the pleasure of writing this book.

IAN JAMIESON

How to Use this Book

This book is divided into three sections: introductory chapters, an A–Z section and a map section. The introductory chapters cover the background and structure of German wine, and ideally should be read first as scene-setters. In order to look up an estate, a vineyard or a wine term, etc., turn to the A–Z section which begins on page 24. The maps, starting on page 136, show the basic geography of the German wine regions and list some of the estates in these regions. For guidance to important growers of, say, Rheingau wines, turn to the map on pages 138–139. The names can then be looked up in the A–Z section.

In the A–Z section the top line of geographical entries – regions, rivers, towns, villages, vineyard sites and so forth – is printed in colour so that locations can be easily distinguished from entries for wine producers, grape varieties, general wine terms and other categories of information.

The top line of the geographical entries gives the following information, where applicable, in abbreviated form:
1. The wine region in which the entry is located. The 11 wine regions (and their abbreviations) are:

Ahr	Mosel-Saar-Ruwer (M-S-R)
Baden	Nahe
Franken	Rheingau (Rhg.)
Hessische Bergstrasse	Rheinhessen (Rhh.)
(Hess. Berg.)	Rheinpfalz (Rhpf.)
Mittelrhein (Mrh.)	Württemberg (Würt.)

A map of all the wine regions is on page 10.
2. The type of wine produced: w. for white, r. for red, (w.) or (r.) if the quantity produced is relatively unimportant.
3. A general rating as to quality, a necessarily rough and ready guide based on the following ascending scale:
   ★ everyday wine
   ★★ above average
   ★★★ excellent, highly reputed
   ★★★★ exceptional, prestigious, expensive

The entries for wine producers, export houses and cooperative cellars include as much information as can be condensed into the necessarily limited space available. Production figures are expressed in cases (e.g. approximate annual production 20,000 cases) to indicate the output of wine so that comparisons can be made between entries. A "case", for the purposes of this book, is taken as $12 \times$ 750ml (0.75 litre) bottles, or 9 litres (in the wine trade, the term "case" is being replaced by "carton"). Where prices are given, they are the 1984 retail price per bottle to the consumer in Germany.

All liquid measurements are given in litres, the standard liquid measurement for German wine (1 litre equals 1.76 pints). Alcohol is expressed as % by volume.

Cross-references in SMALL CAPS throughout the A–Z section help to expand the information given in individual entries. However, the wine regions (e.g. Ahr, Baden) and grape varieties (e.g. Riesling) are automatically included in the A–Z and are not cross-referred.

All figures are the most up to date available.

Germany, in all cases, means West Germany.

WINE TERMS

The following terms are described in the A–Z section:

Ansprechend	Flaschenreife	Meaty
Aromatisch	Frostgeschmack	Mild
Ausdrucksvoll	Fruchtig	Muffig
Ausgeglichen	Grasig	Nervig
Blume	Hagelgeschmack	Neutral
Bodengeschmack	Halbtrocken	Plump
Bodenton	Harmonisch	Rassig
Bottle sick	Herb	Reif
Brandig	Herzhaft	Reintonig
Bukett	Holzgeschmack	Slaty
Duftig	Jung	Sortencharakter
Durchgegoren	Kernig	Spritzig
Edelsüss	Korkgeschmack	Stahlig
Elegant	Kratzig	Stumpf
Fassgeschmack	Lebendig	Süffig
Feine, feinste	Leicht	Ton
Firn	Lieblich	Trocken

German Wine Law

Wine production in Germany is as meticulously structured as the wording on a German wine label. This is the result of Germany's own wine laws and those of the European Common Market.

In 1970 the EEC produced regulations for the organization of wine within its borders. These came into immediate effect and took precedence over national laws, so that Germany was obliged to revise its own wine laws forthwith. In 1971 the fifth German Wine Law came into force, replacing the previous law of 1930. Since then there have been further amendments, including a major revision in 1982 that established Landwein as a new category of Deutscher Tafelwein, made Eiswein into a distinct Prädikat (quality category) and altered several other details of the earlier law.

Probably the best-known results of all this legislation – and the most significant to the consumer – are the division of wine into different quality categories and the organization of the wine regions (see following pages).

The Quality Categories

Wine in the EEC is separated into quality wine and table wine. In German terms this means Qualitätswein (QmP, the top quality, and QbA, a middle level); Tafelwein (Deutscher Tafelwein, or DTW, comes entirely from German vineyards; plain Tafelwein is wine from other EEC countries blended in Germany); and Landwein, a superior Deutscher Tafelwein, from one of 15 specified districts.

Quality Wine (QbA, QmP)	
Region	**Bereich**
Ahr	Walporzheim/Ahrtal
Hessische Bergstrasse	Starkenburg, Umstadt
Mittelrhein	Bacharach, Rheinburgengau, Siebengebirge
Nahe	Kreuznach, Schloss Böckelheim
Rheingau	Johannisberg
Rheinhessen	Bingen, Nierstein, Wonnegau
Rheinpfalz	Südliche Weinstrasse, Mittelhaardt/Deutsche Weinstrasse
Mosel-Saar-Ruwer	Zell/Mosel, Bernkastel, Obermosel, Saar-Ruwer, Moseltor
Franken	Steigerwald, Maindreieck, Mainviereck, Bayerischer Bodensee
Württemberg	Remstal-Stuttgart, Württembergisch Unterland, Kocher-Jagst-Tauber, Württembergischer Bodensee
Baden	Bodensee, Markgräflerland, Kaiserstuhl-Tuniberg, Breisgau, Ortenau
	Badische Bergstrasse/Kraichgau, Badisches Frankenland

The chart shows the relationship of the 11 quality-wine regions to the table-wine and Landwein districts. Unlike France, where the grading of quality wines is largely geographical, in Germany exactly the same vineyards that produce quality wine can also produce table wine and Landwein. The source remains the same; only the category of the wine changes, depending on the quality.

Do not expect to meet all the Bereich, district and sub-district names on wine labels – some of them exist more for administrative purposes than for the benefit of the consumer trying to unravel the intricacies of German laws and labelling (see Learning from the Label, pages 12-13).

Table Wine (DTW)		Landwein
District	**Sub-District**	**District**
		Ahrtaler Landwein
Rhein-Mosel	Rhein	Starkenburger Landwein
		Rheinburgen-Landwein
		Nahegauer Landwein
		Altrheingauer Landwein
		Rheinischer Landwein
		Pfälzer Landwein
	Mosel	Landwein der Mosel
	Saar	Landwein der Saar
Bayern	Main	Fränkischer Landwein
	Donau	Regensburger Landwein
	Lindau	Bayerischer Bodensee-Landwein
Neckar		Schwäbischer Landwein
Oberrhein	Römertor	Südbadischer Landwein
	Burgengau	Unterbadischer Landwein

The Wine Regions

Germany lies at the northern edge of that part of Europe in which grapes will ripen. The climate is cool in comparison with that of other European wine-producing countries – a fact recognized by the EEC which divides member states, for administrative purposes, into wine-producing zones that correspond very approximately to the different climatic condi-

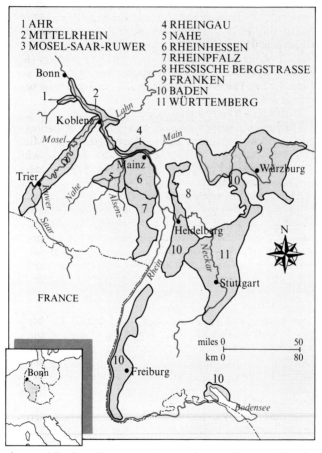

1 AHR
2 MITTELRHEIN
3 MOSEL-SAAR-RUWER
4 RHEINGAU
5 NAHE
6 RHEINHESSEN
7 RHEINPFALZ
8 HESSISCHE BERGSTRASSE
9 FRANKEN
10 BADEN
11 WÜRTTEMBERG

tions. All the German vine-growing regions, with the exception of Baden in the south, are placed in Zone A (with the UK and Luxembourg). Baden shares the warmer Zone B with Alsace, Lorraine, Champagne, Jura, Savoie and the Loire valley.

There are 11 specified regions for quality wine production (Anbaugebiete) in Germany. They are described in the A–Z section and are shown in more detail in the maps that begin on page 136.

In the most northerly regions – the Ahr, Mittelrhein and Mosel-Saar-Ruwer – usually only those sites facing SSE–SW can usefully bear vines, with the very best vineyards facing from S–SSW. An additional rule of thumb is that the average temperature will drop some 0.5°C for every 100m (330ft) above sea level. As a result, 300m (990ft) above sea level is regarded as the maximum height for vineyards on the Mosel near Koblenz. In the sunnier south of Baden, however, on the Bodensee, vines are grown successfully at 530m (1,739ft).

Of the approximate 96,000ha (237,000 acres) under vine in Germany, the Rheinhessen and Rheinpfalz between them account for almost half, with 25.4% and 23.1% respectively, followed by Baden with 14.9%, the Mosel-Saar-Ruwer 12.8%, Württemberg 9.4%, Franken 5%, Nahe 4.8%, Rheingau 3%, Mittelrhein 0.8%, Ahr 0.45%, Hessische Bergstrasse 0.35%.

Each of the wine regions is organized into districts (Bereiche), collections of sites (Grosslagen) and individual sites (Einzellagen). This is where the style and quality of wine begin to be more narrowly defined.

A Bereich is a combination of collective or individual sites. It is usually the largest wine-producing unit within a region and allows a well-known name – Bernkastel in the Mittelmosel, for example – to be applied to wine from anywhere within the Bereich boundaries. Wine marketed solely under a Bereich name is unlikely to be more than a pleasant everyday blend, and this will be reflected in its price.

A Grosslage is a grouping of sites centred on one or more villages or towns (Gemeinden). In the Bereich Bernkastel, for example, the Grosslage Badstube covers five Einzellagen at Bernkastel (see next page). Other Grosslagen may include a number of wine villages, and as the law stands at the moment any of the villages may be linked with the Grosslage name on the wine label, regardless of whether the wine comes wholly or in part from the village vineyards.

Generally speaking, a Grosslage name enables the bottler or wine merchant to offer large quantities of wine of similar quality and style under one name familiar to the customer. Use of a Grosslage name does not mean that the wine will automatically be inferior, but the best quality wines in any grower's or bottler's range will normally be offered under the Einzellage name.

An Einzellage is an individual site, the smallest vine-growing unit recognized by the law. There are currently some 2,600 Einzellagen, varying in size from half a hectare up to about 250ha (618 acres). All Einzellagen are officially registered and in most cases their boundaries are precisely established. Only quality (QbA and QmP) wines may carry an Einzellage name – not table wine (DTW) or Landwein.

The unifying factor within an Einzellage is the flavour and style of wine it can produce. Some sites, because of their inherent qualities combined with the wine-making ability of the growers concerned, have a reputation for producing top-quality wine (e.g. Bernkasteler Doctor). In larger sites, where more growers are involved, the quality will be more variable. In these circumstances, for the consumer the grower's name is more important than that of the Einzellage.

Where all this organization of the wine regions is less than helpful to the consumer is that it is impossible, without memorizing all the 2,600-plus Einzellagen and 152 Grosslagen names, to tell from the information on the label whether a wine comes from an individual site or from a collective site. The entries in the A–Z section of the book, however, will help.

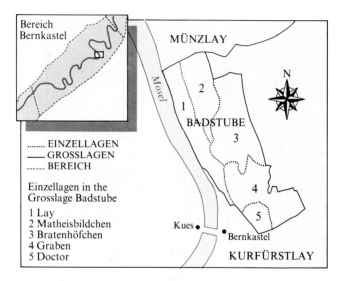

| Bereich Bernkastel |
| MÜNZLAY |
| Mosel |
| 2 |
| 1 |
| BADSTUBE |
| 3 |
| N |

.... EINZELLAGEN
—— GROSSLAGEN
----- BEREICH

Einzellagen in the
Grosslage Badstube

1 Lay
2 Matheisbildchen
3 Bratenhöfchen
4 Graben
5 Doctor

Kues •
• Bernkastel
KURFÜRSTLAY

Learning from the Label

All bottled wines sold to the consumer in the European Common Market must be labelled and all labels must carry certain information.

Most German wines have a main (body) label and a neck label that shows the vintage, if applicable. Some estate bottlers abandon the neck label and include the vintage on the main label. (The famous Karthäuserhof estate on the Ruwer, however, takes the opposite course and uses only a neck label.)

As well as being a legal requirement, labels are considered to be a most important part of the marketing and selling of wine. The use of back labels carrying extra information is increasing and can be very helpful to the consumer. When a wine has won an official award (DLG, etc.), it is usually shown by a strip or circular label.

Labelling regulations are unavoidably complicated for they must provide for all the possibilities of nomenclature and description legally open to wine.

German quality-wine labels bear most of the type of information (where applicable) shown on the sample label that follows. That which is obligatory (specified region of origin, liquid content of the bottle, etc.) must be easily read. The size of the lettering used for the specified region is important, for to it must be related that of the Prädikat (Kabinett, Spätlese, Auslese, etc.), where there is one, and the name of the village or town in which the wine was bottled. For a 700 ml or 750 ml bottle, the liquid content must be indicated in characters at least 4 mm high.

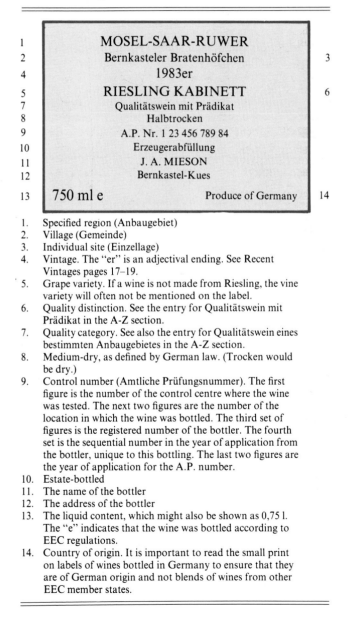

1.   Specified region (Anbaugebiet)
2.   Village (Gemeinde)
3.   Individual site (Einzellage)
4.   Vintage. The "er" is an adjectival ending. See Recent Vintages pages 17–19.
5.   Grape variety. If a wine is not made from Riesling, the vine variety will often not be mentioned on the label.
6.   Quality distinction. See the entry for Qualitätswein mit Prädikat in the A-Z section.
7.   Quality category. See also the entry for Qualitätswein eines bestimmten Anbaugebietes in the A-Z section.
8.   Medium-dry, as defined by German law. (Trocken would be dry.)
9.   Control number (Amtliche Prüfungsnummer). The first figure is the number of the control centre where the wine was tested. The next two figures are the number of the location in which the wine was bottled. The third set of figures is the registered number of the bottler. The fourth set is the sequential number in the year of application from the bottler, unique to this bottling. The last two figures are the year of application for the A.P. number.
10.   Estate-bottled
11.   The name of the bottler
12.   The address of the bottler
13.   The liquid content, which might also be shown as 0,75 l. The "e" indicates that the wine was bottled according to EEC regulations.
14.   Country of origin. It is important to read the small print on labels of wines bottled in Germany to ensure that they are of German origin and not blends of wines from other EEC member states.

Vine Varieties

Of the area under vine, 88% is planted with varieties that produce white wine – although in some cases (the Ruländer, for example) the grape may be "blue" but the wine it produces remains white. 14% of the vines in Germany are 20 years old or more, 36% are 10–20 years old, 41% 3–10 years old and 9% are under 3 years old. (Vines do not become productive until they are 3 years old.) The high proportion of vines under 10 years old is partly the result of the reconstruction and subsequent replanting of the vineyards (Flurbereinigung) over the last 40 years to make vine-growing more efficient.

The chart below shows the percentage grown of the most widely planted varieties and their share of the crop in 1983, followed by a list of the other white-wine and red-wine producing vine varieties. All the varieties are described in the A–Z section of the book.

Approximate % of area under vine	Vine Variety	Approximate % of harvest in 1983
25.8	Müller-Thurgau	30.6
19.4	Riesling	16.2
9.2	Silvaner	9.4
6.3	Kerner	6.4
3.5	Bacchus	4.5
3.0	Morio-Muskat	3.6
3.2	Portugieser	3.3
4.4	Scheurebe	3.3
2.1	Trollinger	3.0
4.0	Spätburgunder	2.3
2.3	Faber	2.0
3.5	Ruländer	1.9
17.7	Others	16.8

Other white-wine varieties

Auxerrois	Muskat	Rotberger
Ehrenfelser	Nobling	Schönburger
Elbling	Optima	Septimer
Freisamer	Ortega	Siegerrebe
Gutedel	Perle	Traminer
Huxelrebe	Regner	Weissburgunder
Kanzler	Reichensteiner	
Klingelberger	Rieslaner	

Other red-wine varieties

Dornfelder	Helfensteiner	Limberger
Frühburgunder	Heroldrebe	Müllerrebe

To grow grapes at all in Germany is a triumph of science, planning and dedication over less than ideal conditions. At these latitudes, local environmental factors take on an importance unknown in places with a more equable climate, and the choice of which variety to plant is crucial. German wine-growing regulations offer a long list of varieties to choose from – varieties that vary considerably in their needs, and yield widely differing types and amounts of wine.

In making his decision, the grower must consider the climate, the site and the soil of his vineyard, and the present and future state of the wine market. The climate is, at best, predictably uncertain: unseasonable rain, hail and frost are constant hazards at different times of the year. Each grower must decide whether to aim for quality or quantity, but often the vineyard site will make the decision for him – a high yield cannot be expected from a 45° slope, and only the return that comes from quality wine production can justify viticulture at such a bizarre angle. Most vines adapt to a wide variety of soils but some have individual preferences. Silvaner, for example, dislikes a dry soil on a sloping site that Riesling will tolerate quite happily.

These being the facts of viticultural life in Germany, there remains the choice of vine.

The choice falls broadly into three categories: first, those vines that have been established in Germany for hundreds of years, in particular Riesling and Silvaner; second, the well-established crossings, developed over 50 or more years ago, such as Müller-Thurgau and Scheurebe; third, the new crossings, such as Kerner and Bacchus.

Riesling is the vine that most consistently provides what we look for in German wine: freshness and fruitiness of flavour and a clean bouquet. In spite of Flurbereinigung (see facing page), 21% of today's Riesling vines are more than 20 years old. A mature vine produces the best wine but yields a small crop. However, the Germans have greatly improved their vines through work at their viticultural institutes; the point at which increasing yield results in decreasing quality has been steadily raised, and Riesling has benefited.

For a greater yield still, or for more exotic flavours, the grower must turn to the crossings, which now account for more than half the total area under vine. The object of their development over the last 100 years has been to achieve improved resistance to disease and adverse weather conditions, greater suitability for different sites and soils, and a higher must weight and increased yield.

Wines from new crossings, with their sometimes rather outré smell and style, are welcome as an addition to the traditional, more neutral flavours. A disadvantage of some crossings is that they can often achieve sufficient must weight to be called Spätlese or Auslese without having the quality found in a Riesling or Silvaner in these categories. The established crossings, however, are steadily being improved, and Müller-Thurgau, once regarded solely as a mass producer of rather ordinary wines, can now occasionally add elegance and style to its other qualities.

The most important crossings are Bacchus, Ehrenfelser, Faber, Huxelrebe, Kerner, Morio-Muskat, Müller-Thurgau, Optima, Ortega, Reichensteiner, Scheurebe and Siegerrebe.

In some cases these names are unfamiliar to consumers as they seldom appear on labels. It is easy for the estate bottler to introduce new crossings by name to his private customers, as the lines of communication are short and explanations can be given. To launch them into the general wine trade is more difficult and therefore, in many cases, the crossings lose their identity but provide useful constituents of commercial blends.

Anatomy of the German Wine Market

Over the last decade the trend has been for the number of growers to decline and the viticultural area to increase. The cooperative movement has become stronger, and the number of growers bottling their own wine has risen. More and more sales are being made directly to the consumer, with the grower benefiting from the additional profit they offer – and, let it be said, from a less exacting buyer. The fragmentation of German wine producers is very slowly disappearing.

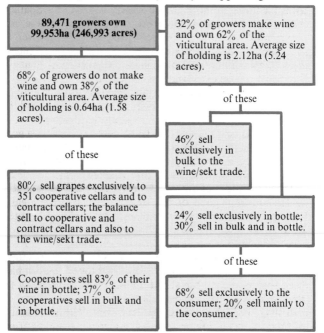

89,471 growers own 99,953ha (246,993 acres)

32% of growers make wine and own 62% of the viticultural area. Average size of holding is 2.12ha (5.24 acres).

68% of growers do not make wine and own 38% of the viticultural area. Average size of holding is 0.64ha (1.58 acres).

of these

46% sell exclusively in bulk to the wine/sekt trade.

of these

80% sell grapes exclusively to 351 cooperative cellars and to contract cellars; the balance sell to cooperative and contract cellars and also to the wine/sekt trade.

24% sell exclusively in bottle; 30% sell in bulk and in bottle.

Cooperatives sell 83% of their wine in bottle; 37% of cooperatives sell in bulk and in bottle.

of these

68% sell exclusively to the consumer; 20% sell mainly to the consumer.

Source: Statistisches Bundesamt Wiesbaden

Recent Vintages

A perfect German vintage seldom happens more than twice in a decade. It will usually be the result of an early flowering, allowing the grapes as long as possible to ripen. Adequate rain in summer will prevent the inhibiting effect of drought on the formation of sugar, and in a warm and sunny autumn noble rot (Edelfäule) may well appear.

More usually, by harvest time, while some grapes are very ripe others are still distinctly sour. To judge the true potential quality of the crop, care is taken to see that the samples of grapes gathered before the main picking starts are truly representative. Except in great years, such as 1971 and 1976, it is only when the pressing has started and the must weight and acidity have been measured that the real value of the harvest can be accurately assessed.

The quality of cheap German wine maintains a steady level, almost regardless of vintage, as blending and skilful vinification smooth away the bumps. Most everyday wine is made to be drunk within two years of the harvest, so there is little point in storing it longer.

On the other hand, Riesling QbA and the better, usually estate-bottled QmP wines improve with bottle age (see page 36 in the A–Z section of the book).

Because of the predictability of much QbA wine, vintage assessments refer more to the QmPs – Kabinett, Spätlese, Auslese, Eiswein and, in great years, Beerenauslese and Trockenbeerenauslese. A poor year for the grower in Germany is one that produces little or no Spätlese wine. In a good vintage the sugar and acid contents are high, but this is a theme with many variations.

Nevertheless, the following are generally accepted as the top-quality vintages since 1970: the 1971, '73, '75, '76 and '83. The Mosel also did well in 1979, '81 and '82.

In almost every vintage it is possible for the effect of a good microclimate to produce wines of above the average quality, but it is only in the really great years that fine wine is made throughout Germany.

Often the wines of any one year will have a particular style or flavour, be it good or otherwise, that makes them easily identifiable. This was the case in 1972 (high malic acid content from unripe grapes) and in 1976 (musts with high sugar content). The differences often fade with bottle age.

It is not obligatory for a wine of one year to bear a vintage, but if it does, 85% of the grapes used for the wine must have been grown in the year stated and the wine must show the characteristics of the vintage.

The qualities that can be expected from the various grades of German wine in poor, average and great years are set out on the following page. Of course, within any region there can be many exceptions to the general standard of the harvest, brought about by site, microclimate and the wine-making. Paradoxically, a great year can be too good for Riesling QbA: the wines can lack acidity and show a certain coarseness, although these deficiencies are less common than they once were. In mediocre years interesting and enjoyable German wines can still be produced, as their attraction does not depend on a high alcohol content.

Eiswein can be made in small amounts in most years when the weather is sufficiently cold from November onwards.

Poor Year

QbA Riesling	Good, sound wine
Kabinett	Light, agreeable. Lacks real quality
Spätlese	None, except for small quantities of non-Riesling wines
Auslese	None

Average Year

QbA Riesling	Good, balanced wine
Kabinett	Light, stylish, typical of vine variety and site
Spätlese	Sound, reflecting regional character well, but limited in quantity
Auslese	Rare except from non-Riesling

Great Year

QbA Riesling	Many good wines, but also some that are coarse and lack acidity
Kabinett	Good quality, but some can miss the charm of those in an average year
Spätlese	Splendid wines of great depth of flavour
Auslese	Superb, unique wines
Beerenauslese and Trockenbeerenauslese	Rarities. Only possible in significant quantities in great years

---

Although the percentage of Spätlese and Auslese in the Mosel-Saar-Ruwer and Nahe in 1983 was less than in 1979, the quality of the Riesling wines made them the best since 1971 or 1976. For the Rheingau, 1983 was the most successful year since 1979. In 1982 the Mosel-Saar-Ruwer again did well.

1981 produced attractive fruity wines in all the regions.

1980 was a little better in the Rheinhessen than in the northern regions. The Rheinpfalz seldom has a poor year, but a true successor to the 1976 vintage is still awaited in the Rheinland.

The table that follows shows the percentage of wine in the most common quality categories produced by the five main exporting regions. These are the official figures declared after the harvest during the five years to 1983, and can be compared to the record of the great 1976 vintage. It should be noted that each year some wine will be downgraded from one category to another, either because it fails to meet the standards expected by the producer or simply to fulfill a commercial need for more wine of a lower (and cheaper) category.

SUMMARY OF RECENT VINTAGES
IN THE FIVE MAIN EXPORTING REGIONS

Total quantity of wine declared at harvest, in hectolitres

	Mosel-Saar-Ruwer hl	Nahe hl	Rhein-gau hl	Rhein-hessen hl	Rhein-pfalz hl
1983	1,829,000	612,000	298,825	3,400,000	3,252,000
1982	2,365,000	716,700	485,000	3,773,000	3,847,000
1981	1,113,500	249,900	171,500	1,724,500	2,166,700
1980	571,500	132,600	101,500	1,145,000	1,593,900
1979	1,090,000	265,000	280,000	1,480,000	2,550,000
1976	1,040,000	366,000	228,000	1,960,000	2,310,000

Percentage of quality wine, by category

		Mosel-Saar-Ruwer %	Nahe %	Rhein-gau %	Rhein-hessen %	Rhein-pfalz %
1983	QbA	43	48	30	46	52
	Kabinett	12	15	50	19	23
	Spätlese	31	25	19	25	16
	Auslese	9	8	0	2	3
1982	QbA	61	67	74	73	72
	Kabinett	30	24	25	18	12
	Spätlese	4	5	0	7	4
	Auslese	2	1	0	0	0
1981	QbA	63	54	71	54	54
	Kabinett	28	35	25	35	33
	Spätlese	9	10	2	10	11
	Auslese	0	1	0	1	2
1980	QbA	75	60	83	57	62
	Kabinett	15	24	15	23	20
	Spätlese	2	9	0	17	12
	Auslese	0	1	0	3	2
1979	QbA	37	16	59	16	46
	Kabinett	14	25	32	21	28
	Spätlese	38	48	7	58	17
	Auslese	11	11	0	5	3
1976	QbA	8	11	11	6	20
	Kabinett	10	26	22	8	30
	Spätlese	34	38	46	64	33
	Auslese	46	25	20	22	15
	Beeren-auslese	2	1	1	2	2

Visiting the Vineyards

The ideal way to discover German wines is, of course, to visit the wine regions. Indeed, the only way to enjoy many German wines is in the setting of the vineyards that produce them, because they may seldom be seen beyond their place of origin.

By happy circumstance the vineyards encompass some of the most picturesque countryside in Germany, even without the attraction of the wines to be tasted in the restaurants and wine bars. "Wine roads" (Weinstrassen) are marked by appropriate signs with such symbols as a bunch of grapes or a wine glass. For the more energetic there are also well-marked footpaths (Weinlehrpfade) in many of the vineyards, punctuated at timely intervals by rest stops where the local wines can be sampled.

Visiting wine cellars is not quite as simple as it is in France, and the equivalent sign to *"Visitez nos caves"* is absent. Nevertheless, most estate and cooperative cellars are happy to welcome interested visitors during business hours – usually between 9 a.m. and 5 p.m. on week days – although they do expect advance warning, either by letter or by telephone. Some cellars set a firm maximum and minimum to the number of persons they will receive in any one party. If a tasting is provided free of charge, it is courteous to buy a few bottles when leaving. The Germans are, by nature, very hospitable, but the visitor to a small estate should remember that although tasting in a producer's cellar is one of the most enjoyable aspects of visiting a wine region, it may be occupying a large part of the estate owner's working day and the welcome should not be overstayed.

Many estates sell almost all their wines directly to the consumer and have a wine bar or tasting room set aside for this purpose. While customers sit around tables the wines are served to them. Facilities for spitting at "sitting" tastings are not normally offered. General comment on the wines is made, after each has been introduced by the cellar master (Kellermeister) or by the estate owner (Weingutsbesitzer). Such tastings quickly become a social occasion, although the wines still receive proper attention. Their relatively low alcohol content makes it possible to taste many wines in this way and remain clear headed. (In the course of his duties the professional taster will willingly tackle 70 or more German white wines in one session. For wines with a higher alcohol content this would hardly be possible.)

Each region has a number of wine festivals of varying sizes, especially in the months of August and September – in the Mosel-Saar-Ruwer alone there are 45 local festivals in August. There are also a number of wine museums, among the best known being that housed in the Historisches Museum der Pfalz in Speyer, which traces vine-growing in Germany back to its origins, and the important Deutsches Weinbaumuseum in Oppenheim. Small local wine museums also have much to tell about the history of wine-making in Germany.

More information can be obtained from the regional wine information offices (see Useful Addresses, page 23) or from the central wine information office, the Deutsches Weininstitut, Gutenbergplatz 3–5, 6500 Mainz, telephone 06131 (the area code for Mainz) 14071.

GERMAN PRONUNCIATION

The German language is often more daunting in appearance than in practice, thanks largely to the German fondness for combining into one eye-numbing word what might be an entire sentence in English (a Gebeitswinzergenossenschaft, for example, is simply the cooperative cellar of a district). Fortunately, in spoken German every word is clearly articulated and never runs into the following word, as happens in French officially and in English colloquially, so at least it is usually possible to distinguish where words begin and end.

A few ground rules are worth bearing in mind, to which of course there are always exceptions.

The main variations in pronunciation between German and English arise from the following differences:

"j"	as in Juffer	pronounced as in English "y"
"v"	as in Vollrads	,, ,, ,, ,, "f"
"w"	as in Winkel	,, ,, ,, ,, "v"
"z"	as in Zwierlein	,, ,, ,, ,, "ts"
"ch"	as in Enkirch	prounced as in "loch" by a Scot (i.e. not "lock")
"d"	as in Boppard, at the end of a word, is pronounced as a "t"; elsewhere as in English
"eu"	as in Neumagen	is pronounced "oi" as in "rejoice"
"g"	as in muffig, following an "i" at the end of a word, is soft, almost like "ch"; elsewhere as in English
"Sch"	as in Schönhell	pronounced as the English "sh"
"sp"	as in Spiegelberg	,, ,, ,, ,, "shp"
"st"	as in Stuttgart	,, ,, ,, ,, "sht"
"s"	as in Siegerrebe	,, ,, ,, ,, "z" before a vowel

In addition, the pronunciation of German vowels is altered by an Umlaut:

"ä"	as in Spätlese	"Spät" rhymes, more or less, with the English "ate"
"ö"	as in Östrich	"Ö" rhymes with the English "fur"
"ü"	as in Mühlheim	no equivalent English sound; similar to the French "u" as in "tu"

The general rule on "ei" and "ie" is:

"ei"	as in Wein	pronounced as "i" as in "vine"
"ie"	as in Riesling	,, ,, "e" as in "geese"

Consonants are always pronounced, and so is the "e" at the end of a word, e.g. in Auslese the "Aus" is pronounced as the English "house" without the "h", "lese" is pronounced as in "laser".

Food and Wine
in Germany

With food, as with wine, in Germany, the best policy is usually to ask for the local speciality. And while the food, in general, may lack the light touch that characterizes much of the wine, there is ample compensation in the form of diversity, quality and quantity.

The main meal of the day is Mittagessen, served from about 12.30–2.00 p.m. A Gaststätte, or restaurant, will provide a full menu, usually fairly international in style. A Gasthof or Gasthaus is an inn where sound but more modest meals of the Wiener Schnitzel and salad variety can be enjoyed. In large towns, the Ratskeller or Rathauskeller – a restaurant in the cellar or basement of the town hall – often serves traditional and local specialities of very good quality at reasonable prices, well worth trying. And throughout the vine-growing regions there are Weinstuben, or wine bars, where simple food is available and wine is served by the glass (Pokal) and bottle.

In the wine regions, in any but the smartest restaurants, local wines will dominate the list, and these are certainly the ones to drink.

The Speisekarte is the regular printed menu; the Tageskarte lists the dishes of the day. Key menu words include Vorspeisen: hors d'oeuvre; Suppen: soups (Tagesuppe is the soup of the day); Eierspeisen: egg dishes; Fisch: fish; Fleisch: meat; Geflügel: poultry; Wild: game; Kartoffeln: potatoes; Gemüse: vegetables; Salate: salads; Nachtisch: dessert. Nudeln and Spätzle are noodles; Knödeln are dumplings.

The undoubted heaviness of much German food can be offset by a light white wine. Some wine producers like to be very specific in their suggestions for partners in the marriage of food and wine, but the choice of happy matches is considerable. In general, wine of Kabinett quality, light and delicate, accompanies most first courses well, except those which have a very sharp flavour, from which no wine would benefit. Riesling Spätlese marries with white meats or fish dishes. With roast game or red meat, a good-quality red wine (probably a Spätburgunder) would drink splendidly. In contrast, a full, powerful Ruländer or Traminer tastes excellent when served with game in a rich sauce. The finest German wine, of Auslese quality or better, is best enjoyed on its own, away from the table, with its possible conflict of flavours.

These, of course, are only guidelines. Enjoyment is what eating and drinking in Germany is about, and nobody need worry too much if a choice of wine is gastronomically correct or not.

Guten Appetit!

Useful Addresses

More information about visiting the wine regions, including details of wine festivals, wine museums, etc., may be obtained from the Wine Information Office in each region:

Ahr
Gebietsweinwerbung Ahr e.V.
Schülzchenstrasse 12
5483 Bad Neuenahr-Ahrweiler
West Germany

Baden
Weinwerbezentrale Badischer
Winzergenossenschaften
Ettlingerstrasse 12
7500 Karlsruhe
West Germany

Franken
Frankenwein-Frankenland e.V.
Postfach 58 48
8700 Würzburg 1
West Germany

Hessische Bergstrasse
Weinbauverband Hessische
Bergstrasse e.V.
Königsbergerstrasse 4
6148 Heppenheim/Bergstrasse
West Germany

Mittelrhein
Mittelrhein-Burgen & Weine e.V.
Postfach
5423 Braubach
West Germany

Mosel-Saar-Ruwer
Weinwerbung Mosel-Saar-Ruwer
Neustrasse 86
5500 Trier
West Germany

Nahe
Weinland Nahe e.V.
Brückes 6
6550 Bad Kreuznach
West Germany

Rheingau
Der Rheingau-Der Weingau
Geisenheim
Im alten Rathaus
6225 Johannisberg
West Germany

Rheinhessen
Rheinhessenweine e.V.
117er Ehrenhof 5
6500 Mainz
West Germany

Rheinpfalz
Rheinpfalz-Weinpfalz e.V.
Postfach 53
6730 Neustadt/Weinstrasse
West Germany

Württemberg
Werbegemeinschaft
Württembergischer
Weingärtnergenossenschaften
Heilbronnerstrasse 41
7000 Stuttgart 1
West Germany

A-Z of German Wine

Abfüllung

Bottling. Top-quality (QmP) wine is bottled as soon as it is micro-biologically and chemically stable, normally between March and June following the vintage. Cheaper wines are usually stored in bulk and bottled when an order has to be despatched. Most German wine retains residual sugar, so a necessary part of the bottling operation is the removal of all yeast and undesirable micro-organisms. To achieve this "wine sterility", approx. 70% of German wine is bottled by the cold sterile method, in which the bottling machinery and other equipment is sterilized with steam. The remaining 30% is either warm-bottled (the wine is heated before bottling to between 45° and 60°C) and/or bottled with the addition of the sterilizing agent sorbic acid.

"Abteihof", Weingut M-S-R

300-year-old family-owned estate with small holdings in top-quality steep sites: Graacher DOMPROBST and HIMMELREICH, Wehlener SONNENUHR, Brauneberger JUFFER. 100% Riesling. Fresh and fruity wines, made by careful vinification, some 20% bottled dry or medium-dry. Average annual production is 2,500 cases. Address: Otto-Ulrich Pauly, Gestade 32, 5550 Graach/Mosel.

Abtsberg M-S-R w. ★★★

Einzellage on the upper slopes of the great hill of vines at GRAACH in the heart of the MITTELMOSEL, 100% steep, facing SSW and planted mainly with Riesling. The wine has good, firm acidity; usually less full than that of the HIMMELREICH lower down the hill. Grosslage: MÜNZLAY. Growers: Kesselstatt, Schorlemer (Meyerhof).

Acidity

See Säure

Adelmann, Weingut Graf Würt.

Small, quality-conscious estate of 15ha (37 acres), two-thirds on steep slopes, n.e. of Stuttgart. The v'yds are known to date from AD 950. Average annual production is 8,300 cases divided equally between red (Trollinger, etc.) and white (Riesling, etc.) wines. Many successes in national and international competitions. Address: Burg Schaubeck, 7141 Steinheim-Kleinbottwar.

Affaltrach, Schlosskellerei Würt.

Estate dating from the 13th century, owned since 1928 by the family of Dr Reinhold Baumann. 7.5ha (19 acres) in Affaltrach and Willsbach near HEILBRONN, and at GUNTERSBLUM in the Rhein-hessen, planted with a wide range of red and white vine varieties. The wines are mainly dry or medium-dry, designed to accompany food and sold principally in the region. A 1973 EISWEIN from the Zeilberg site at Affaltrach reached 292° Oechsle (40% potential alcohol!). The estate also takes in grapes and makes wine for 250 local growers. Address: 7104 Obersulm 1.

Affental, Affentaler Spätburgunder Rotwein

Certain villages immediately s. of Baden-Baden have the right to produce "Affentaler Spätburgunder Rotwein", either as QbA or QmP. Affental, which translates as "monkey valley", is a corruption of Ave Maria Tal. Affentaler Spätburgunder ROTWEIN is sold in a normal slim German wine bottle, embossed with a monkey clinging to its sides.

Ahr r. (w.)

Second-smallest of the wine regions with 424ha (1,048 acres) of v'yds on both sides of the R. Ahr, which flows into the Rhein just s. of Bonn. In spite of its northerly position 66% is planted with red-wine varieties, mainly Spätburgunder and Portugieser, which at this latitude produce wines that incline to the pale, light and pleasant. The white wines from Riesling and Müller-Thurgau are attractive but cannot compare in quality to the finest from regions further south. The best Rieslings, from slaty soil, recall the wines of the nearby Mittelrhein, with their somewhat earthy, occasionally steely flavour. For many vine-growing in the Ahr valley is a part-time occupation and more than half the crop is made into wine by cooperative cellars.

Ahr wine does not attempt to compete with the best that can be found on the international market and therefore the place to meet it is in the valley itself. The region is exceedingly pretty and the steep vineyards are easily accessible through the "Rotweinwanderweg", a well-signposted footpath some 30km (19 miles) in length, which can be joined at many different points. The valley is a great attraction for tourists, especially those from Köln and the Ruhr district. Its narrow roads are often crowded but there are many places to eat and to enjoy the local wines. The capital is BAD NEUENAHR.

Alcohol

Alcohol level is not so significant as a quality factor in wines from Germany as it is in those from elsewhere. For example, a Riesling QbA from the M-S-R region must contain a minimum of actual alcohol (alcohol that is actually present as opposed to total alcohol which takes into account unfermented sugar) of 7% by volume. A BEERENAUSLESE may contain as little as 5.5% and the cheapest German table wine (DTW) not less than 8.5%. The importance of alcohol in German wine lies mainly in its relationship to the acidity, and usually to the sugar content. See also ANREICHERUNG.

Alf M-S-R W. ★★

One of the better-known small wine villages in the Bereich ZELL, on the Lower Mosel near COCHEM. The steep vineyards are planted mainly with Riesling.

Allendorf, Weingut Fritz Rhg.

Noted Winkel estate owned by a family established in the Rheingau since 1192, with 40ha (99 acres) in ASSMANNS-HAUSEN, RÜDESHEIM, JOHANNIS-BERG, GEISENHEIM, WINKEL, OESTRICH, ELTVILLE, HOCHHEIM, etc. Vines are 80% Riesling, 10% Spätburgunder. The largest holding is in the Winkeler JESUITENGARTEN, of which Allendorf owns a quarter. The estate makes the full range of regional wines, matured in wood. Annual production is 33,300 cases, sold in Germany and abroad. Address: Georgshof, Winkel.

Alsenz Nahe w. ★★

Secluded wine village on a Nahe tributary of the same name.

Alsheim Rhh. w. ★★★

Attractive village between WORMS and OPPENHEIM, making distinguished Riesling wines. The best-known Einzellage is the large FRÜHMESSE in the Grosslage RHEINBLICK, which is restricted to the sloping sites. Alsheim's flatter land is in the larger Grosslage KRÖTENBRUNNEN.

Altärchen M-S-R w. ★★→★★★

Large Einzellage of some 245ha (605 acres) lying on both sides of the Mosel at TRITTENHEIM. 60% is on steep slopes facing SSE-W,

25

producing good-quality wines from Riesling and Müller-Thurgau. Grosslage: MICHELSBERG. Growers: Bischöfliche Weingüter, Milz, Reh (Josefinengrund), Ronde.

Altenahr Ahr r. (w.) ★★
Small town on the R. Ahr, near the upstream end of the vine-growing region. It almost sinks under the weight of the well-behaved tourists who arrive in coachloads from the Ruhr district. Some 54ha (133 acres) of vineyard are planted with Riesling, Spätburgunder, Müller-Thurgau, etc., producing typical Ahr wines that are drunk almost exclusively in the region.

Altenbamberg Nahe w. ★★
Secluded village on the R. ALSENZ where excellent wine is made from Riesling grown on porphyritic soil. Grosslage: BURGWEG.

Altenberg M-S-R w. ★★→★★★
Altenberg is a frequently used site name – there are at least 20 scattered across Germany. The Einzellage Altenberg at KANZEM is a steep site typical of the best in the Saar, producing wines of quality and charm, mainly from Riesling. Grosslage: SCHARZBERG. Growers: Bischöfliche Weingüter, Schorlemer (Schlangengraben).

Altenkirch, Weingut Friedrich Rhg.
Family-owned estate dating from 1826 with 18.5ha (46 acres) of vineyards, mainly in LORCH but also in RÜDESHEIM and OESTRICH. Vines are 85% Riesling, 6% Spätburgunder. The present energetic owner, Peter Breuer, is proud of the fruity acidity of his wines from steep sites, matured in the 300m (984 ft) long cellars that lie deep beneath his vineyards. Annual production is some 18,000 cases, of which a third is sold on the export market. Address: Binger Weg 2, 6223 Lorch/Rheingau.

Alzey Rhh. w. ★★
Town first mentioned in AD 223, set in rolling country deep in the Rheinhessen. Very much a centre for the local wine trade, it is best known for its Landesanstalt für Rebzüchtung – the viticultural institute whose first director, in 1909, was Georg Scheu, who bred the Scheurebe and other well-known vines. The town also has its own wine estate, the Weingut der Stadt Alzey (see next entry). It is the home of the wine exporting house SICHEL.

Alzey, Weingut der Stadt Rhh.
Estate of 18ha (44 acres) owned by the town of ALZEY, established in 1916 and producing some 17,000 cases a year. 18 different vine varieties are in commercial production, with Müller-Thurgau and Riesling each occupying 17% of the area under vine. The administrator, Herr U. Kaufmann, aims to make balanced, positive, elegant wines, which are sold only in Germany. The estate is one of the few in Germany to be owned by a town. Address: Schlossgasse 14, 6508 Alzey.

Amtliche Prüfung
Official testing. Quality German wines (approx. 95% of the annual harvest) of all categories must submit to an official "blind" tasting and chemical analysis. If successful, a wine will be granted an Amtliche Prüfungsnummer (A.P. number) which must be displayed on the label. Usually 93-97% of applications for an A.P. number are successful. This countrywide system of quality control, operating through nine centres, is claimed to be unique to West Germany. Its effectiveness, however, has not always been considered beyond reproach.

Anbaugebiet, bestimmtes
A designated wine region, of which there are 11 in Germany (shown on the map on page 10). It is the largest geographical unit for quality wine and the Anbaugebiet name must always appear on the label of a quality (QbA or QmP) wine. The differences between the wines of the various regions are clear, although they naturally tend to be less pronounced in the vineyards at the boundaries of adjoining regions. The maps at the back of the book show the individual regions.

Anheuser, Weingut Ökonomierat August E. Nahe
Large estate of some 60ha (148 acres) founded in 1869 by the Anheuser family, to whom the exporting house Anheuser & Fehrs

also belongs. Sites incl. BRÜCKES. KRÖTENPFUHL and NARRENKAPPE at BAD KREUZNACH; DELLCHEN at NORHEIM; HERMANNSHÖHLE at NIEDERHAUSEN and Königsfels at SCHLOSSBÖCKELHEIM. 70% of the vines are Riesling, the rest are mainly Müller-Thurgau and Silvaner plus some Kerner, Ruländer and Scheurebe. High-quality wine-making with an annual production of some 66,600 cases. Address: Brückes 53, 6550 Bad Kreuznach.

Anheuser, Weingut Paul Nahe

Estate est. in 1888 by the vine-growing Anheuser family, also responsible for the American brewery Anheuser-Busch. 76ha (188 acres), of which more than a quarter is at present being reconstructed. Vines are 70% Riesling in leading sites at ALTENBAMBERG, BAD KREUZNACH. NIEDERHAUSEN, NORHEIM, ROXHEIM and SCHLOSS-BÖCKELHEIM. No Grosslage names are used. Cool fermentation and maturation in cask produces the full range of Nahe flavours. 25% of the wines are dry. 10% of production is exported. Address: Strombergerstr. 15-19, 6550 Bad Kreuznach.

Anheuser & Fehrs, Weinkellereien Nahe

Wine merchants established in 1869, under the same family ownership as Weingut Ökonomierat August E. Anheuser, selling quality wines on the home and export markets. Address: Brückes 41, 6550 Bad Kreuznach.

Annaberg Rhpf. w. ★★★★

Famous little Einzellage owned by Stumpf-Fitz'sches Weingut (see next entry). Until 1971 the wine was sold simply under the site name Annaberg but now the label must include the village name KALLSTADT.

Annaberg Stumpf-Fitz'sches Weingut Rhpf.

Small but important estate (see previous entry) dating from the 16th century or earlier – the site itself was a Roman settlement. The grapes are harvested late and produce top-quality, powerful, concentrated wines that can last for years. Approx. 5,000 cases of Kallstadter Annaberg Riesling, Scheurebe and Weissburgunder are produced each year, sold mainly in Germany but with some exports. Address: 6702 Bad Dürkheim-Leistadt.

Anreicherung

Enrichment. The addition of sugar in various forms (saccharose, concentrated grape juice, etc.) to increase the actual alcohol content and thus produce a balanced wine has been practised for some 200 years in many countries. In Germany only QbA and DEUTSCHER TAFELWEIN, incl. LANDWEIN, may be enriched. This means that wines of KABINETT quality and upwards will never have sugar added, as their superior quality depends on freshness and elegance, not on enhanced alcohol content. See also ALCOHOL.

Ansprechend

Attractive. A somewhat imprecise but useful term for describing a wine, often used as in Ansprechende Süsse ("attractive sweetness") or Ansprechende Säure ("attractive acidity").

A.P.

See Amtliche Prüfung

A.P. Nr.

Abbreviation of Amtliche Prüfungsnummer (A.P. number).

Äpfelsäure

Malic acid. With tartaric acid (WEINSÄURE) it forms approx. 90% of the acidity in German grape MUST (it is also found in many other fruits). The process of malolactic fermentation, in which malic acid is converted into lactic acid and carbon dioxide, does not normally occur in the relatively acidic German wines. If the malic acid content of a wine is excessive it may legally be chemically reduced. See also SÄURE.

Apfelwein

Wine made from apple juice by a process that is very similar to grape-wine vinification. Additions of sugar and water are normal. A popular drink in s. Germany.

Apotheke M-S-R w. ★★→★★★

Einzellage lying on both sides of the Mosel at TRITTENHEIM, prod. good-quality, elegant Rieslings. Grosslage: MICHELSBERG. Growers:

Bischöfliche Weingüter, Friedrich-Wilhelm-Gymnasium, Hain, Kesselstatt, Milz, Reh (Josefinengrund), Ronde.

Arnet, Wilhelm Rhg.
Small 2.6ha (6.4 acre) estate est. in 1632, producing powerful, full wines (90% Riesling) at ELTVILLE, MARTINSTHAL and WALLUF, all sold to private customers. Address: Mühlstr. 96, 6229 Walluf.

Aromatisch
Aromatic. Term used to describe wines with a pronounced bouquet, esp. the wines of the Rheinhessen and Rheinpfalz, from vine varieties such as Morio-Muskat, Traminer and Scheurebe. The strength of the aroma will be affected by the style of the vintage, the soil, vinification and length of maturation in bottle.

Aschrott'sche Erben, Geheimrat Rhg.
Estate dating from 1823 with 16ha (40 acres) of holdings in most of the best HOCHHEIM sites, incl. DOMDECHANEY, HÖLLE and

KIRCHENSTÜCK. The vines are 90% Riesling and the estate makes powerful, spicy wines which have won many awards. Annual production approx. 11,000 cases, sold in Germany and abroad. Address: Kirchstr. 38, 6203 Hochheim am Main.

Assmannshausen Rhg. r. (w.) ★★
Small town some 4km (2½ miles) downstream from RÜDESHEIM, where the river turns n. and the Wagnerian Rhein gorge begins. It is best known for its Spätburgunder and its fine old Krone hotel and restaurant. Wine from Assmannshausen is among the most distinguished red wine in Germany. It improves with bottle age and usually shows clear varietal characteristics. Grosslage: STEIL.

Auctions
See Versteigerungen

Auflangen Rhh. w. ★★
Grosslage of 159ha (393 acres) covering some of the best south-facing sites on the RHEINFRONT above NIERSTEIN, incl. ÖLBERG and ORBEL. Distinguished wines from Riesling and Silvaner, rounded but not flabby, with powerful flavour in good years.

Aus dem Lesegut
On a label this indicates that the wine has been made from grapes grown by the person stated (e.g. Aus dem Lesegut Herr Schmidt). Not a term that is used very often. See also LESE, LESEGUT.

Ausdrucksvoll
Characterful. Suggests that the positive qualities of a wine are strongly pronounced. It might be applied to a well-developed Riesling wine from the Rheingau or Rheinpfalz.

Ausgeglichen
Well balanced. Describes a wine in which the constituent parts, particularly alcohol, acids and residual sugar, are in harmony. Sometimes only achieved after several years' bottle age.

Auslese
Legally established term used to describe quality (QmP) wine made from selected – but not necessarily late-picked – grapes whose MUST weight reached certain minimum levels (e.g. for Rheingauer Riesling Auslese the minimum level is 95° Oechsle = 13% of potential

alcohol). Auslese wines from the Rhein regions are frequently
made from grapes with an increased sugar content caused by
"noble rot" (EDELFÄULE). Such wines will also taste sweeter
(through an enhanced fructose and glycerin content) and will be
darker in colour than wines of lower quality. Auslese wines from
most of the new vine varieties cannot compare in quality with a
Riesling Auslese.

Ausschankwein
German equivalent of the French *vin ouvert* ("open wine"), usually
bottled by the litre and served in a large, 200ml (250ml in
s. Germany) glass in cafés and wine bars. It is never the most
expensive of wines although the quality is by no means always
inferior. Many estates offer their better quality (QmP) wine by the
glass in their own wine bar.

Auxerrois
Vine variety producing a low yield of white grapes with a MUST
weight some 10° Oechsle higher than that of Müller-Thurgau. The
wine is relatively soft, full-bodied and neutral in flavour. Planted
in 83ha (205 acres), 80% in Baden. Varieties bearing a larger crop
are likely to replace it in coming years.

Ayl M-S-R w. ★★★
Rural village in the Saar devoted to viticulture, where great wines
are made in the best years. The finest wines usually come from the
Einzellage HERRENBERGER and the best parts of the KUPP. Grosslage: SCHARZBERG.

Bacchus
White grape variety, a crossing of (Silvaner × Riesling) × Müller-
Thurgau, usually producing a larger crop than Müller-Thurgau
with a greater MUST weight but less acidity. The wine has a slight
Muskat bouquet and is at its best when young and fresh. It blends
well with wines of pronounced acidity, to which it brings body and
flavour. In 1976 Bacchus was planted in 1,447ha (3,576 acres), in
1982 in 3,344 ha (8,263 acres), more than half in the Rheinhessen.

Bacharach Mrh. w. ★★
Attractive old village, known in the past as a marketplace for wine
from the whole of the Rheinland, now respected for its own steely
Rieslings grown exclusively on very steep slopes. The wines are
similarly priced to those from the Nahe.

Bad Dürkheim Rhpf. Pop. 15,700 w. (r.) ★★★
Busy town and spa 25km (15 miles) w. of Mannheim at the foot
of the Pfälzerwald (Pfalz Forest) overlooking the v'yds of the
Bereich MITTELHAARDT/DEUTSCHE WEINSTRASSE, and the site every
September of the largest wine festival in the world, the Dürkheimer
Wurstmarkt (Sausage Market). Excellent white wine is made from
a range of vine varieties, although Dürkheim's wines are probably
not quite as fine as the best from neighbouring FORST or DEIDES-
HEIM. Three Grosslagen: FEUERBERG, HOCHMESS and SCHENKENBÖHL.

Bad Kreuznach Nahe Pop. 41,500 w. (r.) ★★★
The largest town in the Nahe and a spa since the 17th century; the
s. part of the town with its well laid out gardens reflects its pre-1914
heyday. Some of the finest wine of the Nahe is made within the
boundaries of the Grosslage KRONENBERG, surrounding Bad
Kreuznach.

Bad Kreuznach, Staatsweingut Weinbaulehranstalt Nahe
Estate est. in 1900, with an educational and experimental role,
owned by the government of RHEINLAND-PFALZ. It has 31ha (76
acres) of v'yds in BAD KREUZNACH and NORHEIM, 49% Riesling, 18%
Müller-Thurgau, and many new crossings are tested, the best of
which will always reflect the regional wine character. The estate
pioneered controlled fermentation under carbon-dioxide pressure
and aims to produce individual, cask-matured wines with length
and fine acidity. Sales are mainly on the home market. Address:
Rüdesheimerstr. 68, 6550 Bad Kreuznach.

Bad Münster am Stein-Ebernburg Nahe Pop. 3,600 w.
Small and charming spa 5km (3 miles) s. of BAD KREUZNACH near
the distinguished Traisen v'yds which back on to high, warmth-
retaining rocks. Grosslage: BURGWEG.

Bad Neuenahr-Ahrweiler Ahr Pop. 26,000 r.

Principal town in the Ahr valley 30km (18 miles) s. of Bonn. Much damaged in World War II, now skilfully restored and once more the centre of tourism in the Ahr. The wine is red, light in weight and flavour. The best comes from Spätburgunder.

Baden w. (r.)

Most southerly grape-growing region in Germany, covering 14,448ha (35,702 acres) and producing some 15% of the total annual German wine production. The soil is varied, warm and fruitful. Most of the v'yds lie on level or gently sloping ground, although here and there they climb the hillsides, not so much to reach a better exposure to the sun as to avoid the cold air and frosts of the valleys. The EEC recognizes that the climate in Baden is warmer than that elsewhere in West Germany and places the region, for administrative purposes, in wine-producing Zone B, with French regions incl. Alsace and certain parts of the Loire valley. (All other wine-producing regions in Germany are placed in Zone A, together with the UK and Luxembourg.)

85% of the Baden crop is handled by cooperative cellars, incl. the largest wine-producing cellar in Europe, the ZENTRALKELLEREI BADISCHER WINZERGENOSSENSCHAFTEN eG (ZBW) at Breisach, and

it is to the cooperatives that credit must be given for the success of Baden wines in Germany. There are also a number of private estates making top-quality, individual wines.

The range of vines grown is large with Müller-Thurgau, Ruländer and Gutedel heading the list. Perhaps because the region extends over 300km (180 miles) from the R. Main to the Swiss border, there is considerable variation in the style of wine from one Bereich to another. The modern international taste seems to be for lightness and crispness rather than for the heavier, broader flavours favoured in the past. Baden produces both types, and both have their merits. Some wines are allowed to retain sufficient natural carbon dioxide to make them slightly SPRITZIG and most attractive.

The region, which in many places backs on to the Black Forest, is exceptionally pretty and rural, with small v'yds mingling with orchards and meadows covered in wildflowers. Very definitely worth a detour.

Baden-Württemberg

Federal State in which lie the wine regions Baden and Württemberg. Area under vine is 23,548ha (58,189 acres). The capital is STUTTGART.

Badisch Rotgold

Quality rosé wine made in Baden exclusively from mixing Ruländer (Grauburgunder) and Spätburgunder grapes (not wine).

Badstube M-S-R w. ★★→★★★

Small Grosslage of about 51ha (126 acres) that incl. three of the most distinguished sites on the Mosel: DOCTOR, GRABEN and BRATENHÖFCHEN. The sites are sloping or very steep indeed and almost 100% Riesling. Often wines are sold for marketing reasons under the respected Grosslage name Badstube, rather than their individual site names.

Baiken Rhg. w. ★★★→★★★★
Einzellage on sloping ground at RAUENTHAL that makes splendid, balanced, elegant Riesling wines of outstanding quality. Grosslage: STEINMÄCHER. Growers: Eltville Staatsweingut, Simmern'sches Rentamt, Sturm.

Balbach Erben, Bürgermeister Anton, Weingut Rhh.
Great NIERSTEIN estate. The Balbach family, engaged in vine-growing since 1650, cleared woods in the 19th century and laid out the top-quality PETTENTHAL v'yd. Today the estate has holdings in

18ha (44 acres) of prime sites incl. HIPPING, ÖLBERG, etc. Vines are 80% Riesling, the rest mainly Müller-Thurgau (7%) and Kerner (5%). Some 12,500 cases (3,500 from Pettenthal) of good-quality, fresh wines are made and stored in stainless steel and fibreglass before being sold in Germany and abroad. Address: Mainzerstr. 64, 6505 Nierstein.

Base wine
See Grundwein

Bassermann-Jordan, Weingut Geheimer Rat Dr. v. Rhpf.
Estate known to have been in existence in 1250, came into the hands of the Jordan family in 1816. The 47.5ha (117 acres) are divided among the best sites in the Bereich MITTELHAARDT/DEUTSCHE WEINSTRASSE, incl. GRAINHÜBEL, HOHENMORGEN and LEINHÖHLE in DEIDESHEIM, JESUITENGARTEN and UNGEHEUER in FORST, etc. Vines are 92% Riesling; will be 100% by 1987. Wines are matured in oak and the estate aims for fine Riesling acidity and fruit. Sales are worldwide. Address: 6705 Deidesheim, Postfach 120.

Bastei Nahe w. ★★★→★★★★
Mainly steep 2ha (5 acre) Einzellage at the foot of the high rock face near TRAISEN called the Rotenfels, planted entirely with Riesling. The wine has great character and a positive, spicy flavour that comes from the soil. Grosslage: BURGWEG. Growers: Crusius, Niederhausen-Schlossböckelheim Staatl. Weinbaudomäne.

Basting-Gimbel, Weingut Rhg.
Family-owned estate dating from the early 17th century, 86% Riesling. Approx. annual production is 10,000 cases of elegant wines from WINKEL (HASENSPRUNG) and GEISENHEIM, sold in Germany and abroad. Many old vintages, going back to 1950, can be tasted in the estate's own wine bar. Address: Hauptstr. 70-72, 6227 Winkel/Rheingau.

Baumann, Weingut Friedrich Rhh.
Estate founded in 1909, with 10ha (25 acres) in leading sites in OPPENHEIM (e.g. SACKTRÄGER) and NIERSTEIN (FINDLING, PETTENTHAL), producing a large choice of dry and medium-dry wines from Riesling (40%), Silvaner, Kerner, Müller-Thurgau, etc. The wines are fresh and lively, matured in wood, and have won many awards. Sales are in Germany and abroad. Address: Friedrich-Ebert-Strasse 55, 6504 Oppenheim.

Becker, J. B., Weingut Weinkellerei Rhg.
Estate dating from 1893 with 10.61ha (26 acres) of Riesling (80%),
Spätburgunder (12%) and Müller-Thurgau in WALLUF, MARTINS-
THAL, RAUENTHAL and ELTVILLE, producing approx. 8,000 cases
annually. The Spätburgunder is traditionally made, and about 70%
of the white wines are dry or medium-dry. Sales are to the home
and export markets. Address: Rheinstrasse, 6229 Walluf/
Rheingau.

Beeren
Grapes. The structure of the grape has a bearing on wine-making.
Many substances that contribute to the aroma are concentrated in
the skin, as is the colour in red grapes. The content of the outer
and inner areas of the flesh is not the same, with more sugar and
less acid being found near the skin. As a result, the first and second
pressings of the same grapes do not share the same chemical make-
up and produce noticeably different wines.
   Wine grapes vary in size, but small grapes, with their greater
proportion of skin to flesh, will have a powerful bouquet if white
(e.g. Scheurebe), and a good colour if red – all things being equal.
The tightness with which grapes are packed on the bunch has a
direct effect on the rate at which fungus diseases may spread.

Beerenauslese
PRÄDIKAT awarded by the control (AMTLICHE PRÜFUNG) authorities
to wines made from individually selected overripe grapes, probably
attacked by EDELFÄULE, and always intensely sweet. The legal minimum MUST weights vary from 110–128° Oechsle, depending on
where the grapes are grown. Although 128° Oechsle is the equivalent of 18.1% alcohol by volume, most Beerenauslesen will contain
relatively little alcohol (the legal minimum is 5.5%), the rest of the
sugar remaining unfermented. Usually Riesling produces the finest
Beerenauslesen, with a high acid content and pronounced yellow-
gold colour when young, that can turn to deepest amber in old age.
The concentrated flavour of a Beerenauslese tends to mask the
obtrusive characteristics of some new grape crossings, replacing
them with the honey flavour of the Edelfäule.

Beilstein M-S-R W. ★→★★
Picturesque old wine village a few km. upstream from COCHEM,
overlooked by the castle Burg Metternich. A good centre from
which to visit the Bereich ZELL.

Bensheim Hess.Berg. Pop. 33,000 W. ★★
Ancient town s. of Darmstadt. Steep sites produce Riesling wines
with good acidity, drunk mainly in the region. The style of Bens-
heimer wines is similar to that of Rheingau Rieslings but the
quality is less exalted.

Bensheim, Weingut der Stadt Hess.Berg.
One of a few town-owned estates in Germany. 90% is planted with
Riesling and two-thirds of the wine is bottled in litres for consump-
tion in local wine bars and restaurants. The quality is similar to
that from the less well-known parts of the Rheingau. Address: Am
Ritterplatz, 6140 Bensheim 1.

Bereich
Combination of v'yd sites (Grosslagen or Einzellagen) within one
region (Anbaugebiet) with more or less similar growing conditions
and style of wine. In some instances the reason for a Bereich being
created has been to help administration rather than to identify a
particular style of wine. Generally, a wine bearing a Bereich name
must be a quality wine, although in certain areas a Bereich name
can still be used to describe a table wine. The quality of a Bereich
wine should be good within its category (QbA, QmP) but is unlikely to be outstanding.

Berg Roseneck Rhg. W. ★★★→★★★★
Sloping Einzellage on the hill at RÜDESHEIM making top-quality
Riesling wines with a slightly earthy background flavour.
Grosslage: BURGWEG. Growers: Breuer, Eltville Staatsweingut,
Frankensteiner Hof, Groenesteyn, Hessisches Weingut, Holschier,
Mumm'sches Weingut, Nägler, Schlotter, Wegeler Erben (Dein-
hard Oestrich).

Berg Rottland Rhg. w. ★★★→★★★★
Einzellage on the outskirts of RÜDESHEIM producing stylish, fruity, top-quality Riesling wines. Grosslage: BURGWEG. Growers: Altenkirch, Breuer, Eltville Staatsweingut, Frankensteiner Hof, Groenesteyn, Hessisches Weingut, Mumm'sches Weingut, Nägler, Ress, Schlotter, Wegeler Erben (Deinhard Oestrich).

Berg Schlossberg Rhg. w. ★★★
Steep, slaty Einzellage directly overlooking the confluence of the Nahe and Rhein at RÜDESHEIM. Excellent Riesling wines with good acidity. Grosslage: BURGWEG. Growers: Breuer, Eltville Staatsweingut, Frankensteiner Hof, Groenesteyn, Mumm'sches Weingut, Nägler, Ress, Schloss Schönborn, Schlotter, Wegeler Erben (Deinhard Oestrich).

Bergdolt, F. & G. Rhpf.
14ha (35 acre) estate s.e. of NEUSTADT, founded in 1290 and acquired by the Bergdolt family in 1754. Riesling (25%), Müller-Thurgau (20%) and Silvaner (20%) are the main vine varieties, plus some Kerner and other white varieties, producing approx. 13,000 cases of fresh, flowery wines, both dry and sweetish. The most successful are the dry and medium-dry Riesling and Kerner wines. All are sold directly to the consumer in Germany. Address: Klostergut St Lamprecht, 6730 Neustadt-Duttweiler.

Bergstrasse, Staatsweingut Hess.Berg.
Top-quality HESSEN estate of 36ha (89 acres) under the control of the large ELTVILLE STAATSWEINGUT and dating from the early part of the century. Vines are 62% Riesling, 10% Müller-Thurgau, 8% Ruländer, etc., and many new crossings are on trial. The estate is sole owner of the 17.5ha (43 acre) Centgericht site at HEPPENHEIM. Some 25,000 cases are produced annually of fruity, lively wines, 50% dry or medium-dry (TROCKEN, HALBTROCKEN), sold mainly in Germany. EISWEIN is a speciality. A new cellar is to be built in BENSHEIM at the Rodensteiner Hof. Address: Grieselstr. 34-36, 6140 Bensheim.

Bergstrasser Gebiets Winzergenossenschaft eG Hess.Berg.
Cooperative cellar in the smallest wine-producing region. 634 members have holdings in 291ha (719 acres). Vines are 52% Riesling, 18% Müller-Thurgau, 10% Ruländer, 10% Silvaner. Approx. annual production is the equivalent of 297,600 cases, sold entirely in Germany. Address: Darmstädterstr. 56, 6148 Heppenheim.

Bergweiler-Prüm Erben, Zach. M-S-R
Three well-known Mosel families are united in this estate: Prüm, Bergweiler, and Berres from Ürzig. The estate owns 9.5ha (23 acres) with holdings in BERNKASTEL (GRABEN, BRATENHÖFCHEN, SCHLOSSBERG, etc.), GRAACH (HIMMELREICH, DOMPROBST), WEHLEN

(SONNENUHR, etc.) and ZELTINGEN-RACHTIG. Vines are 95% Riesling. Wines are matured in cask and stored in stainless steel, and the individuality of the different sites is well maintained. Approx. annual prod. is 10,000 cases, sold in Germany and abroad. Address: Weingut Dr Pauly-Bergweiler, Gestade 15, 5550 Bernkastel-Kues.

Bernkastel, Bereich M-S-R w. ★
One of five Bereiche in the M-S-R, covering some 9,000ha (22,240 acres). Downstream a few km. from TRIER at SCHWEICH the steep slopes begin to rise from the n. bank of the Mosel. Here the Bereich Bernkastel begins and continues on both sides of the river until it reaches ZELL. The top-quality wines from these v'yds are offered under their own village and Einzellage names. The cheaper wines are often sold under the Grosslage names – Bernkasteler KUR-FÜRSTLAY, Klüsserather ST MICHAEL. Generally speaking, any wine called simply Bereich Bernkastel is likely to be of similar quality to these Grosslagen wines. Today, such wines will probably contain a high proportion of Müller-Thurgau, but when drunk young they should still be fresh and crisp in the proper Mosel manner. Bereich Bernkastel Riesling is likely to be distinctly better.

Bernkastel-Kues M-S-R Pop. 6,800 w. ★★→★★★★
Important wine-producing town on the Mosel. Many of the finest v'yds of the MITTELMOSEL, incl. the Bernkasteler DOCTOR and Wehlener SONNENUHR, are concentrated around Bernkastel on the right-hand river bank. Ancient half-timbered houses, narrow fairy-tale streets and the pleasure of drinking wine at source attract many tourists. In Kues (on the left bank and over the bridge from Bernkastel) several enormous cellars draw their wine from the whole of the Mosel and beyond. Grosslagen: BADSTUBE and KURFÜRSTLAY.

Besenwirtschaft
Name used particularly in Württemberg but also elsewhere for STRAUSSWIRTSCHAFT.

Bestes Fass
Best cask. Term used by some growers before 1971 to identify wines from the best of two or more casks of the same description, e.g. 1953 Oppenheimer Sackträger Riesling Auslese "Bestes Fass". No longer permitted.

Bestimmtes Anbaugebiet
See Anbaugebiet, bestimmtes

Bezner & Fischer
See Sonnenhof, Weingut

Biffar, Weingut Josef Rhpf.
Estate with 12ha (30 acres) in the best sites at DEIDESHEIM and RUPPERTSBERG, 70% Riesling, 20% Müller-Thurgau, producing some 10,000 cases annually. 80% of the wines are usually QmP and all are matured in wood in a deep cellar, developing into the full range of Rheinpfalz quality wine styles. Address: Niederkirchen-erstr. 13, 6705 Deidesheim.

Bildstock Rhh. w. ★★→★★★
Large Einzellage behind the town of NIERSTEIN, that separates it from the Rhein. Most of the site is flat, producing good-quality, fruity wines. Grosslage: SPIEGELBERG. Growers: Balbach Erben, Heyl zu Herrnsheim, Kurfürstenhof, Georg Schneider, Strub, Wehrheim.

Bingen Rhh. Pop. 24,000 w. ★★
Town at the confluence of the R. Nahe and Rhein, severely damaged in World War II but some of the old provincial terraced town houses remain. Several large brandy- and wine-producing companies (Racke, St Ursula, Scharlachberg, Texier) face the Rheingauer RÜDESHEIM v'yds across the Rhein. The best-known individual v'yd site is the Binger SCHARLACHBERG. Grosslage: ST ROCHUSKAPELLE.

Bischöfliche Weingüter, Verwaltung der M-S-R
A combination of four estates of ecclesiastical origin, totalling 105ha (259 acres), their v'yds a roll-call of some of the finest of the M-S-R incl. Erdener TREPPCHEN, Ürziger WÜRZGARTEN, Tritten-heimer APOTHEKE, Kaseler NIES'CHEN, Ayler KUPP, SCHARZHOFBERG, Piesporter GOLDTRÖPFCHEN, Kaseler KEHRNAGEL. The v'yds are mainly steep, 95% Riesling, and produce approx. 83,000 cases annually. The grapes are pressed near the v'yds and the wine is vini-fied in the central cellar in TRIER (part of the cellar is 400 years old), maturing in wood. Top-quality, superbly elegant and characterful

wines, sold all over the world. Address: Gervasiusstr. 1, 5500 Trier.

Black Forest
See Schwarzwald

Blankenhorn K.G., Weingut Fritz Baden
15ha (37 acre) estate in the Bereich MARKGRÄFLERLAND, 30%
Gutedel, 30% Spätburgunder, plus various other varieties, producing true-to-type dry and medium-dry wines that win awards. Sold
only in Germany. Address: 7846 Schliengen.

Blankenhornsberg
See Freiburg, Staatliches Weinbauinstitut, "Blankenhornsberg"

Blauer Frühburgunder
See Frühburgunder

Blauer Limberger
See Limberger

Blauer Spätburgunder
See Spätburgunder

Blend
See Verschnitt

Blume
Translated literally means "flower". As a description of German
wine it is positive and refers to the smell of a fresh, balanced and
stylish white wine, without any unpleasant overtones or excesses
in its make-up. Such a wine is said to have a "schöne (lovely)
Blume". A Riesling Kabinett from the Mosel, a year after the vintage, might be so described.

Bockenheim an der Weinstrasse Rhpf. w. (r.) ★★
Small town near the Rheinpfalz-Rheinhessen border, where Silvaner still predominates. Sound, quality wines.

Bocksbeutel
A green flagon-shaped bottle of ancient design used exclusively in
West Germany for the white and red quality wines of Franken and
certain areas of n. Baden.

Bockstein M-S-R w. ★★★
One of the best-known Einzellagen of the Bereich Saar-Ruwer at
OCKFEN, planted mainly with Riesling. Stylish wines with a lovely
fruity acidity. Grosslage: SCHARZBERG. Growers: Fischer, Geltz,
Reverchon, Rheinart, Schorlemer (Duhr), Trier Staatl. Weinbau-
domäne.

Bodengeschmack
"Taste of the soil". Certain v'yds and their soils transmit a flavour
to the grapes that are grown in them and the flavour is retained
when the MUST becomes wine. Exactly how this happens is not fully
understood. Among the wines with a sometimes pronounced
Bodengeschmack are Mosels (slate taste), Nahe wines from TRAI-
SEN and NORHEIM (rhyolite rock) and Franken wines from various
soils. In all three, the taste of the soil is regarded as a virtue. Bodengeschmack is also known as Bodenton.

Bodenheim Rhh. w. ★★
Small town on the RHEINFRONT producing excellent wine from red
soil. Some attractive old buildings, incl. the town hall and old wine
cellars. Grosslage: ST ALBAN.

Bodensee w. r. ★★
Alias Lake Constance. The v'yds lie within three regions: Baden,
Franken and Württemberg. The steep, high-lying sites are planted
with a number of vine varieties incl. Spätburgunder (frequently
made into WEISSHERBST) and Müller-Thurgau. The reflected light
and additional warmth from the lake help to compensate for a
climate of modest warmth in summer.

Bodenton
See Bodengeschmack

Böhlig Rhpf. w. ★★★
Einzellage of 9ha (22 acres) on mainly level land at WACHENHEIM
making splendid, meaty wines, full of strong regional flavour.
Grosslage: MARIENGARTEN. Growers incl. Bürklin-Wolf.

Boppard Mrh. w. ★→★★
Riverside town on the Rhein, a major anchorage for pleasure boats
and the site of a fine sweep of v'yds – the Bopparder Hamm. Its

steep Einzellagen, more than 90% Riesling, produce racy wines with a good earthy flavour, drunk mainly in the region.

Botrytis cinerea
See Edelfäule

Bottle
Flasche. The typical German wine bottle – ignoring the BOCKSBEUTEL of Franken – is tall, slim and elegant. Since the 18th century, amber-coloured bottles have been used for Rhein wine. Mosel wine has been sold in green bottles for rather longer. Today, clear glass is used increasingly for dry wines, although in the past clear glass in Germany was filled mainly with WEISSHERBST and Ruländer.

Bottle age
Wines with high acidity (e.g. Riesling) require more time in bottle to reach their peak of quality than do softer wines (e.g. Müller-Thurgau). In general, the better the quality the more bottle age is needed, as these very approx. figures for Riesling's development in bottle show. The first column represents the number of years after the vintage before the wine has reached its peak, the second column shows for how many years thereafter the wine will remain at its best.

QbA, Kabinett	1½	1½	Beerenauslese	7	7+
Spätlese	2	2	Eiswein	7	7+
Auslese	5	5	Trockenbeerenauslese	7	7+

These approx. timings can vary widely with different vintages and the conditions under which the wine is stored. Dry Rieslings up to and incl. SPÄTLESE take longer to reach their peak than those with usual amounts of residual sugar, but the sweetness in some wines will often hide the signs of incipient senility. In spite of these general comments, well-made, estate-bottled Rieslings of all qualities may give pleasure, and surprise by remaining fresh and attractive, for many more years than those suggested above.

Bottle sick
Immediately after bottling a wine will sometimes taste "tired" and not show at its best. This is said to be the result of the physical disturbance caused by the bottling operation. The malady normally disappears after a few weeks.

Bottling
See Abfüllung

Bowlen
Wine cups. Those sold commercially must be based at least 50% on wine. If the word"wine" appears in their description the proportion must reach a minimum of 70%. More interesting are the home-made Bowlen spiced with woodruff (Waldmeister) or those with fruits such as strawberries or peaches. Other ingredients are sugar, sometimes brandy, and usually sparkling wine added just before serving, well chilled. There are many variations on this theme.

Branded wine
See Markenwein

Brandig
"Burnt". Describes a wine with a high alcohol and a low acid content, and little sweetness. This characteristic was very common in wines of the 1959 vintage – a year of excessive heat and drought.

Bratenhöfchen M-S-R w. ★★★
Einzellage at BERNKASTEL producing excellent Riesling. Sometimes a little overshadowed by the more luscious wine of the adjacent GRABEN but nevertheless a top-quality site. Grosslage: BADSTUBE. Growers: Bergweiler-Prüm Erben, Deinhard Bernkastel, Kesselstatt, Lauerburg, Pauly, J. J. Prüm.

Braubach Mrh. w. ★→★★
Riverside town, claiming to date from the Stone Age and overlooked by one of Germany's most spectacular castles, the Marksburg. Sound Rieslings from the steepest of sites, not generally as distinguished as those from BACHARACH upstream.

Brauneberg M-S-R w. ★★★
Small village upstream from BERNKASTEL. High percentage of
Riesling and top-quality wines. Grosslage: KURFÜRSTLAY.
Braunfels M-S-R w. ★★★
Steep Einzellage on the Saar. Riesling and Müller-Thurgau pro-
duce good-quality wines. Grosslage: SCHARZBERG. Growers: Kessel-
statt, Koch, Müller-Scharzhof, Vereinigte Hospitien, Bernd van
Volxem, Otto van Volxem.
Breisach am Rhein Baden Pop. 9,300
Small town in s. Germany near the Bereich KAISERSTUHL-TUNIBERG,
known as the home of Europe's largest (110m. litre storage capa-
city) winery belonging to the ZENTRALKELLEREI BADISCHER WINZER-
GENOSSENSCHAFTEN eG (ZBW).
Brentano'sche Gutsverwaltung, Baron von Rhg.
Estate of 10ha (25 acres), family-owned since 1804. Holdings incl.
part of Winkeler HASENSPRUNG. Vines are 97% Riesling, 3% Spät-
burgunder. The estate has romantic associations: its wines were

RHEINGAU
1982er Winkeler Jesuitengarten Riesling
Kabinett

A. P. Nr. 27 017 005 83
Erzeuger-Abfüllung   0,75 L
Baron von Brentano'sche
Gutsverwaltung · Winkel im Rheingau
Qualitätswein mit Prädikat

enjoyed by Goethe, Beethoven, von Arnim and his circle, and the
attractive estate buildings incl. a Goethe museum. The wines are
typical of the region: fruity, fresh and elegant. Annual production
is approx. 5,800 cases, sold in Germany and abroad. Address: Am
Lindenplatz 2, 6227 Oestrich-Winkel.
Breuer, Weingut G. Rhg.
8ha (20 acre) estate dating from 1880 mainly on steep slopes, all
on RÜDESHEIM sites of which BERG SCHLOSSBERG is claimed to be the
best. The owners are partners in the wine-exporting house SCHOLL
AND HILLEBRAND GmbH. Annual production is approx. 4,600 cases
of steely, firm wines with good fruit, sold in Germany and abroad.
Address: 6220 Rüdesheim am Rhein.
Broker
In Germany there are 425 wine brokers (Kommissionäre) who act
as links between grower and buyer. Many broking firms are generations old and have a formidable knowledge of the v'yd area in
which they operate. They know what the growers have to offer,
and their experience of the needs of the wine merchants for whom
they work is the source of their success. At wine auctions in
Germany only brokers are allowed to bid and all sales at auctions
must, by law, be through them.
Brückes Nahe w. ★★★
Einzellage on mainly sloping land close to BAD KREUZNACH. Its
Riesling can produce top-quality, stylish wines in good years.
Grosslage: KRONENBERG. Growers: August E. Anheuser, Paul
Anheuser, Finkenauer, Plettenberg'sche Verwaltung, Schlink-
Herf-Gutleuthof.
Bruderschaft M-S-R w. ★★
Steep Einzellage of some 250ha (618 acres) at KLÜSSERATH, not far
from TRIER, with a high proportion of Riesling. Much good wine
is made but little that compares with the finest from villages such
as PIESPORT or BERNKASTEL. Grosslage: ST MICHAEL. Growers:
Friedrich-Wilhelm-Gymnasium, Reh (Marienhof).

Brut
The French word is also used in Germany to describe a sparkling wine with less than 15 g/l sugar, which will therefore taste dry or very dry depending on the balance of its other constituents. Only a small proportion of German sparkling wine is "Brut".

Brutsekt
Written as one word, Brutsekt is the term given to sparkling wine when it has passed through its second fermentation and has not yet had a final sweetening of beet sugar and wine.

Buhl, Weingut Reichsrat von Rhpf.
Great estate with exciting wines. The property was christened Weingut F. P. Buhl in 1849 but its origins, with family connections to the BASSERMANN-JORDAN estate, reach back into the 15th century. 97ha (240 acres) of v'yds cover parts of most of the best sites in FORST, DEIDESHEIM and RUPPERTSBERG, etc. Vines are 73% Riesling, 14% Müller-Thurgau, 4% Traminer, etc. The grapes are pressed in Forst and the wine is stored in the 2.5km (1½ miles) of cellars at Deidesheim. Annual prod. is approx. 80,000 cases of the full range of top-quality Rheinpfalz wines, sold throughout the world. Address: Weinstrasse 16, 6705 Deidesheim.

Bukett
The "smell" (or literally bouquet) of a wine.

Bukettsorten
Collective noun covering vines that produce wine with a powerful bouquet (BUKETT), e.g. Scheurebe, Morio-Muskat. The attraction for the consumer of a strongly scented wine is often as a brief change from the more neutral Riesling or Silvaner. Wines with an overpronounced smell can quickly cloy, so Bukettsorten will probably remain an interesting diversion rather than become a main part of German wine production.

Bullay M-S-R w. ★★
Typical Lower Mosel village near ZELL with a high proportion of Riesling on steep sites.

Bundesweinprämierung
National wine competition run by the DEUTSCHE LANDWIRTSCHAFT GESELLSCHAFT (DLG), open to QbA and QmP estate bottlings that have passed the regional wine competitions successfully. In 1983 the Bundesweinprämierung was open to wines of the 1979, '80 and '81 vintages. 3,980 wines were entered, representing more than 1m. cases. 1,095 received a Grosser Preis (First Prize), 1,778 a Silberner Preis (Second Prize) and 757 a Bronzener Preis (Third Prize). The winning of an award may be shown on the bottle by means of a strip label running between the neck and body labels, or by a small circular coin-sized label.

Burg
Castle or fortress. EEC law allows the word Burg to be used as part of a wine name if the wine is made solely from grapes grown and vinified by the Burg's estate. In practice, Burg usually appears on a label as part of a community name, e.g. BURG LAYEN.

Burg Layen Nahe w. ★→★★
Small village near DORSHEIM, just s. of BINGEN, probably best known as the home of the direct-selling wine merchants PIEROTH.

Burgberg Nahe w. ★★★
Small, steep Einzellage at DORSHEIM nr. BINGEN, producing well-balanced Rieslings. Grosslage: SCHLOSSKAPELLE. Grower: Nieder-hausen-Schlossböckelheim Staatl. Weinbaudomäne.

Burgeff & Co. GmbH Rhg.
One of the oldest sparking-wine producing companies in Germany, founded in 1836, now owned by Seagram. Leading brands: Burgeff Grün and Schloss Hochheim. Address: 6203 Hochheim/Main.

Bürgermeister
Mayor. In Rheinland-Pfalz the mayor of a community heads the committee that decides when the various stages of the harvest may start. Found in the titles of some estates, e.g. Weingut Bürgermeister Anton Balbach Erben.

Bürgerspital zum Heiligen Geist Franken
Great Würzburg estate, 4th largest in Germany, with 135ha (334

acres) of which 90ha (222 acres) are in production. Riesling, Silvaner and Müller-Thurgau (20% each) plus other varieties incl. Spätburgunder produce an average 66,600 cases annually. The estate is a charitable institution dating from 1319, supporting an old people's home. The romantic buildings incl. a wine bar with places for 500 guests. Most of the wines are "FRÄNKISCH TROCKEN", very dry with less than 4 g/l residual sugar. They are big wines, sold to the wine trade and to private customers in Germany and also abroad. Address: Theaterstr. 19, 8700 Würzburg.

Burgunder
See Frühburgunder, Grauburgunder, Spätburgunder

Burgweg Franken w. ★★
Small Grosslage in s. Franken that incl. the v'yds of IPHOFEN.

Burgweg Nahe w. ★→★★
Grosslage of about 900ha (2,224 acres) incl. top-quality sites such as Schlossböckelheimer KUPFERGRUBE and the 2ha (5 acre) Traisener BASTEI, as well as some very ordinary v'yds. The best sites are 100% Riesling but much Silvaner is also still found. The wine often has a strong flavour given to it by volcanic soil.

Burgweg Rhg. w. (r.) ★★
Grosslage of a little under 700ha (1,730 acres), split in two at the w. end of the Rheingau by the smaller STEIL Grosslage at ASSMANNSHAUSEN. Wines sold under the name Burgweg are not the cheapest – no Rheingau wine is. When made from Riesling they will be, in German terms, full-flavoured, and benefit from a year's bottle age or more, depending on the quality category (QbA, Kabinett, etc.).

Bürklin-Wolf, Weingut Dr Rhpf.
Great family estate, dating back in part to the 16th century. 100ha (247 acres) of top-quality sites at WACHENHEIM, FORST and RUPPERTSBERG. 73% Riesling, 15% Müller-Thurgau, etc., plus some Spätburgunder. Annual production is approx. 100,000 cases. Maturation in wood is still valued and the stylish, well-made wines reflect the care they receive in their vinification. Many trainee wine makers, from Germany and abroad, have studied on this estate, and its wines are found all over the world. Address: 6706 Wachenheim/Weinstrasse.

WEINGUT
Dr·Bürklin-Wolf
WACHENHEIM/WEINSTRASSE

1982er
Wachenheimer Gerümpel
Riesling Spätlese

Qualitätswein mit Prädikat A. P. Nr. 5 142 043 40 85

ERZEUGERABFÜLLUNG
0.75 l **RHEINPFALZ**

Cabinet
See Kabinett

Capsule
A tight-fitting cap enclosing the mouth and part of the neck of a bottle, originally intended to protect the cork. The main job of a capsule today is to complete the "dressing" of a bottle but some estates, notably SCHLOSS JOHANNISBERG and SCHLOSS VOLLRADS, use different coloured capsules to denote different qualities of wine. See LACK.

Carstens KG, Sektkellerei Rhpf.
Sparkling-wine manufacturers, est. in 1959 and wholly owned by HENKELL AND CO. of Wiesbaden. The brand "Carstens SC" is well known on the German market. Price (1984) about DM 6.50. Address. Maximilianstr. 18, 6730 Neustadt/Weinstrasse.

Case
Until the early 1960s German bottled wine was exported in wooden cases, each holding 12 bottles horizontally packed in straw. Today the most usual form of packing is the vertically loaded 12-bottle carton, in which the contents are stored neck downwards. In this book, the term "case" when used as a measure of quantity means 12 0.75-litre bottles, or 9 litres.

Castell'sches Domänenamt, Fürstlich Franken
Great estate dating back to 1258. The family of the owner, Fürst zu Castell-Castell, are bankers, farmers and foresters as well as vine growers. 41ha (102 acres) of v'yds: 35% Müller-Thurgau, 23% Silvaner, 7% Rieslaner – the last is a speciality. The wines can be described as earthy and spicy, with good acidity. Annual prod. is approx. 33,000 cases, sold in Germany and, increasingly, abroad. The estate is also senior partner in a wine-growers' cooperative, taking in and making wine from its members' 61ha (150 acres), greatly increasing the throughput of its own impressive cellar. Address: 8711 Castell/Unterfranken.

Chaptalization
The addition of sugar to MUST or wine (see ANREICHERUNG). A practice developed by Jean Antoine Chaptal (1756-1852) in France.

Charmat-Verfahren
A technique for producing sparkling wine, developed in the 19th century by the French scientist Eugene Charmat. The secondary, sparkle-producing fermentation takes place in bulk instead of in bottle. Today more than 90% of German-made sparkling wine is tank fermented. (See also FLASCHENGÄRUNG.)

Christoffel Jr, Jos. M-S-R
Small family estate that makes award-winning wines from top-quality sites at ERDEN (TREPPCHEN), ÜRZIG (WÜRZGARTEN), WEHLEN (SONNENUHR) and GRAACH (DOMPROBST, HIMMELREICH). 100% Riesling. Christoffels have been vine-growing for more than 300 years; they also own the Christoffel-Prüm estate at GRAACH and WEHLEN. Total annual production is approx. 3,700 cases, sold in Germany and abroad. Address: Moselufer 1-3, 5564 Ürzig/Mosel.

Clevner
See Frühburgunder, Traminer

Coblenz
See Koblenz

Cochem M-S-R Pop. 6,000 w. ★★
Strikingly pretty town and tourist centre on the Rhein, in the Bereich ZELL, overlooked by a dramatically situated castle. Stylish, racy Rieslings.

Constance
See Bodensee

Cooperative cellar
See Winzergenossenschaft

Crusius, Weingut Hans Nahe
Family-run estate with 12ha (30 acres) of prime sites incl. Traiser BASTEI and ROTENFELS, Norheimer Klosterberg, Schlossböckelheimer FELSENBERG. 70% Riesling, 15% Müller-Thurgau, 7.5%

Kerner, etc. Stylish wines, traditionally matured in cask, made under personal family supervision to a high standard. Peter Crusius is a recognized expert on the relationship of quantity to quality in vine-growing. 10,000 cases, sold in Germany and abroad. Address: Hauptstr. 2, 6551 Traisen.

Cuvée

EEC law defines a cuvée as the MUST or wine, or a blend of different musts or wines, destined to be converted into sparkling wine. The making of a cuvée requires organized tasting ability of a very high order. It is exacting work from which the palate can gain little pleasure. The satisfaction lies in the consistency of the end result.

Dahlem Erben, Weingutsverwaltung Sanitätsrat Dr. Dahlem Rhh.

Estate with origins going back to 1702 and holdings in 27ha (67 acres) at OPPENHEIM (incl. SACKTRÄGER), DIENHEIM and GUNTERS-BLUM, 30% Riesling, 25% Silvaner, 23% Müller-Thurgau. Award-winning wines and a considerable choice of vintages, for sale mainly to private customers. Address: Wormserstr. 50, Oppenheim am Rhein.

Daubhaus Rhg. w. ★★

Grosslage covering more than 300ha (741 acres) at the e. end of the Rheingau on the R. Main, often clearly visible when flying into Frankfurt Airport. Its best-known wine-producing village is HOCH-HEIM. A Rheingau Grosslage wine will be a paler reflection of the best wines produced from individual sites within the Grosslage. Nevertheless, the quality of wine from the Daubhaus is high, although it will be more earthy than wine from the central part of the region.

Dautenpflänzer Nahe w. ★★★

6ha (15 acre) Einzellage of the Lower Nahe near BINGEN. The wines are full-bodied, meaty and mainly Riesling. Grosslage: SCHLOSS-KAPELLE. Grower: Niederhausen-Schlossböckelheim Staatl. Wein-baudomäne.

Deacidification

A relatively high acid content is expected and appreciated in German wine. However, in some years when the grapes are not fully ripe the acidity is too high and has to be lowered artificially. When this happens the natural reduction in acidity that occurs in wine-making is complemented by a chemical deacidification with calcium carbonate, or in years of feeble sunshine when the malic acid is particularly high with a double-salt called Acidex. The last nationwide poor vintage was 1972, and even in this year many enjoyable wines were produced with the aid of Acidex. At present, investigations are being made into yeasts that will noticeably reduce the malic acid content during fermentation, but final results are not yet published.

Deckrotwein

Much German red wine is rather pale in colour. Until the end of June 1984 deep-coloured wine from other countries (mainly Spain) could be added to red DEUTSCHER TAFELWEIN (up to 13% of the total) and red QbA (up to 9% of the total) but not to QmP. Attempts are being made to develop new vine varieties in Germany that will produce the necessary colour to darken such traditional wines as Trollinger and Portugieser. (See also FÄRBERTRAUBEN.)

Deidesheim Rhpf. w. ★★ → ★★★★

Attractive small town, recognized for centuries both in Germany and abroad as a source of distinguished wine and the home of a number of fine estates. A high proportion of Riesling in top-quality sites: GRAINHÜBEL, LEINHÖHLE, HERRGOTTSACKER, KIESELBERG, LANG-ENMORGEN. Two Grosslagen: MARIENGARTEN and SCHNEPFENFLUG AN DER WEINSTRASSE.

Deidesheim eG, Winzerverein Rhpf.

Cooperative with 428 members in the well-known wine villages DEIDESHEIM, FORST, RUPPERTSBERG, WACHENHEIM, etc., with 220ha (544 acres). Vines are 70% Riesling, 15% Müller-Thurgau. The wines are sold only in Germany. Address: 6705 Deidesheim/Wein-strasse.

Deinhard & Co. KGaA

Important firm of wine merchants and exporters, founded in the 18th century. Deinhard was one of the earliest producers of sparkling wine in Germany, and at the end of the 19th century acquired its first v'yds. Today the holdings in OESTRICH, DEIDESHEIM and BERNKASTEL make it one of the largest privately owned producers of fine estate-bottled wines. Best-known brands of sparkling wine are the Riesling-based Lila Imperial, and Deinhard Cabinet, selling on the German market for approx. DM 14 and DM 7 respectively. Address: Deinhard Platz 3, 5400 Koblenz.

Deinhard, Weingut Dr Rhpf.

Estate dating from the mid-18th century, separate from but occupying the same premises as the Gutsverwaltung DEINHARD DEIDESHEIM. 40ha (99 acres) in DEIDESHEIM (LEINHÖHLE, GRAINHÜBEL, KIESELBERG, etc.), FORST, RUPPERTSBERG (REITERPFAD, etc.). Vines are 70% Riesling, with small amounts of Müller-Thurgau, Scheurebe, Kerner, Ehrenfelser and others. The wines reflect clearly the variations brought about by site, soil and vine variety. 31,500 cases, sold mainly in Germany. Address: Weinstrasse 10, 6705 Deidesheim.

Deinhard Bernkastel, Gutsverwaltung M-S-R

Estate of 27ha (67 acres), dating from 1900 and owned by DEINHARD & CO. in Koblenz, with holdings in KASEL, GRAACH, WEHLEN (SONNENUHR), BERNKASTEL (DOCTOR, GRABEN), etc. Vines are 88% Riesling, grown mainly on steep or very steep (more than 60% incline) sites. The grapes are pressed in Bernkastel-Kues and the MUST is vinified in Koblenz. The aim is fresh, balanced wines, true to the vine variety, with restrained

amounts of residual sugar. Deinhard has an important holding in the Doctor, probably the finest site on the Mosel. Approx. annual production is 21,200 cases, 60% exported. Address: Martertal 2, 5550 Bernkastel-Kues.

Deinhard Deidesheim, Gutsverwaltung Rhpf.

Estate acquired by DEINHARD & CO., Koblenz, in 1973, with 18.7ha (46 acres) in FORST (UNGEHEUER), DEIDESHEIM (HERRGOTTSACKER) and RUPPERTSBERG (LINSENBUSCH). Vines are 56% Riesling, 26% Müller-Thurgau. Approx. annual production is 14,000 cases. The wines, winners of many competitions, are sold all over the world and reflect the Riesling virtues of freshness, good acidity and the ability to last in bottle. Address: Weinstrasse 10, 6705 Deidesheim.

Deinhard Oestrich, Gutsverwaltung Rhg.

See Wegeler Erben

Dellchen Nahe w. ★★★

Steep, 7.3ha (18 acre) Einzellage at NORHEIM that can produce absolutely top-quality Riesling wines of character with an attractive flavour that comes from the soil. Grosslage: BURGWEG. Growers: August Anheuser, Paul Anheuser, Bad Kreuznach Staatsweingut.

Dernau Ahr w. (r.) ★→★★

Small village of half-timbered houses, making Riesling, Müller-Thurgau and light Spätburgunder from steep v'yds.

Deutelsberg Rhg. w. ★★

Grosslage of some 500ha (1,236 acres) in the neighbourhood of HATTENHEIM, incl. Mariannenau Island (see RHEINHELL) and the famous v'yds of ERBACH. The name Deutelsberg is normally used for the lesser wines, but Rieslings from competent producers will still be well-balanced, stylish, good-quality wines.

Deutsche Landwirtschaft Gesellschaft (DLG)

Society founded in 1885, along the lines of the Royal Agricultural Society of Great Britain, to promote good farming practices. Today the society awards three types of Deutsches Weinsiegel (wine seal): a yellow seal for dry wines, a green for medium-dry, and a red for others that meet with its approval. (The standards set by the DLG tasting panels are higher than those of the AMTLICHE PRUFÜNG authorities.) The DLG also holds an annual national wine competition, open to quality (QbA and QmP) wines that have obtained their A.P. number and have succeeded in an official regional competition. DLG awards are familiar to German consumers and valued by many bottlers.

Deutscher Tafelwein (DTW)
German table wine. Quality category of German wine, below QbA, with an upper section called LANDWEIN. The v'yd area from which a DTW may originate is exactly the same as that which can produce quality wine. There are no areas that can produce table wine only. Whereas a high proportion of French and Italian wine is classified as "table wine", only approx. 5% of the total German wine harvest falls into this category. A DTW does not undergo an examination by the A.P. authorities and therefore does not show an A.P. number on the label. It must be made 100% from German-grown grapes.

Deutsche Weinstrasse
See Weinstrasse

Deutscher Sekt
Quality sparkling wine in which the second fermentation has taken place in Germany. A somewhat controversial definition, for many vine growers maintain that Deutscher Sekt should be made from Deutscher Wein. On the other hand, the view of many sparkling-wine producers is that German wine suitable for conversion into sparkling wine varies too much in price, style and availability to provide continuity of supply.

Deutsches Weinsiegel
See Deutsche Landwirtschaft Gesellschaft (DLG)

Deutsches Weintor, Gebiets-Winzergenossenschaft eG Rhpf.
Huge, expanding cooperative cellar nr. the French border, with some 1,300 members delivering grapes from 960ha (2,372 acres) of the Bereich SÜDLICHE WEINSTRASSE. Storage capacity is 30m. litres (more than 3.5m. cases) and the cellar is well equipped to produce vast quantities of well-made, agreeable, inexpensive wines from many grape varieties, sold mainly but not exclusively in Germany. Address: 6741 Ilbesheim/Südliche Weinstrasse.

Deutz & Geldermann Sektkellerei, Breisach GmbH Baden
Founded in 1838 as producers of Champagne, started sparkling-wine production in Alsace in 1904 and in BREISACH in 1925. The technique used is secondary fermentation in bottle (FLASCHENGÄR-UNG). Deutz & Geldermann Brut at approx. DM17 on the German market is a particularly distinguished wine that retains its sparkle well when opened. Address: 7814 Breisach/Baden.

Dexheim Rhh. w. ★
Village in the Grosslage GUTES DOMTAL which probably benefits from having one large Einzellage called "Doktor", a name (but not the spelling) it shares with the famous DOCTOR at Bernkastel on the Mosel.

Dhron M-S-R w. ★★★
Village linked with NEUMAGEN to form one community of some 2,500 inhabitants nr. PIESPORT, with whom it shares some of its sites. The steep v'yds are planted mainly with Riesling, producing full-flavoured, stylish wines. Grosslage: MICHELSBERG.

Diabetikerwein
Diabetes is such a common complaint in Germany that it has proved profitable to produce diabetic wines on a wide scale. They should be drunk by genuine diabetics, only after medical approval is given. German diabetic wine is subject to a number of restrictions and may contain a maximum of 4 g/l residual sugar, 25 mg/l free sulphur dioxide and 12% alcohol. Since 1970 the DLG has awarded a yellow seal to diabetic wines that meet its standards.

Diefenhardt'sches Weingut Rhg.
Estate dating from 1917, but with a 300-year-old cask cellar. 12.20ha (30 acres) in ELTVILLE, MARTINSTHAL and RAUENTHAL. 85% Riesling, 10% Spätburgunder and – surprisingly – 1.5% Traminer. Typical Rheingauer wine, with the Spätburgunder much in demand. Approximate annual production is 8,300 cases, sold mainly in Germany but also abroad. Address: Hauptstr. 9-11, 6229 Martinsthal.

Diel auf Burg Layen, Schlossgut Nahe
Estate owned by the Diel family since 1806 with 19ha (47 acres)
in BURG LAYEN, DORSHEIM and MÜNSTER-SARMSHEIM. Vines are 40%
Riesling, 20% Kerner, plus many new crossings. A rosé made from
Rotberger, a Riesling × Trollinger crossing of which there are
only 17ha (42 acres) in Germany, is usually sold out before the har-
vest. Sales are mainly to private customers. Address: 6531 bei
Bingen/Rhein.

DLG
See Deutsche Landwirtschaft Gesellschaft

Doctor M-S-R w. ★★★★
Small but outstanding Einzellage above BERNKASTEL. Site, soil and
Riesling vine complement each other perfectly. The MUST weights
are usually the heaviest in Bernkastel; the wine is positive, slaty,
needing time to show its true quality. One of the best-known Einzellagen in Germany. Grosslage: BADSTUBE. Growers: Deinhard
Bernkastel, Lauerburg, Thanisch.

Doktor Rhh. w. ★
Einzellage at DEXHEIM in the Grosslage GUTES DOMTAL.

Domäne
Domain. Name given to estates (Weingüter) owned by old noble
families (e.g. Domänenweingut Schloss Schönborn) or by the
Federal States (e.g. Staatliche Weinbaudomäne Niederhausen-
Schlossböckelheim). Many of the state-owned Domäne have a
training and experimental role as well as operating commercially
as wine makers. They have the advantage over privately owned
estates of state support as well as ownership, and many of them
are superbly equipped.

Domänenamt
Estate office. Found in the title of Fürstlich Castell'sches Domänenamt.

Domblick Rhh. w. ★
Grosslage of more than 800ha (1,977 acres) in s. Rheinhessen, bor-
dering on the Rheinpfalz. V'yds vary from level to steep and face
all points of the compass except e. The wines can have a rather
strong flavour that comes from the mainly clay soil. On a clear day,
from the upper parts of the area, one has a view (Blick) of the cathedral (Dom) of Worms in the distance – hence Domblick.

Domdechaney Rhg. w. ★★★
Einzellage at HOCHHEIM on the R. Main producing full-bodied
Riesling wines with a big flavour. Grosslage: DAUBHAUS. Growers:
Aschrott'sche Erben, Eltville Staatsweingut, Frankfurt am Main
Stadt Weingut, Schloss Schönborn, Werner'sches Weingut.

Domherr Rhh. w. ★
Grosslage in central Rheinhessen covering more than 1,700ha
(4,200 acres). The terrain is mostly sloping or steep, producing
good-quality but usually not the finest wine, displaying the traditional Rheinhessen characteristics: soft, agreeable, pleasant fruity
flavour. The cathedral (Dom) at nearby MAINZ used to own much
land in the area, hence the origin of the name Domherr (Canon
of the Cathedral).

Domprobst M-S-R w. ★★★
Distinguished Einzellage at GRAACH, 100% steep and exclusively
Riesling. The wine is usually crisper than that from the neighbour-
ing Graacher HIMMELREICH and less full-bodied. Grosslage: MÜNZ-
LAY. Growers: "Abteihof", Christoffel, Deinhard Bernkastel,
Friedrich-Wilhelm-Gymnasium, Kies-Kieren, Licht-Bergweiler,
Pauly, J. J. Prüm, S. A. Prüm, Schorlemer, Selbach-Oster, Stephen
Studert-Prüm.

Domthal Rhh.
Once a GATTUNGSLAGENAME, discarded in 1971. See also GUTES
DOMTAL.

Doosberg Rhg. w. ★★★
Large Einzellage of 153ha (378 acres) on mainly level land at OES-
TRICH that makes top-quality, classic Riesling wines. Grosslage:
GOTTESTHAL. Growers: Altenkirch, Eser, Ress, Schloss Schönborn,
Vereinigte Weingutsbesitzer Hallgarten, Wegeler/Deinhard.

Dornfelder

Red grape variety, Helfensteiner (Frühburgunder × Trollinger) × Heroldrebe (Portugieser × Limberger); a new crossing from the Württemberg state viticultural institute at Weinsberg. It ripens earlier than Trollinger and produces a large yield per vine of deep-coloured wine. From an experimental 12ha (27 acres) in 1976, Dornfelder now covers 328ha (810 acres), mainly in the Rheinpfalz and Rheinhessen.

Dorsheim Nahe w. ★★→★★★

One of the best wine-producing villages of the Lower Nahe, nr. BINGEN in the Bereich KREUZNACH. Outstanding meaty Rieslings from steep sites, usually cheaper than the top-quality wines of the Bereich SCHLOSS BÖCKELHEIM further south. Grosslage: SCHLOSS-KAPELLE.

Drathen KG, Ewald Theod M-S-R

Small estate of 6.2ha (15 acres). Also internationally known as wine merchants exporting considerable quantities of inexpensive German wine and EEC table wines. Founded in 1860, the estate holdings are at NEEF, ALF and BULLAY, producing approx. 6,500 cases annually for sale in Germany and abroad. Address: Auf der Hill, 5584 Alf/Mosel.

Dreikönigswein

Three Kings Wine. A description that until 1971 could be given to EISWEIN gathered on 6 January following the main October/November harvest. The word Dreikönigswein may no longer appear on the bottle label, although reference to it may be made in advertising material. In practice, it is a rather charming description that now belongs to the past.

Dry

See Trocken

DTW

See Deutscher Tafelwein

Duftig

Finely scented.

Duhr Nachf., Weingut Franz M-S-R

Estate owned by Hermann Freiherr v. SCHORLEMER GmbH.

Durbach Baden w. ★★→★★★

Attractive village nr. Offenburg, overlooked by steep v'yds. Claims the highest proportion of Traminer (Clevner) of any wine village in Germany and well known for its Riesling (Klingelberger). Produces powerful QbA incl. very successful Halbtrocken (medium-dry) wines.

Durchgegoren

Fermented through. A term used to describe wines in which no fermentable sugar remains. Today most German wines up to and sometimes incl. Auslesen are stored in bulk "durchgegoren", thus avoiding the risk of further fermentation and making it possible to keep the sulphur dioxide content low. Such wines will usually be sweetened with SÜSSRESERVE shortly before bottling.

Edelfäule

"Noble rot": a fungus that in moist and mild conditions sometimes attacks grapes. If the grapes are already ripe the result is beneficial. The grapes shrivel and the water, sugar and acid content is reduced, but the loss of acids is proportionately greater than that of sugar. The result is highly concentrated juice.

Wine made from such grapes will normally have an enhanced MUST weight. In white wine the colour will be deeper and more golden than usual; in red wine there is a browning and loss of colour. The bouquet of the grape variety is to a greater or lesser extent replaced by an aroma reminiscent of honey. The impression of sweetness of flavour is increased, the wine tastes smoother and sometimes also a little honeyed. A Riesling BEERENAUSLESE will nearly always be made from Edelfäule grapes.

1953, '67 and '75 were years in which a considerable amount of Edelfäule occurred. In hot, dry years such as 1959 or '76 the high general level of ripeness partly compensates for a limited amount of Edelfäule.

Edelsüss
Noble sweetness. Term for the sweetness left in a wine of high quality as a result of incomplete fermentation, as is the case with Auslesen, Beerenauslesen or Trockenbeerenauslesen. It is often the result of grapes being attacked by EDELFÄULE ("noble rot") and will contain enhanced amounts of fructose and glycerin. Auslesen to which SÜSSRESERVE has been added should not be described as Edelsüss.

Edenkoben Rhpf. Pop. 5,500 w. ★→★★
Small but locally important wine town in the Bereich SÜDLICHE WEINSTRASSE. More than 500ha (1,236 acres) of v'yds, sprinkled with fig and almond trees, are planted with a wide range of varieties incl. Riesling, Müller-Thurgau and Silvaner. Good, sound, inexpensive wines.

Ediger-Eller M-S-R w. ★★
Two ancient and attractive villages linked in the Bereich ZELL, making elegant, fruity wines.

Ehrenfelser
White grape variety, a crossing of Riesling × Silvaner, from the viticultural institute at Geisenheim. Dating from 1929, it is today planted in 526ha (1,300 acres). Recommended for good sites that do not quite reach the standards required by Riesling. The yield is greater, the MUST weight 5-10° Oechsle heavier than that of Riesling and the acidity slightly lower. The grapes can be harvested late in the season to produce SPÄTLESE and even higher qualities of elegant, fruity wine that will improve in bottle but develop more quickly than Riesling.

Ehrentrudis Spätburgunder Weissherbst
A WEISSHERBST QbA or QmP produced in the Bereich KAISERSTUHL-TUNIBERG in s. Baden, made exclusively from Spätburgunder.

Ehses-Berres, Weingut Geschwister M-S-R
Very small 0.8ha (2 acre) estate owned by Herr Günther Reh of Weingut Reichsgraf von KESSELSTATT, who make the wine. 100% Riesling holdings in Zeltinger SONNENUHR and SCHLOSSBERG produce 650 cases annually, sold in Germany and the USA. Address: Zeltingen-Rachtig/Mosel.

Ehses-Geller-Erben, Weingut M-S-R
Small estate, 2.1ha (5 acres), with an hotel dating from 1880. Holdings are all at ZELTINGEN (SONNENUHR, SCHLOSSBERG, HIMMELREICH, etc.). Vines are 60% Riesling, 30% Müller-Thurgau. Sales in bottle and in bulk to the wine trade. Address: St Stephanstr. 18, 5553 Zeltingen-Rachtig.

Eigeneswachstum
Own growth. Term used before 1971 to describe wines to which no sugar had been added and which were bottled by the grower. Synonyms were Eigenbau, Eigengewächs and Originalabfüllung.

Eitelsbach M-S-R w. ★★★
Small village, overlooked by its v'yds, nr. the point where the little R. Ruwer decants into the Mosel. Forms part of the city of TRIER. Exceptionally racy and stylish wines in good years, great wines in the best years, mainly Riesling. Grosslage: RÖMERLAY.

Einzellage
An individual site, the smallest geographical unit in which vines are planted. Only quality (QbA and QmP) wines may carry an Einzellage name.

Eisheiligen
Ice Saints. The commemoration days of the "Ice Saints" fall between 11-14 May. The saints incl. St Pancras, the patron saint of children, and St Boniface, an English missionary who worked in Germany and founded the Abbey of Fulda that later (in 1775) was said to have been connected with the discovery in the Rheingau of the benefits of late-harvesting grapes. After 15 May, known as the Kalte Sophie, there is virtually no further risk of frost in the v'yds.

Eiswein
Ice Wine. Quality category for wines made from grapes naturally frozen at the time of pressing. The water in the grapes remains in

the press in the form of ice crysals, concentrating the grape acids and sugar wonderfully. The MUST weight, measured in degrees Oechsle, has to reach BEERENAUSLESE level. As the necessary cold weather (approx. $-8°C$) seldom occurs before the third week in November, the risk of failure is serious (in the 1979 vintage, some Rheingau estates did not gather the Eiswein crop until 13 January 1980!). Although Eiswein must be made from ripe grapes, it can be produced in less good years when Beeren- and Trockenbeeren-auslesen are out of the question, hence its commercial interest for the grower. An Eiswein lacks the honeyed tones of a Beerenauslese, but its remarkable acidity and great residual sweetness gives it a "zip" and nervosity quite different to the more solid flavour of normally harvested top-quality sweet wines.

Elbling
One of the oldest white grape varieties growing in Germany, now restricted almost entirely to the M-S-R where it occupies 1,054ha (2,605 acres). Until World War II it was still found in Franken and as a mixed plantation with other vine varieties on the Rhein. On the Mosel above TRIER it produces a high yield (sometimes in excess of 200 hl/ha) of acidic wine, light in body and with a neutral flavour, often converted into sparkling wine.

Elegant
A rather subjective wine description which must be the result of personal judgement rather than of chemical analysis. It may usually be correctly applied to a wine in which the bouquet and flavour are perfectly balanced and no one characteristic is too pre-dominant. Normally, light wines with good acidity around which the other constituents are mustered achieve elegance more easily than heavy, alcoholic wines. In German wine, elegance is found particularly in Rieslings from the M-S-R, Nahe and Rheingau, esp. those of KABINETT quality. Such wines are the equivalent of a good 5th-growth Médoc from Bordeaux. Bigger SPÄTLESE wines can also have tremendous style but their power and weight seem to make the description elegant less appropriate.

Eltville Rhg. Pop. 15,800 w. ★★★
Important wine town, home of the Hessen State Wine Cellars (see next entry) and the Sekt producers Matheus MÜLLER. Good-quality Rieslings, similarly priced to those from other leading Rheingau communities. Grosslagen: HEILIGENSTOCK and STEINMÄCHER.

Eltville, Verwaltung der Staatsweingüter Rhg.
Collection of fine, state-owned holdings covering 160ha (395 acres) in the Rheingau and 36ha (89 acres) in the Hessische Bergstrasse (see Bergstrasse, Staatsweingut). V'yds in many famous sites incl. Rüdesheimer BERG ROSENECK, BERG ROTTLAND, BERG SCHLOSSBERG; Erbacher MARCOBRUNN; Rauenthaler BAIKEN; Hochheimer DOMDE-CHANEY and KIRCHENSTÜCK. Sole owners of the STEINBERG v'yd. 75% Riesling, 10% Spätburgunder, 8% Müller-Thurgau. The variety of holdings indicates a wide range of styles but the goal is to produce wines with backbone, elegance and body. The whole enterprise is under the direction of Dr Hans Ambrosi, leading writer on German wine. Total annual prod. is 100,000 cases, 30% exported. Address: Schwalbacherstr. 56-62, 6228 Eltville.

Engelmann, Weingut Karl Fr. Rhg.
Small family-owned estate dating from 1755 with v'yds in HALL-GARTEN and HATTENHEIM. 85% Riesling. The wines are spicy, fruity, elegant, matured in wood in the old vaulted cellar. 3,300 cases a year, sold in Germany and abroad. Address: Hallgartener Platz 2, 6227 Oestrich-Winkel.

"Engländer"
See Vereinigte Weingutsbesitzer Hallgarten eG

Enkirch M-S-R w. ★★
Village of half-timbered houses and old cellars and, unusually, two parish churches (Protestant and Roman Catholic). The reputation of Enkircher Riesling stands high in Germany but it is not often found abroad. Grosslage: SCHWARZLAY.

Enrichment
See Anreicherung

Erbach Rhg. w. ★★★→★★★★
Small village, home of the SCHLOSS REINHARTSHAUSEN estate, with its gaily painted hotel, and the Einzellage MARCOBRUNN. Its Riesling is among the most full-bodied – and expensive – in the region. Grosslage: DEUTELSBERG.

Erben
Successors. Placed after the name of a company and forming part of the title, e.g. Weingut Bürgermeister Carl Koch Erben. It is similar to the English "& Sons".

Erden M-S-R w. ★→★★★★
Small MITTELMOSEL village, whose PRÄLAT Einzellage is considered one of the best on the river. A high standard of Riesling wine is maintained on other sites. Grosslage: SCHWARZLAY.

Ernte
See Harvest

Erntebringer Rhg. w. ★★
Most widely known Grosslage in the Rheingau, covering more than 300ha (741 acres) in the neighbourhood of JOHANNISBERG, GEISENHEIM and WINKEL. Wines sold as Erntebringer are often slightly lighter in flavour than the most positive wines from individual sites. They have charm and are easy to enjoy, but possibly lack the distinction of the finest Rheingaus.

Erzeugerabfüllung
Estate or producer bottled. A term that appears on labels and in wine lists to indicate that a wine was made and bottled by the grower of the grapes. Cooperative cellars that buy their grapes from their members but have no direct control over the viticulture are also legally entitled to sell their wine as estate bottled. This they do, even for the cheapest QbA, under the names of some of the biggest Bereiche and Grosslagen in Germany. A top-quality producer will usually sell only his QmP and better QbA with the description Erzeugerabfüllung.

Erzeugergemeinschaft
Producers' Association. The formation of such associations became possible for farmers and vine growers when the German Market Structure Law came into force in 1969. As far as viticulture is concerned, they are associations of vine growers who have combined to link their production to the needs of the market. A further aim is to act as marketing groups capable of doing business with large buying organizations on equal terms. Even an estate as famous as the Fürstlich Castell'sche Domänenant in Franken heads a local Erzeugergemeinschaft. More are constantly being formed, and the names of Erzeugergemeinschaften are beginning to appear on wine labels as estate bottlers.

Escherndorf Franken w. ★★→★★★
Charming rustic village lying at the foot of its steep, modernized v'yds, planted mainly with Silvaner and Müller-Thurgau. Powerful wines with lasting flavour.

Eser, Weingut August Rhg.
Family-owned estate with holdings in OESTRICH, HATTENHEIM, WINKEL. etc. Vines are 90% Riesling, 6% Ehrenfelser. A high proportion of dry and medium-dry wines. Each QmP wine is sold with an analysis and a detailed history. No exports. Address: Friedensplatz 19, 6227 Oestrich-Winkel.

Espenscheid, Weingut
See Frankensteiner Hof

Estate bottled
See Erzeugerabfüllung, Erzeugergemeinschaft and Winzergenossenschaft

Etikett
Label.

Ewig Leben Franken w. ★★
Grosslage at RANDERSACKER, nr. WÜRZBURG, covering four sites incl. TEUFELSKELLER. Mainly Silvaner and Müller-Thurgau.

Extract
Term used to describe the non-volatile substances in wine, incl. sugar, glycerin, acids, minerals and tannin. A wine with low extract

will usually be described as hollow and/or short, but a wine high in extract will be full and its flavour will last in the mouth. In theory it might seem that to obtain a scientific, objective judgment of a wine it would only be necessary to determine the extract content. In practice this is not so, and there are many exceptions to the rule that top-quality wines contain more extract than those of lesser quality.

Faber

White grape variety, a crossing of Weissburgunder × Müller-Thurgau from the viticultural institute at ALZEY in the Rheinhessen, created by Dr Georg Scheu (best known for the Scheurebe). It produces a higher MUST weight than Müller-Thurgau with more acidity. Although the grapes ripen very early they can be left on the vine to produce stylish SPÄTLESE wine, before the Silvaner harvest has started. 2,197ha (5,429 acres), 75% in the Rheinhessen, with smaller plantings in the Nahe and Rheinpfalz.

Faber Sektkellerei KG

Founded in 1952, Faber produces approx. 47m. bottles of sparkling wine per year. The best-known brand, Faber Krönung, at about DM 4, is one of the cheapest sparkling wines on the German market. Address: Niederkircherstr. 27, 5500 Trier.

Falkenstein M-S-R W. ★★

Part of the town of KONZ, nr. the confluence of the Saar and Mosel. Fruity, stylish Rieslings. Grosslage: SCHARZBERG.

Färbertrauben

Literally, colouring grapes: grapes for improving the colour of red wine. As dark imported wine may no longer be blended with red German wine (see DECKROTWEIN), interest is being shown in Färbertrauben in which the juice as well as the skin of the grapes is coloured. The MUST from these grapes can be made into SÜSS-RESERVE to help both darken and sweeten otherwise pale, rosé-like "red" wine to the German taste. The most promising of such new vines is probably the Geisenheim-bred, early-ripening Dunkelfelder, planted in 25ha (62 acres), mainly in the Rheinpfalz and Rheinhessen.

Fass

Wooden cask. In Germany, wooden storage casks have, to a great extent, been replaced by vats of stainless steel or other man-made materials. These are more easily maintained and function rather like large bottles, keeping the wine fresh and free from oxidation. Traditionally, Rhein wine used to be sold in Halbstücke (casks) of approx. 610 litres and Mosel wine in the slightly smaller but longer Halbfuder. Today bulk wine is transported in large containers, similar to those used for milk. Sales of Fassweine are declining but remain considerable within Germany. Of the 29,001 growers who make wine, 76% sell in Fass to the wine trade, which relies on such producers for their commercial blends. Few wines sold in this way, however, have ever known the feel of wood, and the term "Fasswein Geschäft" (cask trade) is, strictly speaking, obsolete.

Fassgeschmack

Cask taste, of which there are two entirely different sorts: the flavour that wine can pick up from tannin in the wood of a new cask (much sought-after in Bordeaux but regarded as detrimental in German wine), and the dirty flavour that can appear in wine that has been stored in a poorly maintained cask where mould has developed. A wine from the latter sort of cask can easily be incorrectly thought to be "corked".

Fasswein, Fasswein Geschäft

See Fass

Federweisser

Partially fermented, still very sweet, cloudy young wine, served in wine bars during the harvest and in large helpings to the grape gatherers. It should be treated with caution as its pleasant sweetness and bubbly nature conceal volatile acids, esters, aldehydes and nasty things from the v'yd that can lead to interrupted sleep, heart problems, diarrhoea and skin complaints – according to the medical profession.

Feine, Feinste
Comparative terms meaning fine and finest, used before 1971 to describe superior qualities of SPÄTLESE, AUSLESE and BEERENAUSLESE wines, e.g. feinste Spätlese.

Felsenberg Nahe w. ★★★
Mainly steep Einzellage at SCHLOSSBÖCKELHEIM in the Nahe valley. Its Rieslings are attractive, a little earthy, and can be of top quality in a good year. Grosslage: BURGWEG. Growers: Paul Anheuser, Crusius, Niederhausen-Schlossböckelheim Staatl. Weinbaudomäne, Plettenberg'sche Verwaltung.

Feuerberg Rhpf. w. (r.) ★★
Grosslage of just under 1,000ha (2,471 acres) nr. the town of BAD DÜRKHEIM. Its best-known v'yd is the Kallstadter ANNABERG, but the whole district has a high reputation for its white wine. Red wine is also produced from Portugieser and much is sold under the Grosslage name.

Findling Rhh. w. ★★★
Top-quality Einzellage at NIERSTEIN producing a fine range of wines with considerable elegance. Grosslage: SPIEGELBERG. Growers: Baumann, Guntrum, Heyl zu Herrnsheim, Kurfürstenhof, Georg Schneider, Schuch, Sittmann, Strub, Wehrheim

Finkenauer, Weingut Carl Nahe
Family-owned estate dating from 1828 with 29ha (72 acres), mainly in BAD KREUZNACH (incl. holdings in BRÜCKES and NARRENKAPPE). Also in SCHLOSSBÖCKELHEIM, Winzenheim, etc. 46% Riesling, 16% Müller-Thurgau, 10% Silvaner, plus other varieties incl. some Spätburgunder. Wines show clearly the characteristics of the grape variety. Dry wines are produced to AUSLESE level. Sales mainly in Germany. Address: Salinenstr. 60, 6550 Bad Kreuznach.

Firn
Term used to describe the effect of considerable age on wine, incl. a darkening of colour in white wine, and oxidation noticeable on nose and palate. A somewhat negative description.

Fischer, Weingut Dr M-S-R
Saar estate of 24ha (59 acres) with an 18th-century house lying at the foot of its exclusively owned, steep, 100% Riesling Wawerner Herrenberg site. Other holdings at OCKFEN (incl. BOCKSTEIN) and SAARBURG. Approx. annual production 21,600 cases, The lively, fresh Saar wines with their forceful bouquet are sold in Germany and abroad. Address: Bocksteinhof, 5511 Ockfen-Wawern.

Fitz-Ritter, Weingut K. Rhpf.
Fine old family estate of 22ha (54 acres), dating from 1785. The grounds around the elegant estate house are noted for their fine trees. The v'yd holdings are mainly in BAD DÜRKHEIM (the estate is

sole owner of Dürkheimer Abtsfronhof). Vines are 60% Riesling. Annual production approx. 16,000 cases, almost entirely QmP, sold mainly in Germany. The Fitz-Ritter family (of Scottish descent) also own the Ritterhof-Sektkellerei KG, believed to have been producing sparkling wine since 1828. Address: Weinstrasse Nord 51, 6702 Bad Dürkheim.

Flasche
See Bottle

Flaschengärung
Fermentation in bottle, as opposed to the more common fermentation in vat. Flaschengärung is very suitable for the production of small parcels (say 270 cases) of sparkling wine. For this reason it is the method usually chosen by sparkling-wine producers when making LAGENSEKT (quality sparkling wine from a particular site) for growers. However, almost all the large branded sparkling wines gain their sparkle in vat. In blind tastings at A.P. control centres, no difference in quality has been noted between wines fermented in bottle and those fermented in vat that can be related to the method of second fermentation. (See also CHARMAT-VERFAHREN.)

Flaschenreife
Bottle ripeness. This term has two meanings. It can refer to the moment when a wine has stabilized and the acidity is at the appropriate level, which makes it ready or "ripe" for bottling, or to maturation in bottle.

Flaschenweinverkauf
Sale of wine in bottle. This is the message that is hung outside many cellars in Germany, advertising that wine is sold in bottle to the consumer. It is an increasingly popular form of trading: of the 15,314 growers who bottle their own wine, 88% sell directly to the public.

Flurbereinigung
The reconstruction and reallocation of v'yds among the growers. It is supported by federal and local government and the aim is to improve the competitiveness of German wine by reducing labour costs, improving wine quality, making wine with strong regional and varietal characteristics, and increasing yields. The work of reconstruction, incl. rebuilding hillsides and abolishing old terracing, offers the chance for the best possible vines to be planted. By 1982, 52% of the total area under vine had been "flurbereinigt".

Forst an der Weinstrasse Rhpf. w. ★★★→★★★★
Small but important wine village a few km. s. of BAD DÜRKHEIM, surrounded by top-quality Riesling v'yds and the base of a number of well-known estates with holdings in the famous JESUITENGARTEN and UNGEHEUER sites. Two Grosslagen: MARIENGARTEN (for the best sites) and SCHNEPFENFLUG.

Forster Winzerverein eG   Rhpf.
Cooperative cellar, est. in 1918, owned by 117 members with 60ha (148 acres) of v'yds in top-quality sites (Forster JESUITENGARTEN, UNGEHEUER, etc.). Vines are 67% Riesling. Annual production is the equivalent of 60,000–95,000 cases, half of which is sold in bulk to the wine trade. Distinguished wines with a considerable reputation, sold in Germany and abroad. Address: Weinstrasse 57, 6701 Forst/Weinstrasse.

Forstmeister
Head forester, as in Weingut Forstmeister Geltz Erben.

Franconia
See Franken

Franken w. (r.)
The only wine region belonging to the beer-producing state of Bavaria, covering more than 4,000ha (9,880 acres) n. and s. of the R. Main and centred on the university city of WÜRZBURG. More than half the v'yds have been reconstructed and replanted since 1954. The most widely grown grape is the Müller-Thurgau, followed by Silvaner and the rapidly increasing Bacchus. The winters in Franken are often severe, with temperatures sometimes dropping to −25°C. As a result the yield can vary greatly from year to year (in 1981 it was 31 hl/ha, in 1982 about 170 hl/ha). Half the harvest is processed by cooperative cellars. Among the private growers some have high reputations for wines of outstanding flavour and style. Quality wine is bottled in the flagon-shaped BOCKSBEUTEL.

Wine from Franken is not cheap, and is far more expensive than a wine from the s. Rheinpfalz (Bereich SÜDLICHE WEINSTRASSE). It is, however, good value for money when compared to the price obtained for a simple Mâcon Blanc, for example. It has character in abundance and is never boring. In EEC terms it is often very dry, with a maximum 9 g/l of sugar. When it contains less than 4 g/l of sugar it warrants the description "FRÄNKISCH TROCKEN" (Franken Dry). The regional, slightly earthy flavour is almost always

1982 0,7 ℓ e
Würzburger Stein
Riesling Kabinett
Qualitätswein mit Prädikat
A. P. Nr. 3001 070 83
FRANKEN

present, no matter from what grape variety the wine is made.

In spite of the damage caused by wars over the centuries, medieval buildings in many of the old towns and villages still stand. In the countryside, inns and cellars provide opportunities to taste and buy wines in seductively rustic surroundings.

Franken eG, Gebietswinzergenossenschaft Franken
Seven cooperative cellars combined in 1959 and now produce approx. 1m. cases a year. Vines are 58% Müller-Thurgau, 32% Silvaner, etc. Most of the wines are dry, sold mainly in Germany. Address: 8710 Kitzingen-Repperndorf.

Frankensteiner Hof Rhg.
Estate with origins going back to the 18th century. The holdings, covering 4.5ha (11 acres), are at RÜDESHEIM (BERG ROSENECK, BERG ROTTLAND, BERG SCHLOSSBERG), WALLUF, MARTINSTHAL and RAUENTHAL. Vines are 85% Riesling, 6% Ehrenfelser, 5% Spätburgunder, 4% Kerner. The wines are clean, crisp and fruity, typical of the Rheingau, and have been very successful in regional and national competitions.Sales are mainly in Germany but also in East Africa. Address: Weingut Espenscheid, 6229 Walluf 2/Rheingau.

Frankfurt am Main, Weingut der Stadt Rhg.
The original owners of this 25ha (62 acre) estate were Carmelites and Dominicans. The estate was taken over by the city of Frankfurt in 1803. Holdings are in important sites at HOCHHEIM (DOMDECHANEY, KIRCHENSTÜCK, etc.) and the small 1.25ha (3 acre) residue of once-extensive v'yds in the suburbs of FRANKFURT, the Lohrberger Hang, producing lively Riesling wines. The v'yds are 82% Riesling. Approx. annual production is 21,000 cases, much of which is sold in the estate's two attractive and well-situated wine bars. Address: Aichgasse 11, 6203 Hochheim a. Main.

Fränkisch trocken
Term used to describe Franken wine with less than 4 g/l residual sugar. In 1982, 21% of wines that passed through the Franken A.P. control centre in Würzburg was Fränkisch trocken.

Freiburg Baden Pop. 175,000 w. (r.) ★★
University city, severely damaged in World War II but carefully rebuilt. V'yds are in the three Bereiche of Breisgau, KAISERSTUHL-TUNIBERG and MARKGRÄFLERLAND. The Grosslage name LORETTOBERG is probably more widely known than any other name associated with Freiburg wine.

Freiburg, Staatliches Weinbauinstitut Baden
Founded in 1920, the Freiburg holdings of the state viticultural institute amount to 7.8ha (19 acres) planted with a range of varieties incl. Riesling, Traminer, Freisamer, Müller-Thurgau. The aim is powerful, balanced wines. Approx. 5,000 cases a year are sold

in Germany and abroad. The Baden-Württemberg State owns four separate estates, with an investigative viticultural role: Blankenhornsberg at Ihringen, the largest (see next entry), Hecklingen and Durbach, each 3ha (7.4 acres) and Freiburg itself. Address: Merzhauserstr. 119, 7800 Freiburg.

Freiburg, Staatliches Weinbauinstitut, "Blankenhornsberg" Baden
One of four estates owned by the state of Baden-Württemberg. Founded as a private estate in 1824, it was sold to the state in 1919. Its 25ha (62 acres) of v'yds lie on steep volcanic slopes in splendid country in the extreme s.w. of the Bereich KAISERSTUHL-TUNIBERG. The wines (18% Müller-Thurgau, 17.8% Spätburgunder, plus many others) are sold under the village name Blankenhornsberg without mention of the Einzellage. They are full in weight and flavour and have pronounced acidity. 40–70% are dry. Annual production is approx. 20,800 cases, sold in Germany, half to private customers. Address: Blankenhornsberg, 7817 Ihringen.

Freiherr
Baron. Found in some estate names, e.g. the Baden estate of Weingut Freiherr von Gleichenstein. A Freiherr would inherit the title from a REICHSFREIHERR, but the Reichs or "imperial" description could not be bequeathed.

Freisamer
White grape variety, a crossing of Silvaner × Ruländer from FREIBURG in Baden, with a small plantation of 76ha (188 acres) that has hardly varied in size for the last 10 years. Produces a crop of similar yield and MUST weight to the Ruländer and wine that is neutral in flavour, full-bodied and stylish. If the must weight is less than 80° Oechsle the wine tastes "woody", so overcropping must be avoided and ripeness is all.

Friedelsheim eG, Winzergenossenschaft Rhpf.
Cooperative cellar with 120 members and 140ha (346 acres) of holdings on the e. edge of the finest v'yds of the Bereich MITTELHAARDT/DEUTSCHE WEINSTRASSE, incl. Forster Bischofsgarten. Vines are 26% Riesling, 16% Müller-Thurgau, plus a host of other varieties. Annual production is claimed to be the equivalent of 262,000 cases, sold solely in Germany. Address: Hauptstr. 97-99, 6701 Friedelsheim a.d. Weinstrasse.

Friedrich-Wilhelm-Gymnasium, Stiftung Staatliches M-S-R
Distinguished estate, founded in 1563 by Jesuits, with 45ha (111 acres) of holdings spread along the Mosel (DHRON, GRAACH, ZELTINGEN/RACHTIG, BERNKASTEL, etc.) and the Saar (OBEREMMEL, OCKFEN, etc.). Many of the sites are very steep, planted with 87%

Riesling, 13% Müller-Thurgau and new crossings. Maturation in wood is still valued, and the estate's cellars under TRIER produce racy wines with restrained sweetness. Annual production is approx. 39,000 cases, sold mainly in Germany but also abroad. Address: Weberbachstr. 75, 5500 Trier.

Frostgeschmack
Frost taste. Flavour acquired by unripe grapes attacked by frost in autumn (e.g. in 1972). It can usually be removed with treatment

but not always entirely successfully. The ripeness of grapes used in EISWEIN production, on the other hand, prevents them from developing a taste of frost in spite of the very low temperatures at which they are gathered.

Fruchtig
Fruity. Common description of wine that covers smell and flavour. As the word implies, it refers to pronounced grapey characteristics, often reinforced by high acidity. A Saar wine, made from ripe grapes but with good acidity, can well be described as fruity.

Fruchtwein
Fruit wine. Wine made from fruits, other than grapes, with the addition of water and sugar.

Fruchtzucker
Fruit sugar. Colloquial name for fructose, which tastes twice as sweet as dextrose. However, yeast ferments dextrose more easily than fructose, so the unfermented sugar in a fine sweet wine contains a high proportion of the sweet fructose.

Frühburgunder, Blauer
Red grape variety, an early-ripening mutation of Spätburgunder found mainly in Württemberg where it covers 18ha (44 acres), producing a small yield per vine. It is also known by the synonym "Clevner" – a name confusingly reserved in the Bereich ORTENAU in Baden for Traminer.

Frühmesse Rhh. w. ★★★
Large Einzellage on the slopes at ALSHEIM, producing luscious, stylish Rieslings. Grosslage: RHEINBLICK. Growers: Rappenhof, Sittmann.

Fuchsmantel Rhpf. w. ★★→★★★
Mainly level Einzellage, on the outskirts of BAD DÜRKHEIM but shared with WACHENHEIM, producing good wines typical of the region. Grosslage: SCHENKENBÖHL. Growers: Karst, Schaefer.

Fuhrmann, Karl
See Pfeffingen, Weingut

Fürst
Prince, as in Fürst von Metternich-Winneburg'sches Domäne Rentamt at Schloss Johannisberg.

Fürst Löwenstein, Weingut
See Schloss Vollrads

Gallais, Weingut le M-S-R
Small 2.5ha (6 acre) Saar estate with holdings in the 5.8ha (14 acre) Braune Kupp at WILTINGEN. Only wines of QmP class are sold under the Einzellage name. Approx. annual production is 2,100 cases, all Riesling. The estate is administered by Weingut Egon MÜLLER of SCHARZHOFBERG fame. Address: 5511 Kanzem.

Gattungslagename
Predecessor of the GROSSLAGE but much vaguer in geographical definition, abolished by the 1971 Wine Law. It was a site name that could be given to a wine that came, usually, from within 10km (6 miles) of the village name to which the site was attached. Johannisberger (village name) Erntebringer (Gattungslagename), for example, could originate in a village as far away as Hallgarten or even further. Today, as a Grosslage, ERNTEBRINGER is more narrowly and precisely defined.

Gau-Bickelheim Rhh. ★→★★
Small town nr. BAD KREUZNACH (in the Nahe), best known as the home of the large central cooperative cellar that serves the Rheinhessen and Rheingau.

Gebhardt, Ernst, Weingut Weingrosskellerei Franken
Estate founded in 1723, taken over by Georg Jakob Gebhardt in 1761. 15ha (37 acres) of steep, modernized v'yds in SOMMERHAUSEN, RANDERSACKER, etc., 30% Silvaner, 21% Müller-Thurgau, 20% Scheurebe.The wines are sometimes rather sweeter than is usual in Franken but they – and the estate that makes them – have often won awards at state and national competitions. A high proportion of QmP. 14,300 cases, sold almost entirely in Germany. The estate also operates as a wine merchant. Address: Haupstr. 21-23, 8701 Sommerhausen.

Gebiet

District. Not an official EEC designation, for which the word is BEREICH. Appears in ANBAUGEBIET and WEINBAUGEBIET.

Gebietswinzergenossenschaft

District cooperative cellar (Gebiets: district, Winzer: vine grower, Genossenschaft: association). There are approx. 40 in Germany. Sometimes they are known as Bezirkswinzergenossenschaften (Bezirk is a synonym for Gebiet).

Geheimrat, Geheimer Rat

Privy councillor. Can appear in estate names as one word, e.g. Geheimrat Aschrott'sche Erben, or as two, e.g. Weingut Geheimer Rat Dr v. Bassermann-Jordan.

Geilweilerhof Rhpf.

Home of the viticultural institute Bundesforschungsanstalt für Rebenzüchtung, nr. the village of SIEBELDINGEN a few km. w. of Landau in der Pfalz, where the grape varieties Morio-Muskat, Bacchus and Optima were developed.

Geisenheim Rhg. w. ★★★

Famous for its viticultural institute, Geisenheim produces Riesling wines of distinction, but with a slight additional flavour that comes from the soil. Grosslagen: BURGWEG and ERNTEBRINGER.

Geisenheim, Institut für Kellerwirtschaft der Forschungsanstalt Rhg.

Part of a complex of world-renowned institutes dealing with all sides of vine-growing and wine-making. As a result of the research that is continuously in progress, many vine varieties are grown in Einzellagen in Geisenheim (KLÄUSERWEG, ROTHENBERG, MÄUERCHEN, etc.). The wines are matured in wood and vat. Approx. annual production is 16,500 cases, sold mainly in Germany. Address: Blaubachstr. 19, 6222 Geisenheim.

Geltz Erben, Weingut Forstmeister M-S-R

Family estate of 8.6ha (21 acres) that dates back to 1742, but it was the one-time Master Forester of the King of Prussia, Ferdinand Geltz (1851-1925), who built up its reputation. Today it is very active, selling its wines via brokers at the various important German wine auctions. The holdings in steep sites at SAARBURG and OCKFEN are 90% Riesling and produce fine, positive wines, from the driest to the sweetest TROCKENBEERENAUSLESE. More than half the annual production of approx. 8,900 cases is exported. Address: Heckingstr. 20, 5510 Saarburg.

Gemeinde

Community or village.

Gemmingen-Hornberg'sches Weingut, Freiherrl. von Baden

The 14ha (35 acre) wine estate of the castle of Burg Hornberg in the n. of Baden. Vines are 30% Riesling, 20% Müller-Thurgau, 15% Silvaner. Red wines are also made from Spätburgunder and from Samtrot, a mutation of the Müllerrebe. The complex of buildings overlooking the v'yds incl. a hotel and wine bar where the estate's wines are offered. The castle was the home of Götz von Berlichingen, the one-handed soldier of fortune immortalized by Goethe's play. Address: Burg Hornberg, 6951 Neckarzimmern.

German Wine Academy

Since 1973 this organization has run five-day seminars in English, based at KLOSTER EBERBACH in the Rheingau. In 1984 there were six such courses and a follow-up course. The basic course (DM 1,420 in 1984) covers all aspects of vine-growing and wine-making, incl. many tutored tastings and visits to six vine-growing regions. Address: PO Box 1705, 6500 Mainz.

Gerümpel Rhpf. w. ★★★

Einzellage at WACHENHEIM producing top-quality, full-bodied wines, mainly from Riesling. Grosslage: MARIENGARTEN. Growers: Bürklin-Wolf, Schaefer, Wachtenburg-Luginsland, J. L. Wolf.

Geschwister

Collective noun meaning brothers and sisters, as in Weingut Geschwister Ehses-Berres.

Gewürztraminer

Opinion is divided as to the exact relationship of this vine to Traminer, but both names are found in Germany.

Gimmeldingen an der Weinstrasse Rhpf. w. ★★
Small town just n. of NEUSTADT producing sound wines. Best
known for its Grosslage MEERSPINNE.

Gleichenstein, Weingut Freiherr von Baden
Estate dating from the 17th century, with buildings going back to
the 15th century. 18ha (44 acres), mainly Spätburgunder and
Müller-Thurgau. 60% of the wines are dry, and in the rest the
sweetness is restrained. The Spätburgunder is fermented on the
skins, a practice no longer common in Germany. Approx. 15,000
cases, sold only in Germany. Address: Bahnhofstr. 12, 7818 Ober-
rotweil.

Glühwein
Mulled wine: a hot drink, welcome in winter, based on red wine,
water and sugar with lemon peel, cinnamon and cloves.

Goldbächel Rhpf. w. ★★★
4.3ha (10.6 acre) Einzellage on mainly level ground on the outskirts
of WACHENHEIM. Planted mainly with Riesling, it produces top-
quality wine typical of the Rheinpfalz. Grosslage: MARIENGARTEN.
Growers: Bürklin-Wolf, J. L. Wolf.

Goldlay M-S-R w. ★★
Steep Einzellage at REIL, producing Rieslings of excellent quality
but usually without quite the distinction of the best from WEHLEN,
BERNKASTEL, etc. Grosslage: VOM HEISSEN STEIN.

Goldloch Nahe w. ★★★
Steep Einzellage at DORSHEIM in the Bereich KREUZNACH, adjacent
to the busy Koblenz-Ludwigshafen motorway. Planted mainly
with Riesling, it produces top-quality, meaty wine. Grosslage:
SCHLOSSKAPELLE. Growers: Diel, Niederhausen-Schlossböckelheim
Staatl. Weinbaudomäne.

Goldtröpfchen M-S-R w. ★★★
Einzellage of some 122ha (301 acres) at PIESPORT and DHRON, by far
the best known of all Mosel sites because its wines are the most
widely distributed. Facing SE-S-SW, it is 100% steep and 100%
Riesling. The wines can be of excellent quality and the best are
superb, with a fine powerful flavour and firm acidity. Cheap and
genuine Goldtröpfchen is not likely to be found. Grosslage:
MICHELSBERG. Growers: Bischöfliche Weingüter, Haag, Haart,
Hain, Matheus-Lehnert, Reh (Marienhof), Vereinigte Hospitien.

Göler'sches Rentamt, Freiherr von Baden
Estate w. of HEILBRONN prod. approx. 16,000 cases of dry and
medium-dry wines. 60% is Riesling. Red wines are made from Limberger and Müllerrebe. The wines, many of them winners of state
and national awards, can be tasted at the estate's Burg Ravensburg
restaurant. Address: Hauptstr. 44, 7519 Sulzfeld.

Gondorf M-S-R w. ★★
Wine village not far from KOBLENZ. The v'yds are extremely steep
and almost entirely Riesling. Attractive old buildings and much
wine-village atmosphere. Grosslage: WEINHEX.

Gottesthal Rhg. w. ★★
Grosslage based on OESTRICH, with a high proportion of Riesling.
The finest wines will always be sold under the names of the Einzellagen – LENCHEN, DOOSBERG,· Klosterberg (shared with the
Grosslage MEHRHÖLZCHEN) – and SCHLOSS REICHHARTSHAUSEN, but
many good (QbA) Gottesthal wines have the acidity necessary for
development in bottle.

Graach M-S-R w. ★★★
Hardly more than a hamlet in size, Graach lies amid its v'yds on
the steep SW-SSW facing slopes above the Mosel nr. BERNKASTEL.
All its Einzellagen (ABTSBERG, DOMPROBST, HIMMELREICH, JOSEPHS-
HÖFER) are capable of producing some of the finest Rieslings of the
Mosel. Grosslage: MÜNZLAY.

Graben M-S-R w. ★★★→★★★★
Top-quality Einzellage on the steep, S-SW facing hill of vines
above the Mosel at BERNKASTEL. 100% Riesling. The wines are elegant, racy and very "classy", not the cheapest of Bernkasteler
wines but realistically priced. Grosslage: BADSTUBE. Growers: Bergweiler-Prüm, Deinhard Bernkastel, St Johannishof.

Graf

Title equivalent to a count or an earl. Often appears in the names of wine estates, usually of noble origin, e.g. Weingut Graf von Kanitz.

Gräfenberg Rhg. w. ★★★

Einzellage in a side valley set back from the Rhein at Kiedrich, producing very elegant, spicy Riesling wines. Grosslage: HEILIGEN-STOCK. Growers: Groenesteyn, Sohlbach, Weil.

Grainhübel Rhpf. w. ★★★

One of the best of the distinguished ring of Einzellagen around DEI-DESHEIM, producing top-quality wine. Its 12ha (30 acres) of v'yds are virtually in the town and (unusually for Deidesheim) 40% of the site is steep. The main grape is Riesling. Grosslage: MARIEN-GARTEN. Growers: Bassermann-Jordan, Biffar, Dr. Deinhard, Hahnhof, Kern, Spindler.

Grasig

Literally "grassy". Used to describe wines that are very "green" (presumably herein lies the connection with "grassy"). Such wines will have a high malic acid content and will have been made from unripe grapes, as happens in vintages such as 1972. They are not necessarily unattractive and can benefit from bottle age.

Grauburgunder

Synonym in Baden for the Ruländer grape (see BADISCH ROTGOLD).

Groenesteyn, Weingut des Reichsfreiherrn von Ritter zu Rhg.

See Schloss Groenesteyn

Grosser Herrgott M-S-R w. ★★

Einzellage at WINTRICH on the Mosel making stylish, lively Rieslings. Grosslage: KURFÜRSTLAY.

Grosser Ring

A "ring" in the English auction world has sinister implications. Not so in Germany, where the Grosser Ring (the large ring) consists of 34 fine Riesling-growing estates in the M-S-R. Each autumn they hold an auction in TRIER to promote their own wine and the reputation of M-S-R wines as a whole.

Grosslage

A combination of individual sites (EINZELLAGEN) within one region (ANBAUGEBIET) producing quality (QbA and QmP) wines of similar style. See page 11.

Grosslagefrei

Free of a GROSSLAGE. In some small areas there are EINZELLAGEN but no Grosslagen. Common in Franken.

Grün

Green. Similar to GRASIG but less strong in meaning.

Grundwein

Base wine. Still wine from which sparkling wine is made and all-important in deciding the quality of the final product. The ideal Grundwein will have 9-11° alcohol, a high acid content and no residual sugar. It must be fresh and youthful. As a wine it is austere to the point of unpleasantness, but converted into sparkling wine it becomes balanced and refreshing.

Güldenmorgen Rhh. w. ★★

Grosslage of some 430ha (1,166 acres) on the RHEINFRONT, upstream from OPPENHEIM. The name Güldenmorgen was once reserved for an individual v'yd site but now, as a Grosslage, it includes within its boundaries such distinguished Oppenheimer sites as SACKTRÄGER and KREUZ.

Gunderloch-Usinger, Weingut Rhh.

Estate dating from 1890 with 11ha (27 acres) around NACKENHEIM, incl. the Rothenberg site. Vines are 55% Riesling, 30% Silvaner, 10% Müller-Thurgau, etc. The wines are elegant and well defined. Approx. annual production is 5,000 cases, sold in Germany and abroad. Address: 6506 Nackenheim.

Guntersblum Rhh. w. ★★★

Small town at the s. end of the RHEINFRONT, known for fine wines. It has a number of old cellars, patrician houses and the "Kellerwegfest", a wine festival, at the end of August. Two Grosslagen: KRÖTENBRUNNEN and Vogelsgärtchen.

Gunterslay M-S-R w. ★★

Steep Einzellage at PIESPORT producing good, fresh, fruity Rieslings, not quite in the class of Piesporter GOLDTRÖPFCHEN. Grosslage: MICHELSBERG. Growers: Haag, Haart, Reh (Marienhof).

Guntrum-Weinkellerei GmbH, Louis Rhh.

Company operating as estate owners and wine merchants. 60ha (148 acres) in top-quality sites at NIERSTEIN, NACKENHEIM, OPPENHEIM and Dienheim, 30% Riesling, 25% Müller-Thurgau, 14% Silvaner, etc., producing approx. 42,000 cases a year. Efficient,

modern wine-making with emphasis on retaining fruity acidity and varietal characteristics. The company dates from 1824, although Guntrums were active as coopers and brewers in the 14th century. As wine merchants Guntrum also sell some 250,000 cases a year of non-estate-bottled wines, in Germany and abroad. Address: Rheinallee 62, 6505 Nierstein/Rhein.

Gut

As a noun has several meanings, incl. that of an estate. Frequently found as part of the word Weingut – wine estate.

Gutedel, Weisser

An ancient vine variety (known in France as the Chasselas) producing white grapes for the table and the press house, covering 1,255ha (3,100 acres), mainly in the Bereich MARKGRÄFLERLAND in Baden. It is most respected in Switzerland where it is known as Fendant. The wine is light in weight and low in acidity – a pleasant SCHOPPENWEIN, best drunk young.

Gutes Domtal Rhh. w. ★

Grosslage of more than 1,300ha (3,212 acres) behind the RHEINFRONT at NIERSTEIN. It covers the v'yds of 15 villages and 31 Einzellagen, the best known being the DOKTOR at Dexheim because of its similarity (in name only) to the famous DOCTOR at Bernkastel on the Mosel. After LIEBFRAUMILCH, Gutes Domtal has the widest distribution of any Rhein wine. It is frequently very cheap, and drunk within the year following the vintage it can provide a pleasant glass of wine. Unfortunately, with the accepted market price set so low, there seems little incentive to produce simple-quality wine with much character under the name Gutes Domtal.

Gütezeichen für Badischen Qualitätswein

Award given by the Baden Winegrowers Association to quality (QbA and QmP) wines in standard-size (no litre) bottles, that have already won their A.P. Nr. and achieved a sufficiently high level of marks to qualify for the Gütezeichen. A special yellow award can be won by dry wines. The Badisches Gütezeichen is officially recognized by the state of Baden-Württemberg.

Gütezeichen Franken

Award first given to Franken quality wines in 1981, under the auspices of the Bavarian government, based on a tasting and analytical examination. Since 1983 only available to wine in BOCKSBEUTEL. To qualify, dry wines must be FRÄNKISCH TROCKEN.

Haag, Weingut Fritz M-S-R

Small, 3.8ha (9 acre) family-owned estate dating from 1605 with holdings at BRAUNEBERG and GRAACH. Vines are 90% Riesling, 10% Müller-Thurgau. Approx. annual production is 4,300 cases of typical, good-quality, crisp Mosel wine, sold in Germany and also in California. Address: Dusemonder Hof, 5551 Brauneberg/Mosel.

Haart, Weingut Johann M-S-R
6ha (15 acre) estate belonging to the Haart family, owners of v'yds in PIESPORT since the 14th century. Holdings are in GOLDTRÖPFCHEN, GÜNTERSLAY, etc. Annual production is the equivalent of 8,300 cases of very good quality wine, sold to the wine trade. Much is exported. Address: Trevererstr. 12, 5555 Piesport.

Hagel
Hail. Hailstorms can cause damage at almost any time – they have been known to strip vines of leaf and fruit in mid-summer, destroying the current harvest and severely reducing the following year's crop. If a hailstorm occurs shortly before the vintage, many of the grapes may be knocked to the ground. In these circumstances, an early gathering (VORLESE) is allowed.

Hagelgeschmack
"Taste of hail." Hailstones can damage grapes in such a way that they rot on the vine and later pass on to the wine an unpleasant flavour (Hagelgeschmack), and often excessive volatile acidity as well.

Hahnhof GmbH, Die Weinbau Rhpf.
The wine-estate subsidiary of a large catering company, Hahnhof KG. Hahnhof wine bars are found throughout Germany, selling wine from the estate and from other Rheinpfalz growers. The estate has 27ha (67 acres) of v'yds in top-quality sites in DEIDESHEIM, FORST and RUPPERTSBERG. Vines are 57% Riesling, 25% Müller-Thurgau, 12% Silvaner, etc. The fresh, full and luscious wines are sold mainly through the wine bars. Address: Weinstrasse 1, 6705 Deidesheim.

Hail
See Hagel

Hain, Weingut Dr J. B. M-S-R
2.9ha (7 acre) estate owned by Herr Günther Reh, with small holdings (95% Riesling) at PIESPORT (GOLDTRÖPFCHEN, etc.), DHRON, TRITTENHEIM (APOTHEKE), NEUMAGEN. The wines are made and sold by Weingut Reichsgraf von KESSELSTATT. Production is approx. 2,800 cases a year, sold in Germany and the USA. Address: Neumagen-Dhron.

Halbfuder
The Mosel equivalent of the Rhein HALBSTÜCK, with a capacity of approx. 500 litres. Its disappearance parallels that of the Halbstück and for the same reasons.

Halbstück
Round-shaped (as opposed to oval) wooden cask with a capacity of some 610 litres, used until the mid-1960s for transporting and storing Rhein wine. Still found to a small extent in some cellars, but steadily disappearing because of high maintenance costs and the possible loss of freshness in white wine of relatively low acidity (e.g. Müller-Thurgau) when stored in wood.

Halbtrocken
Medium-dry. When describing still (i.e. non-sparkling) wine, "halbtrocken" indicates that the sugar content is not more than 10 g/l greater than that of the total acid content, with a maximum of 18 g/l. For those who feel that German dry ("trocken") wines too often lack body, and do not want a sweetish wine, Halbtrocken seems an excellent compromise. It allows the true flavour to be easily tasted and can produce most attractive, balanced results. A Halbtrocken sparkling wine in the EEC can contain between 33 and 50 g/l sugar.

Hallgarten Rhg. w. ★★★
Small rural village away from the bustle of the Rhein and protected by the TAUNUS hills that border its n. v'yds. Produces fine Riesling wines. Grosslage: MEHRHÖLZCHEN.

Hallgarten GmbH, Arthur Rhg.
Much-respected firm of wine exporters, formed in 1933, with an

associated company in London. Well-established brands incl. Domgarten Niersteiner Gutes Domtal and Kellergeist Liebfraumilch. Hallgarten also export a full range of estate-bottled wines, bought for quality rather than name, incl. at the lower end an estate-bottled LANDWEIN. Address: 6222 Geisenheim.

Hallgarten/Rhg. eG, Winzergenossesnschaft Rhg.

Cooperative with 200 members supplying grapes from 100ha (247 acres), 85% Riesling, 10% Müller-Thurgau, etc., all in sites at HALLGARTEN. Annual production is some 100,000 cases. No exports. Address: Hattenheimerstr. 15, 6227 Oestrich-Winkel-Hallgarten.

Halsschleife

Neck label. It is common for German wine bottles to be dressed with a neck label, showing vintage or other optional information. Some estates, however, feel that a neck label does not improve the appearance of their bottles and omit its use (e.g. Schloss Reinhartshausen).

Hambach an der Weinstrasse Rhpf. w. ★★

Small wine town near NEUSTADT, well known in the region, producing wines of good quality (Riesling, Silvaner, etc.) but not comparable to the best from a few km. further n.

Hammel & Cie Weingut Weinkellerei, Emil Rhpf.

Estate of 21ha (52 acres), dating from 1723, producing approx. 15,000 cases a year from its own v'yds and selling the equivalent of a further 60,000 cases from bought-in grapes – not, of course, as estate-bottled wine. The Weinkellerei also sells Alsatian wines and those of Ch. Soutard in St.-Emilion. The estate's holdings, all in n. Rheinpfalz, are planted with a wide range of vine varieties. The aim is to produce pleasant "drinking" wines, i.e.  with a gentle acidity and agreeable fruitiness. In recent years more than half the estate-bottled wines have been dry or medium-dry. Address: 6719 Kirchheim/Weinstrasse.

Hammelburg Franken Pop. 12,700 w. ★★

On the R. Saale, one of the oldest wine towns of Franken, with a tradition of 1,200 years of viticulture. Some fine old buildings and one of the earliest cooperative cellars in the region. Produces wines of good acidity from Müller-Thurgau and Silvaner.

Hammelburg, Stadt. Weingut Franken

In 1964 the town of HAMMELBURG bought the ancient v'yds around Schloss Saaleck, now covering 23ha (57 acres). Vines are 50% Müller-Thurgau, 20% Silvaner, 10% Bacchus, etc., producing approx. 7,800 cases a year of powerful, dry wines bottled in the Franken BOCKSBEUTEL and 2,700 cases in litre bottles. Sales are mainly in Germany. Address: 8783 Hammelburg/Bayern.

Harmonisch

Balanced. Describes wine in which alcohol, sugar and acidity are in harmony. Fine wines, by definition, must be balanced; lesser wines may be balanced.

Harvest

The German grape harvest (Ernte) usually takes place over a period of two months from mid-September onwards. It starts with grapes such as Ortega and Siegerrebe, continues with Müller-Thurgau, Bacchus and Morio-Muskat and finishes with Riesling, the very last of which may not be gathered until January if EISWEIN is being made. (See also HAUPTLESE.)

Growers have to consider many factors when organizing their harvest, incl. the rate at which the grapes can be picked and pressed and the risks involved in leaving them on the vine to increase their sugar content. Because of the varying pace at which different grapes ripen, the gathering of SPÄTLESE Müller-Thurgau, for example, will often be finished before the main picking of Riesling has begun.

The timing of the harvest is officially controlled and the v'yds are put out of bounds except during the hours when picking is permitted. In recent years in the Rheinpfalz and Rheinhessen, mechanical harvesters have appeared in some force but their use, even in these regions, is not nearly as widespread as in France.

Hasensprung Rhg. w. ★★★→★★★★

Large, 100ha (247 acre) Einzellage at WINKEL producing top-quality, refined Riesling wines that are among the best in the region. Grosslage: HONIGBERG. Growers: Basting-Gimbel, Brentano'sche Guts., Hessisches Weingut, Hupfeld, "Johannisberger Rosenhof", Johannishof, Mumm'sches Weingut, Ress, Schloss Schönborn, Wegeler/Deinhard.

Hattenheim Rhg. w. ★★★→★★★★

Village with fine old half-timbered houses; produces some of the best Riesling wines in the region. Grosslage: DEUTELSBERG.

Hauptlese

Main harvest; takes place when the overall ripeness of the grapes has reached the desired maturity. The main harvest of any one wine will last about 7–10 days, after which it may be followed by a SPÄTLESE harvest. Theoretically, all qualities can be picked during the main harvest with the sole exception of Spätlesen. (From an early-ripening vine such as Optima, BEERENAUSLESE can be gathered even before the main Riesling harvest has begun.) Because the weather is not sufficiently cold during the main harvest, EISWEIN picking will also take place, in practice, after the start of the Spätlese harvest. (See also HARVEST.)

Haustrunk

"Drink of the house." Usually a low-quality wine provided by a producer from the "left-overs" of his vintage, free of charge, for the everyday consumption of his workers.

Heckenwirtschaft

Term used in parts of Franken for STRAUSSWIRTSCHAFT.

Hectare

2.471 acres. The standard unit of measurement of v'yds.

Heddesdorff, Weingut Freiherr von M-S-R

One of the most distinguished estates of the Bereich ZELL, with origins in the 15th century. 3.6ha (6 acres) of holdings, all at WINNINGEN, are 100% Riesling, producing approx. 4,300 cases of carefully made, often steely wine, with restrained amounts of residual sugar. Since its formation in 1981 the estate has been a

member of the ERZEUGERGEMEINSCHAFT Deutsches Eck. Heddesdorff wines are not cheap but are well worth their price and less expensive than those from comparable estates in the Bereich BERNKASTEL. Sales are mainly directly to the consumer in Germany. Address: 5406 Winningen/Mosel.

Hegemann & Co. GmbH M-S-R

Since 1969 a subsidiary exporting company of Franz REH & Sohn, concentrating on selling inexpensive wine in the UK. Address: 5559 Leiwen/Mosel.

Heidelberg Baden Pop. 129,000 w. ★★
Famous old university town astride the R. NECKAR, escaped damage in World War II. Has many old buildings and the vast Heidelberger Fass (cask), dating from 1751, with a capacity of 220,000 litres (314,286 bottles). Produces sound wines from a wide range of vine varieties incl. Müller-Thurgau, Riesling, Silvaner and Weissburgunder, grown on steep or sloping sites.

Heilbronn a. Neckar Würt. Pop. 113,000 r. w. ★★
Severely damaged in World War II, the rebuilt town as a whole lacks charm but produces Trollinger and Riesling wines to a good standard at the Heilbronn-Erlenbach-Weinsberg Cooperative.

Heiligenhäuschen M-S-R w. ★★
100% steep Einzellage on the edge of the Ruwer vine-growing area, shared by three communities incl. WALDRACH. Produces lively, fruity Rieslings in good years. Grosslage: RÖMERLAY.

Heiligenstock Rhg. w. ★★
Small Grosslage covering the v'yds of KIEDRICH. Mainly Riesling.

Heissen Stein, vom M-S-R w. ★★
First Grosslage of the top-quality Middle Mosel, travelling upstream from KOBLENZ. 628ha (1,552 acres), much of it on steep slopes, incl. the GOLDLAY site at REIL. The main grape is Riesling.

Helfensteiner
Red grape variety, a Frühburgunder × Trollinger crossing from the viticultural institute at WEINSBERG. 66ha (163 acres), almost exclusively in WÜRTTEMBERG. It dislikes lime in the soil, ripens early and produces pleasant but undistinguished wine.

Henkell & Co., Sektkellereien
Est. in 1856 as Sekt producers, the family-owned Henkell group of companies has the largest turnover in sparkling wine in Germany. It can also claim 50% of the export market, where "Henkell Trocken", which sells for about DM 9 a bottle in Germany, is particularly well distributed. Sales of Rüttgers Club, a Sekt at about DM 5 a bottle produced by a Henkell subsidiary company, amount to some 30m. bottles a year. (See also CARSTENS KG.) Address: Biebricher Allee 142, 6202 Wiesbaden-Biebrich.

Heppenheim Hess.Berg. Pop. 24,000 w. ★★
Town 28km (17 miles) n. of Heidelberg, with some attractive old half-timbered buildings. Lively wines, mainly Riesling. Largest producer is the local cooperative cellar.

Herb
Austere. Sometimes used in restaurants as a synonym for "trocken". Elsewhere generally describes the effect of tannin in red wine, without residual sugar.

Hermannsberg Nahe w. ★★★★
Small Einzellage on the slopes at NIEDERHAUSEN producing charming Riesling wines of great finesse. Grosslage: BURGWEG. Owner: Niederhausen-Schlossböckelheim Staatl. Weinbaudomäne.

Hermannshof
See Schmitt, Weingut Hermann Franz

Hermannshöhle Nahe w. ★★★→★★★★
One of the best Einzellagen on the Nahe, at NIEDERHAUSEN. 100% steep and 100% Riesling. In a good vintage great wine of immense elegance is made. Grosslage: BURGWEG. Growers: August E. Anheuser, Niederhausen-Schlossböckelheim Staatl. Weinbaudomäne, Jacob Schneider.

Heroldrebe
Red grape variety, a crossing of Portugieser × Limberger. Like the Helfensteiner it originated in WEINSBERG. Can yield as much as 140 hl/ha of light red wine of no special quality. Needs to be picked late in the season, even later than Trollinger, to avoid an unripe flavour and an excess of tannin. 241ha (596 acres), almost half in the Rheinpfalz.

Herrenberg Franken w. (r.) ★★
Small Grosslage at Castell prod. full-bodied Silvaner and Müller-Thurgau, and a small quantity of red wine.

Herrenberg M-S-R w. ★★★
Herrenberg is a common site name, but the Herrenberg Einzellage at OCKFEN on the Saar is one of the best known outside Germany. It is an excellent sloping site producing well-balanced, full wines in good years. Grosslage: SCHARZBERG. Growers: Fischer, Rheinart, Solemacher, Trier Staatl. Weinbaudomäne.

Herrenberg, Weingut
See Simon, Bert

Herrenberger M-S-R w. ★★★→★★★★
Einzellage of outstanding quality at AYL on the Saar, 100% steep and exclusively Riesling. In good years the wine shows great class: it is stylish, well structured and will keep for years. Grosslage: SCHARZBERG. Growers incl. Bischöfliche Weingüter.

Herrgottsacker Rhpf. w. ★★★
Largest, 120ha (296 acres), Einzellage at DEIDESHEIM. Produces racy Rieslings, lighter than some in the district but stylish, with a balance more often found in the Rheingau. Grosslage: MARIENGARTEN. Growers: Bassermann-Jordan, Josef Biffar, Bürklin-Wolf, Deinhard Koblenz, Hahnhof, Kern, Mosbacher, E. Spindler, J. L. Wolf.

Hersteller
The producer of a wine, not the grower of the grapes. Often found as in "hergestellt in", i.e. "produced in".

Herzhaft
Hearty. In Germany, describes a wine with pronounced flavour and bouquet, and usually good acidity. A term that might be applied, for example, to a Riesling from MÜNSTER-SARMSHEIM in the Nahe, or from LORCH in the Rheingau.

Hessen
Federal state encompassing the vine-growing regions of the Rheingau and Hessische Bergstrasse. The capital is WIESBADEN. Not to be confused with Rheinhessen in Rheinland-Pfalz. Area under vine 3,319 ha (8,202 acres).

Hessische Bergstrasse w.
Smallest of the wine-producing regions, with 380ha (939 acres) under vine. Riesling covers 199ha (492 acres). Müller-Thurgau is widely planted in the n. near Darmstadt. The v'yd holdings are

exceptionally small and in most cases vine-growing is very much a weekend occupation. More than 90% of the harvest is delivered to cooperative cellars. For all that, the wines can be excellent and compare in quality with many from the Rheingau, to which they are similar in style. They are seldom found outside the region.

Hessisches Weingut, Landgräflich Rhg.
30ha (74 acre) estate taken over by the Prince and Landgrave of Hessen in 1958, 85% Riesling, in well-known sites at RÜDESHEIM, GEISENHEIM, JOHANNISBERG, WINKEL, RAUENTHAL, ELTVILLE and KIEDRICH. The estate is enthusiastic about the Scheurebe plantations in the Winkeler Dachsberg, that have produced many award-winning wines. Annual yield is claimed to be some 41,000 cases, sold in Germany and abroad. Address: 6225 Johannisberg/Rheingau.

Heyl zu Herrnsheim, Weingut Freiherr Rhh.

Important NIERSTEIN estate, with buildings dating from the 16th century. 30ha (74 acres) in the best sites (PETTENTHAL, HIPPING, ÖLBERG, etc.), 55% Riesling, 18% Silvaner, 18% Müller-Thurgau, etc. The estate also owns all the 1.3ha (3.2 acres) of the Niersteiner

Bruderberg. Approx. annual production is the equivalent of 24,000 cases. The estate is totally dedicated to producing character-ful Riesling and Silvaner wines as well as flavoury wines from Müller-Thurgau. Sales in Germany and abroad. Address: Mathil-denhof, Langgasse 3, 6505 Nierstein/Rhein.

Himmelreich M-S-R w. ★★★

100% steep, SW-facing Einzellage of nearly 90ha (222 acres) at GRAACH. The site forms part of the great sweep of v'yds that stretches from BERNKASTEL to ZELTINGEN-RACHTIG. Among Mosel wines, those from the Graacher Himmelreich seem full, fruity, with a stylish acidity. Prices are similar to those of nearby Wehlener SONNENUHR. Grosslage: MÜNZLAY. Growers: "Abteihof", Bergweiler-Prüm, Jos. Christoffel, Deinhard Bernkastel, Friedrich-Wilhelm-Gymnasium, Haag, Kesselstatt, Kies-Kieren, Lauerburg, Otto Pauly, J. J. Prüm, S. A. Prüm, Richter, St Johannishof, Schorlemer, Stephan Studert-Prüm, Thanisch.

Himmelreich M-S-R w. ★★→★★★

Like the site of the same name at Graach (see previous entry), the Himmelreich Einzellage at ZELTINGEN-RACHTIG forms part of the continuous v'yd that stretches from BERNKASTEL to Zeltingen-Rachtig. Classic Mosel Riesling wines, although the general stan-dard is probably not quite so high as that set by the Graacher Himmelreich. Grosslage: MÜNZLAY. Growers: Bergweiler-Prüm, Ehses-Geller, Nicolay'sche Weinguts., Selbach-Oster.

Hipping Rhh. w. ★★★

Mainly steep Einzellage overlooking the Rhein at NIERSTEIN, pro-ducing top-quality wines of depth and much flavour. Grosslage: REHBACH. Growers: Balbach, Kurfürstenhof, Hermann Franz Schmitt, Georg Schneider, Sittmann, Strub.

Hitzlay M-S-R w. ★★★

Einzellage on the rural R. Ruwer at KASEL. Like all the Kasel sites, of excellent quality and capable of producing tremendously fresh, well-constructed wine in good years. Grosslage: RÖMERLAY.

Hochheim a. Main Rhg. Pop. 15,200 w. ★★★

Small town 5km (3 miles) e. of MAINZ, but one of the largest wine-growing communities of the Rheingau. The best sites (DOMDE-CHANEY, KÖNIGIN VICTORIA BERG, KIRCHENSTÜCK) produce powerful Rieslings with a distinct earthy flavour. The English word "HOCK" derives from Hochheim. Grosslage: DAUBHAUS.

Hochmess Rhpf. w. ★★

Small Grosslage of some 100ha (247 acres) on the n. edge of BAD DÜRKHEIM, incl. the well-known SPIELBERG site. The best wines are sold under the Einzellagen names but the quality of wine produced by the Grosslage as a whole is high. The Riesling and Scheurebe wines are often excellent.

Hock
Abbreviation for Hochheimer, originally described wines from HOCHHEIM but became a generic term for all white Rhein wine. The heading "Hocks and Moselles" still appears on many restaurant wine lists in the UK. Now defined by the EEC as (1) any German table wine that bears the description "Rhein", (2) a German quality wine from any of the following regions: Ahr, Hessische Bergstrasse, Mittelrhein, Nahe, Rheingau, Rheinhessen, Rheinpfalz.

Hoensbroech, Weingut Reichsgraf & Marquis zu Baden
12ha (30 acre) estate nr. HEIDELBERG, incl. sole ownership of the Michelfelder Himmelberg site. Vines are 40% Weissburgunder, 30% Riesling, 20% Müller-Thurgau, etc., producing approx. 14,000 cases a year of powerful dry and medium-dry wines sold exclusively in Germany. Address: 6921 Angelbachtal-Michelfeld.

"Hof Sonneck", Weingut Rhg.
8ha (20 acre) family-owned estate dating from 1756 with holdings in the HÖLLE, Mittelhölle and Goldatzel sites at JOHANNISBERG. Vines are 85% Riesling and the wines are, to a large extent, matured in cask. Approx. annual production 6,500 cases, sold in Germany and abroad. Address: 6225 Johannisberg/Rheingau.

Höfer, Weingut Dr Josef Nahe
35ha (86 acre) family-owned estate est. in 1775 with holdings at BURG LAYEN, DORSHEIM, MÜNSTER-SARMSHEIM, etc. Vines are mainly

Silvaner, Müller-Thurgau, Riesling and Ruländer; the wines are soft yet fresh and sold mainly to the consumer in Germany. Address: 6531 Burg Layen.

Hofstück Rhpf. w. (r.) ★★
Grosslage that covers some 1,250ha (3,089 acres) of scattered v'yds nr. DEIDESHEIM and RUPPERTSBERG. Most of the sites are on level land on clay or sandy soil, producing good-quality white wines from the standard Rheinpfalz vine varieties (Riesling, Müller-Thurgau, etc.) and red from Portugieser.

Hohenlohe Langenburgsche Weingüter, Fürstlich Würt. and Franken
26ha (64 acre) estate, 30% Müller-Thurgau, 17% Riesling, 15% Kerner, etc. Sole owners of the 17ha (42 acre) Karlsberg site on the slopes at Weikersheim in Württemberg. The wines are Franconian in style, with a pronounced earthy flavour. Annual production is approx. 14,300 cases, all sold in Germany. Address: 6992 Weikersheim/Württemberg im Schloss.

Hohenlohe-Ohringen'sche, Fürst zu Würt.
Estate first mentioned in 1360, covering the 22ha (54 acres) of the sloping Verrenberger Verrenberg site (sole ownership) e. of HEILBRONN. Vines are 50% Riesling, 15% Limberger, 15% various types of "Burgunder" (Pinot), etc., and the wines, both red and white, are mainly dry, racy and typical of the grape variety. Approx. annual production is 16,700 cases, sold to private customers and restaurants. Address: 7110 Ohringen. Schloss.

Hohenmorgen Rhpf. w. ★★★
One of several excellent Einzellagen at DEIDESHEIM producing

top-quality, weighty Rieslings from sloping ground. Grosslage: MARIENGARTEN. Growers: Bassermann-Jordan, Bürklin-Wolf.

Hölle Rhg. w. ★★★
Einzellage at HOCHHEIM, overlooking the R. Main. Produces full, rounded, slightly earthy wines of excellent quality. Grosslage: DAUBHAUS. Growers: Ashcrott'sche Erben, Eltville Staatsweingut, Frankfurt am Main Stadt Weingut, Schloss Schönborn, Werner'sches Weingut.

Hölle Rhg. w. ★★★
Sloping Einzellage at JOHANNISBERG making balanced, classic Rheingau Riesling wines. Grosslage: ERNTEBRINGER. Growers: Hessisches Weingut, "Hof Sonneck", Hupfeld, "Johannisberger Rosenhof", Johannishof, Mumm'sches Weingut, Wegeler/Deinhard.

Höllenberg Rhg. r. ★★
Steep Einzellage overlooking the village of ASSMANNSHAUSEN, planted mainly in Spätburgunder. The wine is usually stylish and shows the vine characteristics well. Somewhat expensive. Grosslage: STEIL.

Holschier, Weingut Nikolaus Jakob Rhg.
Small, 2.34ha (5.8 acre) estate with holdings mainly in GEISENHEIM. Vines are 80% Riesling. Production has been limited while the v'yds have been reconstructed and modernized. A small quantity of sparkling wine is made for the estate, using base wine from its holding in the Geisenheimer Mönchspfad site. Vinification is traditional and increasingly meeting a demand for drier wines. Sales are exclusively in Germany, some via STRAUSSWIRTSCHAFT. Address: Hermannstr. 11, 6222 Geisenheim/Rheingau.

Holzgeschmack
"Taste of wood." The flavour picked up by a wine that has been stored in a new cask, that has not been properly prepared.

Honigberg Rhg. w. ★★
Grosslage of some 250ha (618 acres), incl. the Winkeler HASENSPRUNG site and SCHLOSS VOLLRADS. Production of good-quality Rheingau Riesling is endemic in Honigberg, so a Riesling sold under the Grosslage name will be closely related to wines sold with an Einzellage name. Good value for money but not cheap.

Honigsäckel Rhpf. w. ★★
A relatively small Grosslage of about 170ha (420 acres) covering three sites near the village of UNGSTEIN (Weilberg, Herrenberg and Nussriegel). Full-bodied wines, typical of the region, from varied soil on steep or gentle slopes.

Hövel, Weingut von M-S-R
Important Saar estate, nearly 200 years old, with cellars dating back to the 12th century. A holding in the SCHARZHOFBERG and sole ownership of the Hütte in OBEREMMEL, total 12ha (33 acres) of steep v'yds, 95% Riesling. Approx. annual production is 9,100 cases, 37% from the Scharzhofberg, of typical high-quality Saar wines with pronounced acidity. Sales are in Germany and abroad. Address: Agritiusstr. 5-6, 5503 Konz-Oberemmel.

Hubertuslay M-S-R w. ★★
Mainly steep Einzellage at KINHEIM producing good-quality, charming Riesling wines, possibly lacking the personality of the best of the region. Grosslage: SCHWARZLAY. Growers: Kies-Kieren, Nicolay'sche Weinguts.

Huesgen GmbH, A.
Wine merchants, est. 1735, known on the export market particularly for cheap QbA, DTW and EEC table wine. Huesgen has offices in the USA and UK. Turnover is in excess of DM 40m. Address: 5580 Traben-Trabach.

Hupfeld Erben, Weingut Rhg.
5ha (12 acre) estate, dating in its present form from 1907, with holdings in OESTRICH, WINKEL, JOHANNISBERG, etc. Vines are 85% Riesling. Approx. annual production is 3,300 cases of wines with restrained sweetness, sold entirely in Germany. The KABINETT wines are particularly successful and have won many regional awards. Address: Rheingaustr. 113, 6227 Oestrich-Winkel.

Huxelrebe
White grape variety, a crossing of Weisser Gutedel × Courtillier musqué by Dr Georg Scheu of Alzey, dating from 1927. If the vine is prevented from its tendency to overcrop the MUST will be above average in weight, with more acidity than Müller-Thurgau. Because of the high sugar content of the grapes the wine will often reach potential AUSLESE quality, with a light MUSKAT bouquet. Planted in 1,687ha (4,169 acres), mainly in the Rheinhessen and Rheinpfalz.

Hybriden
Hybrid vines: crossings of American and European vines that may be grown only under controlled conditions for experimental purposes. Hybrids are not the same as the popular new crossings (NEUZÜCHTUNGEN) of one European vine with another.

Ice Saints
See Eisheiligen

Ice Wine
See Eiswein

Ihringen Baden w. (r.) ★★
Village in the Bereich KAISERSTUHL-TUNIBERG producing positive wines from a variety of vines, esp. Silvaner, which covers 37% of the area under vine. Müller-Thurgau and various members of the Burgunder (Pinot) family are also grown.

Immich-Batterieberg, Carl Aug. M-S-R
Small estate with sites at ENKIRCH, incl. sole ownership of the steep 1ha (2.5 acre) Batterieberg v'yd. 100% Riesling. Approx. annual production 3,300 cases of elegant, racy wine, sold exclusively in Germany. Address: 5585 Enkirch/Mosel.

Ingelheim am Rhein Rhh. Pop. 19,300 r. ★★
Small town known for many years for its agreeable but somewhat expensive Spätburgunder wine.

Innere Leiste Franken w. ★★★
Steep site at WÜRZBURG and one of the relatively few internationally known Franken Einzellagen. Produces splendid, rather earthy Riesling wines with positive, firm style. Not in a Grosslage (see GROSSLAGEFREI). Growers: Bürgerspital, Juliusspital, Würzburg Staatl. Hofkeller.

Invertzucker
Invert sugar. A mixture of glucose and fructose which until 1971 could be used with water to enrich and deacidify cheaper wines. Achieved notoriety in the early 1980s for having been used in the falsification of wine.

Iphofen Franken w. ★★★
Fine old town with many noble and ecclesiastical wine-related buildings dating back to the 16th century. Silvaner, Müller-Thurgau and other vines produce top-quality wines, full of flavour and character. Grosslage: BURGWEG.

Itschner-Sittmann, Dr L.
Wine merchants, owned by Dr Liselotte Itschner of the adjacent Weingut Carl SITTMANN, selling a range of wines incl. estate bottlings. Sales in the UK and USA are particularly strong. Address: Wormserstr. 59, 6504 Oppenheim am Rhein.

Jahrgang
Vintage. Not used in the sense of "harvest", for which the German word is Ernte, but simply to denote wine of any one year. (See pages 17–19 for vintage information.)

Jahrgangssekt
Vintage, quality sparkling wine. A vintage may be given to a quality sparkling wine if at least 85% of the grapes used to make its base wine come from the year stated. Jahrgangssekt is not necessarily either better or worse than non-vintage sparkling wine, but in the eyes of the consumer it has a certain added individuality.

Jesuitengarten Rhg. w. ★★
Einzellage close to the R. Rhein at WINKEL producing well-balanced wines, mainly from Riesling. Grosslage: HONIGBERG. Growers: Allendorf, Brentano'sche Guts., Hessisches Weingut, Hupfeld, Johannishof, Wegeler/Deinhard, Zwierlein.

Jesuitengarten Rhpf. w. ★★★
Only 6ha (15 acres) in extent, this Einzellage at FORST has a reputation for refined, well-balanced Riesling wines. More elegant and
less fat in flavour than some from the Rheinpfalz, their quality is
undenied. The site is widely known outside the region. Grosslage:
MARIENGARTEN. Growers; Bassermann-Jordan, Buhl, Bürklin-
Wolf, Forster Winzerverein, Hahnhof, E. Spindler, J. L. Wolf.

Johannisberg Rhg. w. ★★→★★★
Through its Schloss (castle), one of the most famous German wine-
producing villages, lying in a fold in the v'yds. Distinguished Riesling wines are made and the Grosslage, ERNTEBRINGER, is probably
the best known in the region.

Johannisberg, Bereich Rhg. w.
The Rheingau region and the Bereich Johannisberg cover exactly
the same territory – a little under 3,000ha (7,413 acres), alongside
the Rhein and Main rivers between LORCHHAUSEN and Wicker,
beyond WIESBADEN. Johannisberg has been known for many years
as a wine-producing village and its name has become legally
attached to the whole of the Bereich. The use of the name Bereich
Johannisberg for still wine has been limited, as in many instances
the Grosslage name (ERNTEBRINGER, BURGWEG, STEINMÄCHER, etc.)
preceded by the appropriate village name has seemed more attractive. Nevertheless, the name has proved popular as a description for
sparkling wine made from grapes grown in the district.

Johannisberg, Schloss
See Schloss Johannisberg

"Johannisberger Rosenhof", Weingut Rhg.
5ha (12 acre) estate with holdings in GEISENHEIM, WINKEL and
JOHANNISBERG. Vines are 75% Riesling, 10% Spätburgunder, 5%
Kerner, etc. The typical Rheingauer wines have been very successful both in regional and national competition, and can be tasted
in the estate's wine bar. Approx. annual production is 4,600 cases.
No exports. Address: Rosengasse 7, 6225 Johannisberg.

Johannishof, Weingut Rhg.
Estate dating from 1790. 18ha (44 acres) of modernized v'yds
in JOHANNISBERG, WINKEL and GEISENHEIM, 95% Riesling, produce
some 12,900 cases a year of powerful wine: deep cellars ensure
correct conditions for maturation. Sales in Germany and abroad.
Address: 6222 Johannisberg/Rheingau.

Josefinengrund, Weingut M-S-R
Estate owned by Franz REH & Sohn.

Josephshof, Der
See Kesselstatt, Weingut Reichsgraf von

Josephshöfer M-S-R w. ★★★
Small, prestigious Einzellage at GRAACH, owned by the Weingut
Reichsgraf von KESSELSTATT. 6ha (15 acres), 90% steep, produce
stylish, full-bodied wines that benefit from maturation in bottle.
Grosslage: MÜNZLAY.

Jost, Weingut Toni Mrh. and Rhg.
Family-owned estate, est. in 1832, with 10ha (24 acres) on steep or
sloping sites at BACHARACH and STEEG in the Mittelrhein and at
WALLUF and MARTINSTHAL in the Rheingau. Vines are 65% Riesling,
15% Müller-Thurgau, etc. On average, half the wine is of KABINETT
quality and matured in wood. Approx. annual production is 8,300
cases. Much is sold in the estate's wine bar, some is exported.
Address: Hahnenhof, Oberstr. 14, 6533 Bacharach.

Juffer M-S-R w. ★★★
One of the best-known Einzellagen on the Mosel, at BRAUNEBERG.
100% steep. Produces elegant Riesling wines, less steely than some
from BERNKASTEL and more gentle in flavour. Very appealing and
can certainly be of top quality. Grosslage: KURFÜRSTLAY. Growers:
"Abteihof", Bergweiler-Prüm, Haag, Karp-Schreiber, Kesselstatt,
Licht-Bergweiler, Richter.

Julius-Echter-Berg Franken ★★★
Einzellage at IPHOFEN producing wines with firm acidity and much
flavour from Riesling, Silvaner and Müller-Thurgau. Growers:
Juliusspital, Wirsching.

Juliusspital-Weingut Franken

Great WÜRZBURG charitable estate, dating from 1576, owned by the Julius hospital. Its 156ha (386 acres) of v'yds incl. holdings in many of Franken's most famous sites: Würzburger STEIN and INNERE LEISTE, Randersackerer TEUFELSKELLER, Escherndorfer LUMP, Rödelseer KÜCHENMEISTER, and at IPHOFEN. Vines are 43% Silvaner, 24% Müller-Thurgau, 13% Riesling, plus 20 other vine varieties incl. a small amount of Spätburgunder. Maturation in wood in the old 150m (492 ft) long cellar helps to produce wines with depth and body. Annual production is the equivalent of some 95,000 cases, most of it bottled in the flagon-shaped BOCKSBEUTEL. Sales are in Germany and abroad. The wines can also be tasted in the estate's own wine bar. Address: Juliuspromenade 19, 8700 Würzburg.

Jung

Young. Implies freshness if applied to a QbA and immaturity in the case of a fine wine.

Jungfernwein

Literally virgin wine: the first wine to be produced from vines in their second year after being planted. The term is no longer allowed to be used.

Jungwein

Young wine. Defined by the EEC as a wine with an incomplete fermentation, not yet separated from its yeast deposit.

Kabinett

Before 1971 spelt "Cabinet", originally a description given to wines considered to be particularly fine and worthy of storage in a grower's private cellar, or Cabinet. Since 1971 Kabinett has been the legally established term for the first category of PRÄDIKAT (QmP) wine, the lightest and most delicate of German wines. However, the old spelling is still permitted as a brand name for sparkling wines, e.g. Deinhard Cabinet, Schloss Wachenheim Grün-Cabinet, Schloss Koblenz Cabinet.

Kaiserstuhl-Tuniberg, Bereich Baden w. (r.)

The warmest and driest BEREICH, facing v'yds of Alsace across the Rhein. Although the wines are not widely known outside Germany, the Spätburgunder and Ruländer have a good reputation in their homeland. The volcanic soil gives the white wine a positive flavour that is easily recognized.

Kaiserstühler Winzergenossenschaft, Ihringen eG Baden

Largest local cooperative cellar in Germany, with 920 members owning approx. 450ha (1,112 acres) in the Bereich KAISERSTUHL-TUNIBERG. Vines incl. a high proportion of Silvaner (34%) plus Müller-Thurgau (24%), Ruländer (18%), Spätburgunder (17%), etc. Annual production is 476,200 cases of full-bodied wine, with the lower acid content (compared to the wines of the n. regions) expected in Baden. No exports. Address: 7817 Ihringen.

Kalb Franken w. ★★★

Well-known Einzellage on the slopes at IPHOFEN producing stylish, firm Müller-Thurgau and Silvaner wines. Grosslage: BURGWEG. Growers incl. Wirsching.

Kallstadt Rhpf. w. ★★→★★★

The northernmost of the string of top-quality Rheinpfalz villages. Splendid, full-flavoured, essentially fruity wines from Riesling, Silvaner, Scheurebe, etc., similar in price to those of FORST and DEIDESHEIM further s.

Kallstadt eG, Winzergenossenschaft Rhpf.

Small cooperative cellar with 200 members owning 120ha (297 acres) of v'yds at KALLSTADT, 25ha (62 acres) at BAD DÜRKHEIM and 55ha (136 acres) at the lesser-known Freinsheim. Vines are 18% Riesling, 17% Silvaner, 13% Portugieser, 11% Müller-Thurgau, etc. 27% of production is sold to the wine trade; approx. 4% is exported. Address: Deutsche Weinstrasse, 6701 Kallstadt.

Kalte Ente

"Cold duck": a corruption of "Kalte Ende", the cold end to a meal. A drink which, sold commercially, must contain at least 25% sparkling wine or PERLWEIN. Other ingredients are still wine, lemon peel and sugar to taste. In home-made Kalte Ente the proportion of sparkling wine will probably be much higher and will be added, very chilled, immediately before serving.

Kalte Sophie
See Eisheiligen

Kanitz, Weingut Graf von   Rhg.
Estate dating from the 13th century or earlier with 19.5ha (48 acres) of v'yds, all on steep sites at LORCH. Vines are 95% Riesling, organically manured. The wines are elegant, full of flavour and softer than many in the Rheingau. They can be tasted in the wine bar in the estate's 16th-century buildings. Sales are almost exclusively in Germany. Address: Rheinstr. 49, 6223 Lorch/Rheingau.

Kanzem   M-S-R   w.   ★★★
One of a number of very small, pretty, rustic villages on the Saar that can make superb Riesling wines in good years.

Kanzemer Berg, Weingut   M-S-R
Small, 5ha (12 acre), high-quality estate, dating from the 16th century or earlier, with a holding in the modernized Kanzemer ALTENBERG site, 95% Riesling. Superb, flowery wines with lingering fruity acidity, that last for years in bottle. The great 1976 vintage produced only 2,000 cases, incl. two different Trockenbeerrenauslesen. Sales in Germany and abroad. Address: 5511 Maximilian v. Othegraven, 5511 Kanzem.

Kanzler
White grape variety, a crossing of Müller-Thurgau × Silvaner from Dr Scheu of ALZEY, planted in 115ha (284 acres), mainly in the Rheinhessen and Rheinpfalz. The yield is often small but the MUST weight is usually higher by about 20° Oechsle than that of Müller-Thurgau. The harvest can take place after the Müller-Thurgau has been picked resulting in full-bodied wines, sometimes of AUSLESE quality.

Karp-Schreiber, Weingut Chr.   M-S-R
3ha (7 acre) estate with holdings at BRAUNEBERG (incl. part of the JUFFER site), 66% Riesling, 33% Müller-Thurgau and Kerner. Approx. annual production is 3,300 cases of racy, fruity wines with restrained sweetness. Many successes in regional and national competitions. Sales in Germany and abroad. Address: 5551 Brauneberg/Mosel.

Karst & Söhne Weingut Weinkellerei, Joh.   Rhpf
10ha (24 acre) estate owned by the Karst family, growers for more than 200 years. Holdings are at BAD DÜRKHEIM (SPIELBERG, FUCHS-MANTEL, etc.), 80% Riesling, also 10% highly successful Scheurebe. Approx. annual production is 8,300 cases, 35% exported. Address: Burgstr. 15, 6702 Bad Dürkheim.

Karthäuserhof, Gutsverwaltung   M-S-R
Top-quality Ruwer estate, est. in the 14th century, known for Riesling wines of character and restrained sweetness. The estate owns the 20ha (49 acre) hill, the KARTHÄUSERHOFBERG, from which it produces some 15,000 cases a year, sold in Germany and abroad. Address: 5500 Trier-Eitelsbach.

Karthäuserhofberg   M-S-R   w.   ★★★
Hill of vines overlooking EITELSBACH on the Ruwer, divided into five, mainly steep, Einzellagen: Burgberg, Kronenberg, Orthsberg, Sang and Stirn. All are owned by the Gutsverwaltung KARTHÄUSERHOF. Grosslage: RÖMERLAY.

Kasel   M-S-R   w.   ★★→★★★
Small village in the compact little Ruwer valley, making top-quality Riesling wines in good years.

Kehrnagel   M-S-R   w.   ★★★
One of several excellent Einzellagen at KASEL on the Ruwer, mainly steep and planted with Riesling and Müller-Thurgau. Racy, elegant wines, esp. the Rieslings. Grosslage: RÖMERLAY. Growers: Bischöfliche Weingüter, Deinhard Bernkastel, Kesselstatt, Simon.

Kellerbesichtigungen
"Cellar visits". For details on visiting cellars, see page 20.

Kellermeister
Cellar master. Responsible for the wine-making and all cellar activity, incl. training apprentices. Today, the younger generation

of cellar masters will almost certainly have trained at a viticultural institute.

Kendermann GmbH, Hermann

Export house, est. in 1947. Leading brands are Black Tower Lieb-fraumilch and a QbA Mosel, Green Gold. Very successful in the USA. Address: Mainzerstr. 57, 6530 Bingen/Rhein.

Kern, Weingut Dr. Rhpf.

Estate dating in its present form from the start of the 19th century, with holdings in top-quality sites in DEIDESHEIM (HERRGOTTSACKER. KIESELBERG. LANGENMORGEN. LEINHÖHLE. GRAINHÜBEL, etc.), RUPPERTSBERG (LINSENBUSCH. REITERPFAD) and in FORST (UNGE-HEUER). Production is some 4,750 cases of cask-matured, mainly dry and medium-dry wines, many sold in the estate's wine bar. Address: Schloss Deidesheim an der Weinstrasse, 6705 Deidesheim.

Kerner

White grape variety, a crossing of Trollinger × Riesling from the viticultural institute in WEINSBERG. From 5ha (12 acres) in 1964, plantings had increased to 6,121ha (15,126 acres) in 1982 and Kerner is now found in all 11 wine-producing regions. It grows well in middle-quality sites, suitable for Silvaner, and can ripen late into the season, producing wine in all the quality (QmP) categories. The crop is large and the MUST weight usually 10–15° higher on the Oechsle scale than that of Riesling. Its acidity often causes it to be likened to Riesling, although its flavour is less fine. It is fruity, with a slight MUSKAT bouquet.

Kernig

Term used to describe a wine that has good body and acidity. Associated particularly with Rheingau Rieslings, often with a certain amount of bottle age.

Kesselstatt, Weingut Reichsgraf von M-S-R

Great estate, dating in its present form from 1820 but it has oper-ated as a Weingut for more than 600 years. Consists of four different estates, all owned by Herr Günther Reh, at GRAACH ("Der Josephshof"), PIESPORT. KASEL and OBEREMMEL. virtually 100% Riesling and covering 85ha (209 acres) in some of the best sites of the M-S-R: Graacher JOSEPHSHÖFER (sole owner) and HIMMEL-REICH. Bernkasteler BRATENHÖFCHEN. Zeltinger SONNENUHR, Pies-porter GOLDTRÖPFCHEN and Brauneberger JUFFER on the Mosel; at KASEL on the Ruwer and at WILTINGEN and SCHARZHOFBERG on the Saar. Annual prod. is approx. 76,500 cases of fine, classic Riesling, matured in wood, sold in Germany and abroad. The estate also has close commercial ties with a number of other top-quality estates incl. KOCH and Felix MÜLLER at Wiltingen, Otto van VOLXEM at Oberemmel and EHSES-BERRES at Zeltingen-Rachtig. Address: Lieb-frauenstr. 9, 5500 Trier.

G. C. Kessler and Co.

Oldest sparkling-wine producers in Germany, at Esslingen nr. Stuttgart, est. in 1826 by Georg Christian von Kessler, who had worked with the Champagne house Veuve Clicquot Ponsardin. Wine sold under the Kessler label is made by FLASCHENGÄRUNG (bottle fermentation) and that of the subsidiary company, Gebrüder Weiss, by vat fermentation. Address: 7300 Esslingen.

Kesten M-S-R W. ★★

Old village near BRAUNEBERG. whose wines are not often found abroad other than under the Grosslage name KURFÜRSTLAY. A high proportion of Riesling is grown.

Kiedrich Rhg. W. ★★★

Small, attractive village on the slopes above ELTVILLE. There has always been a close bond between the vine growers of the region and the remarkable parish church of St Valentin (although it was an Englishman, John Sutton, who restored the church and organ to their present splendour in the 19th century, and established the famous choir). Best-known sites are the GRÄFENBERG and SAND-GRUB. Grosslage: HEILIGENSTOCK.

Kies-Kieren, Weingut M-S-R

Estate of 3.7ha (9 acres) incl. holdings at KINHEIM (HUBERTUSLAY) and GRAACH (DOMPROBST and HIMMELREICH), 90% Riesling. Annual production is some 4,200 cases of racy, light wines, matured in wood in the vaulted cellar built in 1828. Biggest demand is for the KABINETT wines. Sales in the USA and UK. Address: Hauptstr. 22, 5551 Graach/Mosel.

Kieselberg Rhpf. w. ★★★
One of the best sites in DEIDESHEIM, making excellent Riesling wines. Grosslage: MARIENGARTEN. Growers: Bassermann-Jordan, Biffar, Buhl, Dr. Deinhard, Kern, Spindler.

Kinheim M-S-R w. ★★
Ancient wine village nr. TRABEN-TRABACH; the v'yds were established by Benedictine monks in the 12th century. The sites face S and SE, planted mainly with Riesling, and produce stylish, elegant wines. Grosslage: SCHWARZLAY.

Kirchberg Franken w. ★★
Kirchberg is one of the most common site names in Germany. The small, 1.5ha (3.7 acre) Kirchberg site at Castell produces excellent, powerfully flavoured, earthy wines. Grosslage: HERRENBERG. Growers incl. Castell'sches Domänenamt.

Kirchenstück Rhg. w. ★★★
One of the best small Einzellagen at HOCHHEIM, producing elegant Riesling wines with fine, balanced acidity. Grosslage: DAUBHAUS. Growers: Aschrott'sche Erben, Eltville Staatsweingut, Frankfurt am Main Weingut, Schloss Schönborn, Werner'sches Weingut.

Kitzingen Franken Pop. 20,200 w. ★★→★★★
Town 19km (12 miles) s.e. of WÜRZBURG with attractive old buildings, and for centuries a centre of the Franken wine trade. The 8th-century Benedictine abbey claims one of the oldest (more than 1,000 years old) cellars in Germany. Wines with grip, from Silvaner and Müller-Thurgau.

Kläuserweg Rhg. w. ★★★
One of several excellent Einzellagen at GEISENHEIM, on sloping ground, producing full-bodied Riesling wines with firm acidity. Grosslage: ERNTEBRINGER. Growers: Hessisches Weingut, Johannishof, Mumm'sches Weingut, Ress, Schumann-Nägler, Vollmer, Wegeler/Deinhard, Zwierlein.

Klingelberger
Name used in the Bereich ORTENAU in Baden for Riesling, after the one-time Klingelberg site at DURBACH in which it was planted.

Klingenberg a. Main Franken r. (w.) ★★
Small town 23km (14 miles) s. of Aschaffenburg on the Main, first mentioned in connection with wine-growing in AD 776. Well known in Germany for its red wine (Portugieser, Spätburgunder). Also produces Müller-Thurgau.

Kloster
Monastery or convent. In law, Kloster can be included in the title of an estate if the wine is made in the Kloster's own cellar from its own estate-grown grapes. The Cistercian, Carthusian and Benedictine Orders have all been involved in vine-growing in Germany, but the most famous wine-connected Kloster today is undoubtedly the Cistercian KLOSTER EBERBACH in the Rheingau.

Kloster Eberbach
12th-century Cistercian monastery in a valley above HATTENHEIM in the Rheingau. Today, like the Cistercian Clos de Vougeot in Burgundy, it is very much the spiritual home of vine-growing in the region. It is open to the public and provides a venue for many activities promoting wine. It is also a base for the GERMAN WINE ACADEMY.

Klostergut St Lamprecht
See Bergdolt, F. u. G.

Klüsserath M-S-R w. ★★
Long, narrow village on the MITTELMOSEL, stretching for 250ha (618 acres) between the BRÜDERSCHAFT Einzellage and the river. Good-quality Riesling wines. Grosslage: ST MICHAEL.

Knebel, Weingut Erwin M-S-R
Small estate nr. KOBLENZ, in the vine-growing Knebel family since 1727. Holdings in all the Einzellagen at WINNINGEN, 80% Riesling. Depending on the vintage, Erwin Knebel will produce the full

range of award-winning Mosel wines up to EISWEIN and TROCKEN-BEERENAUSLESE level. Sales are to private customers and visitors to the estate's wine bar. Approx. production 3,750 cases a year. Address: Am Markt 5, 5406 Winningen/Mosel.

Knoll & Reinhart, Weinbau-Weinkellerei Franken
Estate dating from 1925 with 3ha (7 acres) in SOMMERACH, RÖDEL-SEE and IPHOFEN. 33% Silvaner, 30% Kanzler. The success of recent years has been the Kanzler wine. Sales are directly to the German consumer. Grapes are also bought in from neighbouring growers to increase the throughput. Address: Alte Poststr. 6, 8710 Kitzingen 2.

Knyphausen, Weingut zu Rhg.
Estate founded in the 12th century by the Cistercians from KLOSTER EBERBACH, acquired by the Knyphausen family in 1818. 16ha (40 acres) incl. holdings at ERBACH (MARCOBRUNN, SIEGELSBERG, etc.), HATTENHEIM (WISSELBRUNNEN) and KIEDRICH. 80% Riesling, 10% Spätburgunder. Approx. annual production 13,000 cases of good-quality wine, typical of the region, sold in Germany and abroad. Address: Klosterhof Drais, 6228 Eltville/Rheingau.

Kobern M-S-R w. ★★
Charming old village nr. KOBLENZ in the Bereich ZELL. Very steep v'yds planted mainly with Riesling give powerfully flavoured, fruity wines. Grosslage: WEINHEX.

Koblenz Pop. 117,000 w.
Founded in the 1st century after Christ as "Confluentes", Koblenz stands at the meeting point of the Rhein and Mosel. Badly damaged in World War II, the old part of the town has been expertly restored. Near the centre of the town are the 0.2ha (0.5 acres) of one of the smallest Einzellagen in Germany, the Schnor-bach-Brückstück, planted mainly in Müller-Thurgau. In the Ehrenbreitsteiner Kreuzberg site, in a charming side valley of the Rhein, good Mittelrhein Riesling wines are made. Koblenz is an important administrative centre for the local wine trade and is the home of v'yd owners, wine exporters and Sekt producers DEINHARD.

Kobnert Rhpf. w. (r.) ★★
Grosslage of some 1,500ha (3,707 acres) that spreads n. from the village of KALLSTADT. As throughout the Bereich MITTELHAARDT/DEUTSCHE WEINSTRASSE, the quality of wine is high, the range of vine varieties wide and the soil varied.

Koch, Weingut Appolinar Joseph M-S-R
8.6ha (21 acre) estate administered by Weingut Reichsgraf von KESSELSTATT and owned by Herr Günther Reh, with holdings at SCHARZHOFBERG and WILTINGEN. Vines are 92% Riesling. An elegant park surrounds the Victorian estate buildings, whose origins go back several centuries. Approx. annual production is 7,400 cases of stylish wines with balanced fruit and acidity, sold in Germany and abroad. Address: 5511 Wiltingen/Saar.

Koch Erben, Weingut Bürgermeister Carl Rhh.
Estate dating from the 16th century, owned by the Koch family since 1824. 11ha (27 acres) in OPPENHEIM (SACKTRÄGER, etc.) and Dienheim, 35% Riesling, 15% Müller-Thurgau, 15% Silvaner, etc. Approx. 7,100 cases a year. Dry wines from QbA level up to AUSLESE, sold mainly in Germany. Address: Postfach 40, 6504 Oppenheim.

Koehler-Ruprecht, Weingut Rhpf.
8.5ha (21 acre) KALLSTADT estate, incl. holdings in STEINACKER. Vines are 65% Riesling, plus some Traminer and Scheurebe, producing concentrated wines full of flavour and character. Spät-burgunder is also grown. Maturation is in oak casks and only QmP is sold. Because of the micro-climate, AUSLESE can be made every year from one or more of the vine varieties. Approx. annual pro-duction is 5,000 cases, sold in Germany and abroad. Address: Weinstr. 84, 6701 Kallstadt an der Weinstrasse.

Koenen Ltd., A. J.
Small exporting house based in London, but with an office in BERNKASTEL-KUES, offering a range of estate- and German-bottled wines. Address: 83 Windmill Street, London W1.

Kommissionär
See Broker

Königin Victoria Berg Rhg. w. ★★★
Small, 5ha (12 acre) Einzellage at HOCHHEIM. named after Queen Victoria and owned by the Weingut Königin Victoria Berg. Grosslage: DAUBHAUS.

Königin Victoria Berg, Weingut Rhg.

Estate concentrated entirely in one site, the Königin Victoria Berg (see previous entry), owned by the Weingut, to which Queen Victoria allowed her name to be officially given in 1857, following a visit to HOCHHEIM in 1850. Production is approximately 3,300 cases a year of firm, full-bodied Riesling wines with a positive, earthy character. Much is exported to the English-speaking countries via the Koblenz wine shippers DEIN-HARD & COMPANY, under the original Victorian oval label. Address: Rheinstrasse 2,6203 Hochheim.

Königswinter Mrh. Pop. 35,000 w.
Today a tourist attraction, Königswinter, nr. Bonn, is known to have produced wines since the 11th century. Its small – and only – Einzellage, Drachenfels, accounts for more than half the 19ha (47 acre) viticultural area of the state of NORDRHEIN-WESTFALEN, producing Müller-Thurgau and Riesling wines with pronounced acidity.

Konsumwein
Wine for everyday drinking. The term is not defined in law but refers to cheap wine blended to a particular style.

Konz M-S-R Pop. 14,700 w. ★★
Town at the confluence of the Saar and Mosel. A high proportion of Riesling is grown, producing fruity, racy wines. Grosslage: SCHARZBERG.

Korkgeschmack
Corked. Term used to describe wines with an unclean smell. The causes are not fully understood but they include infection of the cork on the tree by fungus, incorrect storage and inadequate cleaning of cellar equipment.

Kratzig
Describes a wine that "scratches" (kratzt) the throat through too much volatile acid. Such a wine would be in very poor condition and liable to deteriorate further.

Kreuz Rhh. w. ★★★
Einzellage shared by OPPENHEIM and Dienheim, next to the well-known SACKTRÄGER site and almost as distinguished. Grosslage: GÜLDENMORGEN. Growers: Baumann, Guntrum, Heyl zu Herrnsheim, Koch Erben, Oppenheim Staatsweingut, Schmitt'sches Weingut, Sittmann.

Kreuznach, Bereich Nahe w.
Bereich that covers the v'yds of what used to be known as the Lower Nahe (Untere Nahe) from Bingerbrück upriver to BAD KREUZNACH. The Bereich name is probably used more for administrative purposes than as a description of wine. The type of simple quality wine likely to be sold as Bereich Kreuznach will usually be a little more full in flavour than a wine from the adjacent Bereich SCHLOSSBÖCKELHEIM.

Kronenberg Nahe w. ★★
1,300ha (3,212 acre) Grosslage surrounding the town of BAD KREUZNACH. The top-quality sites concentrate on Riesling but many other grapes are grown on a wide variety of soils. The best

Riesling wines will normally be sold under an Einzellage name, but a Kronenberg wine should still show the blend of body and racy flavour expected from the Nahe.

Krötenbrunnen Rhh. w. ★→★★

Large Grosslage covering nearly 1,800ha (4,448 acres). It encompasses some of the v'yds of the well-known wine villages of Dienheim, GUNTERSBLUM, ALSHEIM and UELVERSHEIM, as well as four of the sites at OPPENHEIM – Schlossberg, Schloss, Paterhof, Herrengarten. The Krötenbrunnen name is mainly used for inexpensive simple-quality wine (QbA), very much on the same level as that from the adjacent Grosslage GUTES DOMTAL.

Krötenpfuhl Nahe w. ★★★

Small Einzellage at BAD KREUZNACH planted mainly in Riesling, from which excellent, positive, stylish wines are made. Grosslage: KRONENBERG. Growers: August E. Anheuser, Paul Anheuser.

Kröv M-S-R w. ★→★★

Village near TRABEN-TRABACH, probably best known outside the region for the wines of its Grosslage NACKTARSCH.

Küchenmeister Franken w. ★★★

Einzellage at RÖDELSEER producing spicy wines, full of flavour, that can rise to considerable heights in a good vintage. Grosslage: Schlossberg. Growers: Juliusspital, Wirsching.

Kupferberg & Cie., KGaA., Christian Adalbert

Est. in 1850 as producers of sparkling wine, Kupferberg quickly moved into the export market, selling, in particular, a "Sparkling Hochheimer Domdechaney", an early forerunner of LAGENSEKT. At the same time, in the 1850s, the brand "Kupferberg Gold" was launched. About two-thirds of Kupferberg's production gains its sparkle in vat, one-third in bottle. For the latter, the yeast deposit from the second fermentation is removed by filtration, avoiding the regular and expensive shaking of each bottle to force the deposit onto the cork for later removal. Address: Kupferberg-Terrasse, 6500 Mainz.

Kupfergrube Nahe w. ★★★→★★★★

Undoubtedly one of the finest Riesling Einzellagen of the Nahe, and therefore of the whole of Germany. It was created by convict labour in the early part of this century, and literally hewn out of the rocky hillside. In the best years great wines of incredible distinction and complexity are made from the 100% steep slopes. Rightly expensive. Grosslage: BURGWEG. Growers: Niederhausen-Schlossböckelheim Staatl. Weinbaudomäne, Plettenberg'sche Verwaltung, Schlink-Herf-Gutleuthof.

Kupp M-S-R w. ★★★

100% steep Riesling Einzellage at AYL on the Saar, capable of producing great wines in fine vintages. Grosslage: SCHARZBERG. Growers: Bischöfliche Weingüter, Nell, Rheinart.

Kupp M-S-R w. ★★★

One of two good Einzellagen on the Saar of the same name, the small, mainly steep Kupp at WILTINGEN produces elegant Riesling wine. Grosslage: SCHARZBERG. Growers: Bischöfliche Weingüter, Felix Müller.

Kurfürstenhof, Weingut Rhh.

Centuries-old estate, aquired by the Seip family in 1950, with 35ha (86 acres) in many of the best sites at NIERSTEIN (PATERBERG, BILDSTOCK, FINDLING, PETTENTHAL, HIPPING, ÖLBERG, etc.), and at NACKENHEIM, Dienheim and OPPENHEIM. The estate is also sole owner of the small, 0.6ha (1.5 acre) Goldene Luft site at Nierstein. Fresh, lively wines, showing the grape characteristics well, and incl. surprising quantities of BEERENAUSLESE and TROCKENBEERENAUSLESE from many new vine crossings (e.g. 2,140 cases of Beerenauslese in 1976). Sales in Germany and abroad. Address: 6505 Nierstein.

Kurfürstlay M-S-R w. ★

Large Grosslage of more than 1,600ha (3,954 acres), incl. the top-quality wine-producing village of BRAUNEBERG. Wines sold under the Kurfürstlay name should be of adequate quality, reflecting the expected fresh Mosel characteristics, but are unlikely to be very distinguished.

Lack

Lac or varnish. Originally a resinous substance secreted by an insect, the *Coccus lacca,* which yields a fine, red dye. Before the arrival of the capsule, coloured wax seals (Siegellack) were used to protect the corks in bottled wine. The different colour capsules used by Schloss Johannisberg today for its various qualities of wine are still referred to as Rotlack, Grünlack, etc.

Lactic acid

See Milchsäure

Lage

Site: a v'yd that has been recorded in the official v'yd register (the Weinbergsrolle). The smallest unit is the EINZELLAGE, which should be not less than 5ha (12 acres) in size, although there are exceptions. A GROSSLAGE comprises a number of Einzellagen. Only quality (QbA or QmP) wines may bear site names. If they do, at least 85% of the wine must come from the site stated. In the case of a QbA the remaining 15% must have originated in the same region, or for a QmP from the same BEREICH.

Lagensekt

Quality sparkling wine from an EINZELLAGE or GROSSLAGE. There is an increasing interest in Germany in sparkling wines bearing site names, often offered by well-known estates. Lagensekt is usually made by a specialist contract cellar, using a second fermentation in bottle (FLASCHENGÄRUNG) to produce the sparkle. See also MARKENSEKT, RIESLINGSEKT.

Lahn   Mrh.

Small river that joins the Rhein at Lahnstein, just below KOBLENZ. The v'yds, now much reduced in size and number, are planted mainly with Riesling.

Laible, Weingut Andreas   Baden

Long-established family-owned estate of 3.8ha (9 acres) with holdings on the hilly slopes around DURBACH. Vines are 26% Riesling,

18% Traminer, etc. The estate has new cellars, set in the midst of the v'yds, and produces a low yield of fresh, full-bodied and often slightly SPRITZIG wine, sold mainly to private customers in Germany. Address: Am Buehl 71, 7601 Durbach.

Lamm-Jung, Weingut   Rhg.

Estate est. in 1948 by Herr Josef Jung from two separate holdings at ERBACH and KIEDRICH. 8.21ha (20 acres) of vines, 72% Riesling. Fruit trees are also grown commercially. Good-quality winemaking, 60% dry or medium-dry. Most of the annual production of some 5,800 cases is collected by private customers directly from the cellars. Address: Eberbacherstr. 50, 6229 Erbach im Rheingau.

Landau in der Pfalz   Rhpf. Pop. 36,500 w. ★→★★

Attractive town in the Bereich SÜDLICHE WEINSTRASSE, suffered much through wars and political upheavals over the centuries. Wines are sound but seldom outstanding when compared to the finest in the region. Grosslage: Königsgarten.

Landgräflich

Belonging to a landgrave, as in Landgräflich Hessisches Weingut at Johannisberg. A landgrave was a count of a country district (his urban counterpart was a burgrave).

Landwein

"Country wine": a German table wine, the equivalent of *vin de pays,* with a natural alcohol content (before enrichment) at least 0.5% higher than the minimum set for DEUTSCHER TAFELWEIN. A Landwein cannot be sweeter than HALBTROCKEN (i.e. it will contain at most 18 g/l sugar). It is a rustic wine, to be enjoyed in large quantities, accompanying food.

Lang, Weingut Hans Rhg.

11.5ha (28 acre) estate with holdings in KIEDRICH and HATTENHEIM (incl. WISSELBRUNNEN). Herr Lang's initial interest was grafting vines; he moved into wine-making in 1959. Annual production is some 8,800 cases of wines of character and pronounced acidity, very successful at national competitions. Sales in Germany and abroad. Address: Rheinallee 6, 6228 Eltville-Hattenheim.

Langenlonsheim Nahe w. ★★

Small agricultural town between BAD KREUZNACH and BINGEN. could be described as top of the second division in the Nahe. Old-established estates produce good, wholesome wines, seldom found outside Germany.

Langenmorgen Rhpf. w. ★★★

Small, 7ha (17 acre) Einzellage on the slopes at DEIDESHEIM. making excellent Riesling wine. Grosslage: MARIENGARTEN. Growers: Bassermann-Jordan, Bürklin-Wolf, Kern.

Laubenheim Rhh. w. ★★

Small town, now within the boundaries of MAINZ. The first well-known name in wine-making travelling s. along the RHEINFRONT.

Lauerburg, Weingut J. M-S-R

4ha (10 acre) Mosel estate, in the Lauerburg family since 1700. Holdings are 100% Riesling in top-quality sites incl. Wehlener SONNENUHR. Graacher HIMMELREICH, Bernkasteler BRATENHÖFCHEN and the Bernkasteler DOCTOR. Approximate annual production is 5,800 cases of elegant, correct, well-made wine that benefits from ageing in bottle. Sales are in Germany and abroad – much through the Alzey wine shippers H. Sichel Söhne. Address: 5550 Bernkastel/Mosel.

Lauffen a. Neckar Würt. r. w. ★★

Small town 10km (6 miles) s.w. of HEILBRONN. esp. well known in the region for its gentle Schwarzriesling (Müllerrebe) wine, but other red and white vine varieties are also grown.

Lay M-S-R w. ★★

Small Einzellage at BERNKASTEL, planted exclusively in Riesling. Grosslage: BADSTUBE.

Lebendig

Lively. Describes a fresh wine with good acidity and often an above-average amount of carbon dioxide (slightly SPRITZIG).

Lehmen M-S-R w. ★★

One of many small villages in the Bereich ZELL producing sound, crisp Riesling wines from very steep v'yds.

Lehranstalt

Teaching institute. Germany's teaching institutes for viticulture and wine-making are respected throughout the world. Among the best known are those at GEISENHEIM and WEINSBERG.

Leicht

Light. Describes a wine that is light in alcohol and low in extract.

Leinhöhle Rhpf. w. ★★★

Mainly sloping Einzellage at DEIDESHEIM from which full-bodied, top-quality Riesling wines are made. Grosslage: MARIENGARTEN. Growers: Bassermann-Jordan, Josef Biffar, Buhl, Dr Deinhard, Hahnhof, Kern, E. Spindler, J. L. Wolf.

Leiwen M-S-R w. ★★

Small, pleasant village in the MITTELMOSEL. probably best known as the home of wine merchants and v'yd owners Franz REH & Sohn. Racy, fruity Rieslings.

Lemberger

See Limberger

Lenchen Rhg. w. ★★★

Large, 145ha (358 acre), mainly level Einzellage at OESTRICH making flowery, balanced Rieslings with much finesse. Grosslage: GOTTESTHAL. Growers: Eser, Hupfeld, Vereinigte Weingutsbestizer, Wegeler/Deinhard.

Lese

HARVEST

Lesegut

The grapes from which wine is made. Most often found in the phrase "AUS DEM LESEGUT".

Licht-Bergweiler Erben, Weingut P. M-S-R

Mosel estate, in the Licht family for more than 200 years, with holdings at BRAUNEBERG (incl. JUFFER), Wehlener SONNENUHR, Graacher DOMPROBST and at BERNKASTEL, producing some 11,000 cases a year of balanced, elegant wine, matured in wood. Sales in Germany and abroad. Address: Bernkastelerstr. 33, 5551 Brauneberg/Mosel.

Liebfrauenkirche Rhh.

The Church of Our Lady in Worms: the v'yd from which the world-famous LIEBFRAUMILCH originally came adjoins the Gothic church. The v'yd is largely on the site where a convent once stood – a writer in the early 19th century noted that the soil was much mixed with rubble and therefore somewhat artificial. Today it forms the Liebfrauenstift-Kirchenstück Einzellage, itself part of the LIEBFRAUENMORGEN Grosslage.

Liebfrauenmorgen Rhh. w. ★★

Grosslage of more than 1,000ha (2,471 acres) scattered around the cathedral city of WORMS in the extreme s. of the Rheinhessen. V'yds are on level or slightly sloping land. The name Liebfrauenmorgen shares its origin with LIEBFRAUMILCH: both relate to the LIEBFRAUENKIRCHE (Church of Our Lady) in Worms. A Morgen is an obsolete measure of land, being that which could be worked in a Morgen (a morning).

Liebfrauenstift-Kirchenstück

See Liebfrauenkirche

Liebfraumilch

Also spelt Liebfrauenmilch, meaning the "milk of Our Lady", after the v'yd of the LIEBFRAUENKIRCHE (Church of Our Lady) in Worms from which the wine originally came. A white QbA, produced mainly in the Rheinpfalz and Rheinhessen regions, to a lesser extent in the Nahe and theoretically also in the Rheingau. It must derive predominantly from Riesling, Silvaner, or Müller-Thurgau and should taste of these grapes. It may not, however, bear a grape name and must contain more than 18 g/l of residual sugar (the upper limit for HALBTROCKEN wines). Liebfraumilch is the most widely exported of German wines, and since the early 1970s has become among the cheapest. In as much as it is a German quality wine and must pass through a control centre, Liebfraumilch should be at least pleasant and agreeable. However, the quality of the cheapest will bear little relationship to the standards set by old established brands, such as "Blue Nun" and "Crown of Crowns".

Lieblich

Medium-sweet. Describes a wine with 18–45 g/l residual sugar. Can often be applied to Rheinhessen QbA with low acidity and a gentle, sweet flavour. Such wines contain relatively little alcohol and are, for many, the archetypal German wines, so widely appreciated (esp. as LIEBFRAUMILCH) on the export market.

Lieser M-S-R w. ★★

Small village nr. BERNKASTEL-KUES making racy, elegant wines. It takes its name from the stream that flows into the Mosel. The castle at Lieser is the family seat of the v'yd-owning von SCHORLEMER family.

Limberger, Blauer

Red grape variety, also spelt Lemberger, occupying 412ha (1,018 acres) in Württemberg (also widely grown in Austria where it is known as Blaufränkisch). It ripens late in the season, shortly before the Spätburgunder, compared to which its wine is lighter, has a higher acid content and is usually inferior in quality. Often sold blended with Trollinger.

Linsenbusch Rhpf. w. ★★→★★★
Large, 175ha (432 acre), level Einzellage at RUPPERTSBERG, in which various vine varieties are grown. Its Müller-Thurgau is exceptionally stylish. Grosslage: MARIENGARTEN. Growers: Bassermann-Jordan, Buhl, Bürklin-Wolf, Deinhard Koblenz, Kern, Ruppertsberger Winzerverein "Hoheburg", E. Spindler.

Loeb GmbH, Sigmund
Exporters, a subsidiary company of London-based wine merchants O. W. Loeb and Co. Ltd., est. in 1874. Loebs are known for traditional estate-bottled wines of absolute top quality and impeccable origin. Their list must be almost incomparable. Address: Engelstr. 18, 5500 Trier/Mosel.

Longuich M-S-R w. ★★
Small village e. of TRIER, nr. the upstream boundary of the MITTEL-MOSEL, making distinguished, fruity Rieslings.

Loosen-Erben, Weingut Benedict M-S-R
Small Mosel estate with holdings at ERDEN (TREPPCHEN and PRÄLAT), ÜRZIG (WÜRZGARTEN) and ZELTINGEN-RACHTIG, etc. Over the years many fine wines have been made, incl. BEERENAUSLESEN and EISWEINE. Many of the wines can be tasted at the estate's "Alter Klosterhof" wine bar in Ürzig. Address: Würzgartenstr. 1, 5564 Ürzig/Mosel.

Lorch Rhg. w. ★★
Village in the Rhein Gorge, opposite the v'yds of the Mittelrhein, at the downstream end of the Rheingau. Riesling predominates. Quality is good, prices are similar to those from villages such as JOHANNISBERG and WINKEL, although the wines probably cannot quite compete with the finest in the region. Grosslage: BURGWEG.

Lorchhausen Rhg. w. ★★
Attractive village immediately adjacent to the v'yds of the Mittelrhein, producing light, elegant Riesling wine. Grosslage: BURGWEG.

Lorettoberg Baden w. ★★
Grosslage s. of FREIBURG in the Bereich MARKGRÄFLERLAND. Many vine varieties (esp. Gutedel) and a high proportion of simple quality wine (QbA), made to modern high standards of vinification. Much of the wine is sold by the vast Central Cooperative Cellars (ZBW) at BREISACH.

Löwenstein-Wertheim-Rosenberg'sches Weingut, Fürstlich Franken
Estate that has been producing wine since the 12th century; acquired by the Löwenstein-Wertheim-Rosenberg family nearly 200 years ago. 27ha (67 acres), many in very steep sites, incl. the terraced Homburger Kallmuth by the R. Main. Vines are 47% Silvaner, 20% Müller-Thurgau, 9% Bacchus, etc. Annual production is approx. 14,500 cases of traditional dry Franken wines, and a small amount of red wine sold in Burgundy bottles. No exports. Address: Kreuzwertheim a. Main.

Lump Franken w. ★★★
Steep, well-known Einzellage at ESCHERNDORF making powerful, soft, Silvaner and Müller-Thurgau wines. Grosslage: KIRCHBERG. Growers incl. Juliusspital.

Maikammer Rhpf. w. ★
Small town in the n. of the Bereich SÜDLICHE WEINSTRASSE, well known in the region. Sound but not top-quality wines. Grosslage: Mandelhöhe.

Main
River 483km (300 miles) long that flows into the Rhein at MAINZ. En route it provides an erratic line around which the Franken v'yds are planted. It also passes the small but important sites at HOCH-HEIM in the Rheingau.

Mainz Rhh. Pop. 186,500
Capital of RHEINLAND-PFALZ and headquarters of many institutions concerned with wine. It lies mainly in the Bereich NIERSTEIN and much of its sound wine is sold under the Grosslage names ST ALBAN and DOMHERR. Birthplace of the printer Johannes Gutenberg.

Mainzer Weinbörse
A fair held each year in MAINZ for the wine trade. In 1984 more than 600 wines, incl. sparkling wines, from 52 leading estates in Rheinhessen, Rheinpfalz, Nahe, Mosel-Saar-Ruwer, Franken, Rheingau, Baden and Württemberg were available for tasting. The fair is an important event in the German wine-trade year.

Maische
The pulp of the grape, after it leaves the crusher and before it is pressed.

Malic acid
See Äpfelsäure

Marcobrunn Rhg. w. ★★★
One of the best-known Einzellagen in the Rheingau, covering some 5ha (12 acres) nr. ERBACH. The mainly Riesling wines need time in bottle to show their very considerable best, but are somewhat expensive compared to those from neighbouring sites. Grosslage: DEUTELSBERG. Growers: Eltville Staatsweingut, Knyphausen, Oetinger, Reinhartshausen, Schloss Schönborn, Simmern'sches.

Mariengarten Rhpf. w. ★★
Grosslage of some 400ha (988 acres) in the heart of the Bereich MITTELHAARDT/DEUTSCHE WEINSTRASSE. It covers v'yds in three well-known wine villages – WACHENHEIM, FORST and DEIDESHEIM. A high percentage of Riesling is grown. Although the Grosslage wines are not expected to be in the same class as those from the best Einzellagen, they should still show similar characteristics of Riesling style with a slightly earthy Rheinpfalz flavour.

Marienhof, Weingut M-S-R
Estate owned by Franz REH & Sohn.

Marienhof, Weingut Rhpf.
See Minges, Rudolf

Marienthal, Staatliche Weinbaudomäne Ahr
The RHEINLAND-PFALZ state-owned cellars in the Ahr valley, with 20ha (49 acres) of v'yds. Vines are mainly Spätburgunder and Portugieser. Wines are matured in cask and no wine from warmer climates is added to deepen their colour. In Germany they have a loyal following, but their relatively low alcohol and tannin content limits their appreciation abroad. Approx. annual production is 6,700 cases. Address: Klosterstrasse, 5481 Marienthal/Ahr.

Markensekt
Quality sparkling wine sold under a brand name. Most German sparkling wine is Markensekt, and the number of consumers who ask for a sparkling wine with a regional or site name (LAGENSEKT) is still relatively small. Unlike the wine lover who will want, and find, endless variations in still wine, the German sparkling-wine drinker prefers consistency of price and quality. For him, geographical origin is unimportant. He will ask for a RIESLINGSEKT when he wants a top-quality sparkling wine, but it, too, will probably bear a brand name, such as Deinhard Lila Imperial, Jubilar Brut from Rilling or Riesling Brut from Kupferberg & Cie.

Markenwein
"Branded wine": wine sold under a (usually) registered name by one company or group of companies. The aim is to supply the same style of wine year after year, even if the blend varies from one market to another. The large number of German branded wines reflects the attempts over many years to overcome the difficulties of the German language, particularly in English-speaking countries. Some of the best-known brand names are applied to a range of wines (e.g. Goldener Oktober). Others, such as Black Tower and Green Label, and to a lesser extent the famous Blue Nun, are more closely associated with one wine. The efforts of the leading brand owners on the export markets, and the finanical support they have given to their wines, are largely responsible for the success of German wine abroad.

Markgräflerland, Bereich Baden w. (r.)
Bereich that stretches from FREIBURG to Lörrach nr. the Swiss border. Its wines are well known in Germany, esp. those made from Gutedel.

Martinsthal Rhg. w. ★★
Small, out-of-the-way village at the WIESBADEN end of the Rheingau producing admirable Riesling wines, somewhat overshadowed by those of neighbouring RAUENTHAL. Grosslage: STEINMÄCHER.

Matheisbildchen M-S-R w. ★★
Einzellage at BERNKASTEL producing full-bodied, firm Riesling wines. Grosslage: BADSTUBE.

Matheus-Lehnert, Weingut J. M-S-R
2.5ha (6 acre) Mosel estate – the Matheus family has been growing vines for many generations. The mainly steep holdings, planted 90% in Riesling, are at PIESPORT (GOLDTRÖPFCHEN) and DHRON. Annual production is almost 3,000 cases of cask-matured wines that have won many prizes at regional and national competitions. Sales are mainly to private customers in Germany. Address: In der Zeil 1, 5559 Neumagen-Dhron.

Mäuerchen Rhg. w. ★★★
Mainly level Einzellage on the outskirts of GEISENHEIM. producing elegant, fruity wines. Grosslage: BURGWEG. Growers: Hessisches Weingut, Holschier, Schloss Schönborn, Schumann-Nägler, Vollmer, Zwierlein.

Maximin-Grünhaus M-S-R w. ★★★
Small hamlet on the Ruwer. All its excellent 32ha (77 acres) of mainly Riesling v'yd is owned by C. V. SCHUBERT'SCHE Gutsverwaltung. Grosslage: RÖMERLAY.

Maximiner Stifts-Kellerei
See Studert-Prüm, Stephan

Mayschoss Ahr w. r. ★★
Village producing spicy Riesling wines, Müller-Thurgau, Spätburgunder, etc., from steep, often terraced v'yds. Home of the first (1868) cooperative cellar in Germany. Grosslage: Klosterberg.

Meaty
Describes a full-bodied, rich but not sweet wine, with sufficient acidity to balance the weight. Might be applied to a Riesling SPÄTLESE from the Rheinpfalz in a good year.

Medium-dry
See Halbtrocken

Meersburg a. Bodensee Baden Pop. 5,100. r. w. ★★
Beautiful old walled town on the banks of the BODENSEE and a major tourist attraction. Steep, lakeside v'yds produce good Spätburgunder, lively Müller-Thurgau and well-balanced Ruländer. See also next entry.

Meersburg, Staatsweingut Baden
60ha (148 acre) estate owned since 1802 by the state of Baden-Württemberg. The v'yds are mainly on the shores of the BODENSEE. facing Switzerland. Vines are 45% Spätburgunder, 40% Müller-Thurgau, 10% Ruländer, etc. The range of wines is impressive, incl. BEERENAUSLESEN and EISWEINE from both red and white grapes. The rule of the estate, laid down in 1801, "non in quanto, sed in quale" ("not in quantity, but in quality"), is followed closely. Annual production is approx. 35,800 cases, sold mainly in Germany. Address: Seminarstr. 6, 7758 Meersburg a. Bodensee.

Meerspinne Rhpf. w. (r.) ★→★★
Grosslage of some 795ha (1,964 acres) at the s. end of the Bereich MITTELHAARDT/DEUTSCHE WEINSTRASSE. The reputation of its wines is inevitably overshadowed by those of the adjacent Grosslage HOFSTÜCK. with its sites at DEIDESHEIM.

Mehrhölzchen Rhg. w. ★★
Grosslage of some 350ha (865 acres) in the central Rheingau covering individual sites at HALLGARTEN and OESTRICH. As usual in the region, the finest wines are sold under the site names. The Grosslage name is used for sound but not top-quality wine. A very high proportion of Riesling is grown.

Mehring M-S-R w. ★★
Village on the Mosel some km. downstream from TRIER. overlooked by its steep or sloping v'yds. In the steep sites, Riesling makes flowery, firm wines with good acidity. Grosslagen: ST MICHAEL for the better, SSW-facing sites; Probstberg for the rest.

Mertes GmbH, Peter
Wine merchants and exporters, est. 1924. Sales concentrate on cheap QbA (Liebfraumilch, Niersteiner Gutes Domtal, Piesporter Michelsberg) and EEC table wine. Main export market is the UK. Address: 5500 Bernkastel-Kues.

Mertesdorf M-S-R w. ★★★
Small Ruwer village whose best-known wines are sold under the name of its satellite hamlet MAXIMIN-GRÜNHAUS. Prestigious Riesling wines of great elegance. Grosslage: RÖMERLAY.

Metternich Sektkellerei GmbH, Fürst von
Sparkling-wine manufacturers founded in 1971 by Söhnlein Rheingold KG to sell wine under the Fürst von Metternich name, a right acquired by Söhnlein in 1934. Vintage "Fürst von Metternich Brut", although based on Riesling wine, has less acidity than some of the best German sparkling wines but is full bodied. Approx. selling price in Germany is DM 15.00. Address: Söhnleinstr. 1-8, 6200 Wiesbaden-Schierstein.

Meyer-Horne KG, Peter
Wine merchants heavily involved in exports to the UK and USA, concentrating on LIEBFRAUMILCH and inexpensive QbA. Owners of the von SCHORLEMER estates. Address: Cusanusstr. 14, 5550 Bernkastel-Kues.

Meyerhof, Weingut M-S-R
Estate owned by Hermann Freiherr v. SCHORLEMER GmbH.

Michelmark Rhg. w. ★★→★★★
Einzellage at ERBACH making Riesling wines with pronounced fruity acidity that benefit from bottle age. Grosslage: DEUTELSBERG. Growers: Nikolai, Oetinger, Reinhartshausen, Richter-Boltendahl, Tillmanns, Wagner-Weritz.

Michelsberg M-S-R w. ★
One of the best-known Grosslagen in Germany, covering more than 1,300ha (3,212 acres) in the neighbourhood of PIESPORT. Some of the individual sites, such as Piesporter TREPPCHEN and Trittenheimer ALTÄRCHEN, extend over 200ha (494 acres) or more; others cover less than a hectare. The quality varies greatly, with much rather ordinary Müller-Thurgau wine being made and sold as Piesporter Michelsberg. However, as soon as the word Riesling appears on the label, one should have a wine with good Mosel style and fruit. No top-quality wine will be sold under the name Michelsberg; its reputation has been somewhat tarnished in recent years.

Milchsäure
Lactic acid. Not normally present in MUST but formed during alcoholic fermentation and, infrequently in German wine, by a malolactic fermentation (see ÄPFELSÄURE).

Mild
Describes a wine that is balanced but has relatively low acidity. It is not a quality definition and is neutral in implication. Might well be applied to a Müller-Thurgau from the Bereich SÜDLICHE WEINSTRASSE (Rheinpfalz).

Milz, Weingut M-S-R
The Milz family has been making wine since 1520. Today the estate has holdings at NEUMAGEN, DHRON, TRITTENHEIM (ALTÄRCHEN, APOTHEKE) and OCKFEN, and enjoys sole ownership of the 0.8ha (2 acre) Neumagener Nusswingert, the 0.5ha (1.18 acre) Trittenheimer Felsenkopf and the 0.25ha (0.6 acre) Trittenheimer Leiterchen – all three sites very steep and 100% Riesling. The wines, matured in the estate's 300-year-old cellar, have won many prizes. Approx. annual production is 8,300 cases, sold in Germany and abroad. Address: Laurentiushof, 5559 Trittenheim.

Minges, Weingut Ernst Rhpf.
Estate in the less fashionable s. part of the Rheinpfalz, whose commitment to good wine-making is total. 8ha (20 acres) of holdings in four surrounding villages, incl. RHODT and EDENKOBEN. Riesling (60%), Silvaner (10%) and Kerner (6%) head the list of wine varieties. All possible styles and quality of Pfälzer wines are made, from dry QbA to luscious EISWEINE – one of which reached a remarkable

252° Oechsle. The wines have won many regional and national awards, and four times in recent years the estate has been given the Staatsehrenpreis (state prize) for its overall performance. 70% of sales are in Germany. Address: 6736 Edesheim/Pfalz.

Minges, Rudolf Rhpf.
6ha (15 acre) estate with all its holdings at Flemlingen, nr. LANDAU IN DER PFALZ. The buildings are modern but the estate, dating from 1285, shares a common origin with Weingut Ernst Minges (see previous entry). Vines incl. Ruländer, Kerner, Huxelrebe, Müller-Thurgau. Annual production is approx. 7,000 cases, sold mainly in Germany. Address: Weingut Marienhof, 6741 Flemlingen/Weinstr.

Mittelhaardt/Deutsche Weinstrasse, Bereich Rhpf. w. (r.)
Bereich that covers some of the best v'yds in Germany. The quality of the wines is very high and most are sold under the Einzellage or Grosslage name. The Bereich name is rarely found on a label.

Mittelheim Rhg. w. ★★
Small village joined to its neighbour WINKEL, looks across the Rhein to INGELHEIM in the Rheinhessen. The proportion of Riesling grown is high. Grosslagen: shares HONIGBERG with Winkel; the remainder is in ERNTEBRINGER.

Mittelmosel M-S-R
Middle Mosel: area almost the same as that covered by the Bereich BERNKASTEL.

Mittelrhein
Region of 748ha (1,848 acres) whose steep v'yds closely follow the course of the Rhein upstream from KÖNIGSWINTER, just s. of BONN. The attractive terraced v'yds have almost all been rebuilt in recent years to form uninterrupted, more easily worked slopes. The romantic and sometimes dramatic scenery is well known to many visitors, but the wine seldom leaves the region except in the back

of tourists' cars. Riesling covers 76% of the area under vine and its wine can reach great heights, but in general the quality is not so distinguished as that from the neighbouring Rheingau, of which it often seems a slightly more steely, earthy version. In the region n. of BRAUBACH the wine resembles that from the Lower Mosel. Mittelrhein Riesling makes excellent sparkling wine.

Mittlere Nahe
Area covering the best v'yds of the Nahe between BAD KREUZNACH and SCHLOSSBÖCKELHEIM. Not an official wine designation, but a description used in the region.

Monsheim Rhh. w. ★
Wine village nr. the border with the Rheinpfalz, with a technically advanced cooperative cellar. Grosslage: DOMBLICK.

Morgen
A measure of land, now obsolete, that varied from region to region but was usually a little less than an acre (.405 hectare): thought to have equalled the amount of land that a man could plough in a Morgen (morning). The word is still recalled in site names such as Güldenmorgen and Hohenmorgen.

Morio Muskat

White grape variety, a crossing of Silvaner × Weissburgunder, grown on 2,933ha (7,248 acres), mainly in the Bereich SÜDLICHE WEINSTRASSE where the vine was developed and in the Rheinhessen. It can yield up to 200hl/ha or more and often forms part of good commercial blends, to which its pronounced bouquet brings a certain attraction. If the grapes are left until after the Silvaner harvest they can make full-bodied, balanced wines. Although Morio-Muskat now accounts for more than 3% of the total area under vine, planting is unlikely to increase. Its particularly strong bouquet and flavour can become cloying and the wine usually lacks true distinction.

Mosbacher, Weingut Georg   Rhpf.

Estate of 8ha (20 acres) with holdings in most of the best sites at FORST (UNGEHEUER, PECHSTEIN, MUSENHANG, etc.) and at DEIDESHEIM (HERRGOTTSACKER) and WACHENHEIM. The percentage of Riesling planted is high (75%) and the wines have had many successes at regional and national competitions. Riesling KABINETT TROCKEN has been much in demand from the estate's private customers in Germany. Approx. annual production is 7,500 cases. Address: 6701 Forst an der Weinstrasse.

Mosel

Famous wine river that rises in the Vosges mountains and flows some 500km (310 miles) later into the Rhein at KOBLENZ, having been joined en route by many tributaries incl. the Ruwer and the Saar. The 130 or so picturesque wine villages that line its banks are easily reached from the Koblenz-Trier motorway or from the Hunsrück Hohenstrasse (B327). Minor roads follow both sides of the river closely for much of the distance from Trier to Koblenz, and much of the riverside journey can also be made by train.

Mosel-Saar-Ruwer   W.

Probably the best known of the wine-producing regions, with 12,361ha (30,545 acres) under vine, mainly Riesling (56%), Müller-Thurgau (23%) and Elbling (9%). Many of the v'yds are on very steep, slaty sites that provide ideal ripening conditions for Riesling. Because of the difficult terrain, viticultural costs are far greater

than in the flat or rolling countryside of the Rheinhessen or Rheinpfalz. However, in recent years most of the old walled terraces that could only bear a small number of vines have been replaced by more economically worked v'yds, and 72% of the vine-growing area has now been modernized. Only 20% of the crop is delivered to cooperative cellars, although this percentage is increasing. The balance is either bottled by the grower or sold in bulk to the wine trade. There are many distinguished estates, most of them upstream from ZELL, either on the Mosel itself or on its tributaries, the Saar and the Ruwer. A Riesling wine from the M-S-R has a high level of tartaric acid which gives it style, freshness and the possibility of developing well in bottle over many years. A "good" year will be one in which these characteristics are pronounced and much late-picked (SPÄTLESE) wine can be made.

Mosel-Saar-Ruwer eG, Zentralkellerei M-S-R
Rapidly growing cooperative cellar with 4,100-plus members, who
deliver to it each year approx. 16% of the M-S-R grape harvest.
Vines are 60% Riesling, 20% Elbling, 20% Müller-Thurgau. The
aim is to produce wines truly representative of the region, at all
quality levels. Annual production is 1.6m. cases, 25% sold on the
export market. Address: 5550 Bernkastel-Kues.

Most, Mostgewicht
See Must

Muffig
Musty. Wines that have been stored in unclean containers or bottled with corks that have also been incorrectly stored can develop
a dirty smell. If the fault is not too serious, the smell can be
removed by treatment in bulk.

Mülheim M-S-R w. ★★★
Village on the Mosel with a high proportion of Riesling in its v'yds,
making elegant, lively wines. Somewhat overshadowed by its neighbours, BERNKASTEL and BRAUNEBERG. Grosslage: KURFÜRSTLAY.

Müller, Weingut Felix M-S-R
Small, 2.4ha (6 acre) estate owned by Herr Günther Reh of the von
KESSELSTATT estate (which makes and sells the wine), with holdings
in the famous SCHARZHOFBERG site and at WILTINGEN. Approx.
annual production 2,100 cases, sold in Germany and abroad.
Address: 5511 Wiltingen/Saar.

Müller KGaA, Mattheus
One of the oldest sparkling-wine producers in Germany, est. in
1838, and taken over by Seagram in 1984. "MM Extra", the best
known of the company's brands today, gains its sparkle in vat.
Mattheus Müller owns Gebrüder Hoehl GmbH, whose best-
known brand is Hoehl Diplomat. Address: 6228 Eltville.

Müller GmbH and Co. KG, Rudolf M-S-R
Wine merchants, sparkling wine producers and owners of v'yds
incl. holdings at OCKFEN. SCHARZHOFBERG. SAARBURG. KANZEM.
ÜRZIG and REIL. 50% of the famous THANISCH estate in Bernkastel
belongs to Rudolf Müller. 96% of the Saar holdings are planted
in Riesling, but at Reil there are also significant amounts of
Kerner, Ehrenfelser and Bacchus. Best known of the Rudolf
Müller wines is the widely exported "Bishop of Riesling", a Bereich Bernkastel Riesling QbA. Address: 5586 Reil/Mosel.

Müller-Dr Becker, Weingut Rhh.
35ha (86 acre) estate nr. the border with the Rheinpfalz, planted
35% Müller-Thurgau, 30% Riesling, etc. Some 39,000 cases are
produced annually. 30-40% of the wines are dry, under the names
Dalsheimer Hubacker or Dalsheimer Sauloch. Sales only in
Germany. Address: 6521 Flörsheim-Dalsheim.

Müller-Scharzhof, Weingut Egon M-S-R
Great estate, owned by Egon Müller, dating in its present form

from 1797 but with origins reaching back over 700 years. 8.5ha (21
acres) of top-quality Saar v'yds incl. 7ha (17 acres) in the heart of
the superb SCHARZHOFBERG. 2ha (5 acres) of the Scharzhofberg

holding is planted in ungrafted Riesling, and only QmP is sold under the Scharzhofberger name. The estate also owns part of the steep BRAUNFELS site at WILTINGEN. 96% of the total area under vine is Riesling. In good years the wines are known for their great finesse and ability to last in bottle. Approximate annual production is 7,100 cases, sold in Germany and abroad. Address: 5511 Wiltingen.

Müller-Thurgau

White grape variety, the great work-horse vine of Germany, covering 23,944ha (61,639 acres) in all 11 wine-growing regions. Named after its developer, Prof. Dr Müller from the Thurgau in Switzerland, it was originally thought to be a crossing of Riesling × Silvaner but is now considered to be a crossing of two clones of Riesling. It regularly produces a large crop, usually with low acidity, early in the autumn. The low acid content and the tendency of the grapes to rot makes a late harvest difficult.

Müller-Thurgau cannot compare in quality with Riesling but it makes perfectly sound, agreeable wine, of no great distinction, and thereby meets the needs of many growers and consumers. It is the backbone of many cheap commercial blends and is best drunk within a year or so of being bottled.

Müllerrebe

Red grape variety, a mutation of Spätburgunder, also deceptively known as Schwarzriesling and found in France as Pinot Meunier. Planted in 1,168ha (2,886 acres), mainly in Württemberg, it produces wine with a good deep colour but rather lacking in acidity and, therefore, elegance.

Mumm'sches Weingut, G. H. v. Rhg.

70ha (173 acre) estate, est. in the early 19th century, lying above SCHLOSS JOHANNISBERG where it owns Burg Schwarzenstein and a restaurant with a fine view of the Rheingau. The estate is also sole owner of the 3.8ha (9 acre) Hansenberg and 5.5ha (14 acre) Schwarzenstein sites at JOHANNISBERG, and has holdings at RÜDESHEIM (BERG ROTTLAND, BERG SCHLOSSBERG, BERG ROSENECK, etc.), ASSMANNSHAUSEN, GEISENHEIM and WINKEL. All wines are cask-matured and more than half are dry or medium-dry. The aim is the Rheingau Riesling virtues of good acidity and fruit. Approx. annual production is 54,000 cases, sold in Germany and abroad. Address: 6225 Johannisberg/Rheingau.

Münster-Sarmsheim Nahe w. ★★★

Small village some 3km (2 miles) s. of BINGEN, producing top-quality Riesling wine from its DAUTENPFLÄNZER Einzellage. The "Sarmsheim" does not appear on the label. Grosslage: SCHLOSS-KAPELLE.

Münzlay M-S-R w. ★★

Grosslage of more than 500ha (1,236 acres) around ZELTINGEN-RACHTIG, GRAACH and WEHLEN, on both sides of the R. Mosel. Most of the v'yds are very steep, producing a relatively small crop from Riesling grown on slaty soil. The best wines will normally be sold under the individual site names (Wehlener SONNENUHR, Zeltinger SONNENUHR, Zeltinger HIMMELREICH, etc.). Wine that is sold carrying only the Grosslage name, Munzlay, should still be quite stylish, but will probably lack the finesse of one of the wines bearing an Einzellage name on the label.

Müsenhang Rhpf. w. ★★★

Sloping Einzellage at FORST making top-quality, stylish, meaty Riesling wines. Grosslage: MARIENGARTEN. Growers: Bassermann-Jordan, Forster Winzerverein, Hahnhof, Mosbacher.

Muskat

Name applied to many different and sometimes unrelated vine varieties. Some are European in origin, others are hybrids. Both red and white Muskat grapes are possible. The common factor of all Muskat wine is a distinctive bouquet that can range from the flowery and delicate to the overblown and sickly. The most widely grown "Muskat" in Germany is Morio-Muskat. Gelber Muskateller with 30ha (74 acres) and Muskat-Ottonel, 25ha (62 acres), have a certain importance in Baden and Württemberg. Although

Muskat is prepared as a single-vine wine, it is also added to neutral-tasting blends based on vines such as Gutedel or Silvaner.

Must

Grape juice. Its quality is judged by weight, which for practical purposes means its sugar (and thus its potential alcohol) content and its degree of acidity. Must weight (Mostgewicht) is measured in Germany against the OECHSLE scale. The legal minimum must weight for each quality of German wine ranges from 44° Oechsle for DEUTSCHER TAFELWEIN in the n. regions to 150° for a TROCKEN-BEERENAUSLESE. Thus, although the importance attached to the actual ALCOHOL content of a wine is not as great in Germany as in other countries, great value is placed on the potential alcohol content as expressed by the sugar content of the must. From must, wine and SÜSSRESERVE are made.

Nackenheim Rhh. w. ★★→★★★

Small town on the Rhein, nr. MAINZ. The area under vine is not large but the red sandstone produces excellent wine with character and style. Grosslagen: SPIEGELBERG, GUTES DOMTAL.

Nacktarsch M-S-R w. ★★

Relatively small Grosslage of some 400ha (988 acres) in the MITTEL-MOSEL, devoted entirely to the v'yds of the village of KRÖV. A high proportion of Riesling is grown on extremely steep sites and the wine, like that from the neighbouring villages, has all the welcome Mosel characteristics of freshness and fruitiness. None of the individual Kröver site names is as well known, particularly to the German consumer, as that of Nacktarsch – a name which, if translated, means exactly what you would expect.

Nägler, Weingut Dr Heinrich Rhg.

5.9ha (15 acre) estate with holdings in RÜDESHEIM (BERG ROTTLAND, BERG SCHLOSSBERG, BERG ROSENECK, Bischofsberg, Drachenstein and Magdalenenkreuz). Vines are 87% Riesling, 8% Ehrenfelser, 5% Spätburgunder. Approx. annual production is 5,000 cases of cask-matured wine, sold in Germany and abroad. Address: Friedrichstr. 22, 6220 Rüdesheim am Rhein.

Nahe w. (r.)

Region of 4,561ha (11,271 acres) with a relatively small number of growers making what is generally accepted as some of the finest wine in Germany. Many of the v'yds are on gentle or steep slopes and Riesling occupies the best sites. Wines made in the attractive area between BAD KREUZNACH and SCHLOSSBÖCKELHEIM resemble those of the Mosel or Saar. They can be extremely elegant, with

a wonderfully balanced fruity acidity. The Nahe is very much an agricultural as well as a viticultural region and many vine-growers are involved in farming as well. Often the growers are also wine-makers and bottle their produce themselves rather than sell their grapes, or their wine in bulk, to others. Some 40% of a vintage is said to be sold directly to the consumer by estate-bottlers. The best-known on the export market, but not the best wine of the region is that of the Grosslage Rüdesheimer ROSENGARTEN. At all quality levels, Nahe wine is normally good value for money.

Nahewinzer eG, Zentralkellerei der Nahe

Central cooperative cellar with 2,000 members supplying grapes from 60 villages spread throughout the Nahe. Unusually high percentage of Silvaner (32%), plus 30% Müller-Thurgau, 26% Riesling, etc. Approx. annual production is 816,000 cases, sold in Germany and abroad. Address: Winzenheimerstr. 30 6551 Bretzenheim/Nahe.

Narrenkappe Nahe w. ★★★

One of several sloping Einzellagen at BAD KREUZNACH producing essentially racy Riesling wines with fine, fruity acidity. Grosslage: KRONENBERG. Growers: August E. Anheuser, Paul Anheuser, Finkenauer, Schlink-Herf-Gutleuthof.

Nassverbesserung

Wet-sugaring: the addition of a solution of sugar and water to QbA and DTW (not QmP), to increase the alcohol content and reduce acidity. Although it is often the most satisfactory way of improving the quality of wine made from unripe grapes in poor vintages, it has been forbidden since March 1984. The EEC objection to Nassverbesserung lies not in the method, or indeed in the quality of the result, but in the fact that the total quantity of liquid is increased (by a maximum of 10% for QbA and 15% for DTW) over its original volume.

Naturrein

According to the 1930 German Wine Law, a wine in which the alcohol content had not been increased by added sugar could be called "naturrein". As a result, wines that would have benefited from more alcohol were sometimes left thin and unbalanced so as to be able to claim "purity". The use of the term was prohibited by the 1971 Wine Law.

Naturwein

A NATURREIN wine.

Neckar

River that rises nr. the Danube and flows, some 402km (250 miles) later, into the Rhein at Mannheim. Its Württemberg v'yds are not as continuous as those of the Mosel but are often equally as steep and as costly to maintain. Many lie well away from the river, diminishing somewhat the river's importance to vine-growing.

Neckerauer, Weingut K. Rhpf.

Old-established estate n. of BAD DÜRKHEIM covering 16ha (40 acres), selling Weisenheimer and Freinsheimer wines from a wide range of vines suitable to the sandy clay soil. The approx. annual production of 12,000 cases shows a low yield, concentrated on QmP. All styles of Pfälzer wine are made, incl. dry and medium-dry, esp. Müller-Thurgau in years with high acidity. Sales are mainly in Germany. Address. Ritter von Geisslerstr. 9, 6714 Weisenheim am Sand.

Neef M-S-R w. ★→★★

Small village between COCHEM and ZELL producing positive Riesling wines. Surprisingly for this part of the river, Elbling is also grown. Grosslage: Grafschaft.

Neipperg, Weingüter u. Schlosskellerei Graf von Würt.

Estate dating back to the 12th century, with the von Neipperg family still in command. 17ha (42 acres) are planted with red vine varieties (Limberger, Schwarzriesling, Spätburgunder, Trollinger), 11.4ha (28 acres) with white vine varieties (Riesling, Traminer, Muskateller, Müller-Thurgau). Emphasis in listing and selling the wines is given to the vine variety and PRÄDIKAT (e.g. Riesling Spätlese Schwaigerne Ruthe). Approx. annual production is 16,600 cases of firm, dry, elegant red wines and characterful white wines, sold exclusively in Germany. The estate also owns Ch. Canon la Gaffelière, Clos l'Oratoire, Ch. La Mondotte and Ch. Peyreau in St-Emilion, Bordeaux. Address: 7103 Schwaigern/Württemberg.

Nell, Georg-Fritz von M-S-R

17ha (42 acres) Trier estate, owned by the von Nell family since 1803, with sole ownership of the Trierer Benediktinerberg and Kurfürstenhofberg sites as well as holdings at WILTINGEN, AYL and BERNKASTEL. The proportion of Riesling grown is high (100% in some sites). The wines are concentrated in flavour and benefit from bottle age. 50% are dry or medium-dry. Approx. annual produc-

tion is relatively low (11,700 cases), sold in Germany and abroad. Address: Weingut Thiergarten, 5500 Trier/Mosel.

Nervig
Nervous. A term similar in meaning to KERNIG. or the French *nerveux*. Describes a wine in which the balance of alcohol, extract and acid is very good. Such a wine will be vigorous (not flat and tired), firm and impress by its style. Not a description that is often used, but could be applied to good Riesling wines.

Neuer Wein
New wine. The consumer in Germany has as yet no great interest in drinking his own Neuer Wein within weeks of the vintage, but is as partial to Beaujolais Nouveau as anybody else. Nevertheless, cheap wines from early-ripening vine varieties are on sale by November, but they are not given any special prominence.

Neuleiningen Rhpf. w. ★★
Fine old fortified village perched on a hilltop in the n. of the Rheinpfalz, overlooking its sloping v'yds. Great wines are not likely to be found but characterful and flavoury wines are made from Riesling and Silvaner. Grosslage: Höllenpfad.

Neumagen M-S-R w. ★★→★★★
Ancient wine village nr. PIESPORT. producing racy wines, mainly from Riesling. Grosslage: MICHELSBERG.

Neus, Weingut J. Rhh.
Mainly red-wine producing estate, founded in 1881, with 10ha (25 acres) of vines in the long-established enclave of Spätburgunder around INGELHEIM. facing MITTELHEIM and OESTRICH across the

Rhein. Approx. annual production is 9,700 cases, incl. 4,750 cases of Spätburgunder and 3,400 cases of Portugieser. The wines are dry and are much admired in Germany, but have a low tannin content compared to those from France. Sales at home and abroad. Address: Bahnhofstr. 96, 6507 Ingelheim/Rhein.

Neustadt Rhpf. Pop. 50,500 w. (r.) ★★
Busy wine-town in the s. of the Bereich MITTELHAARDT/DEUTSCHE WEINSTRASSE. Produces good, meaty, but not outstanding wine. Grosslagen: MEERSPINNE, Rebstöckel, Pfaffengrund.

Neutral
Wine term, used mainly within the trade, often applied to QbA or DTW with no excesses of flavour or bouquet, made from grapes such as Elbling, Silvaner and sometimes Riesling. A neutral flavour is often unrelated to quality, except in a base wine from which sparkling wine is to be made, in which case it is normally considered an advantage.

Neuzüchtungen
New crossings of one European vine with another, e.g. Müller-Thurgau, a crossing of Riesling × Silvaner. (Crossings of European and American vines are HYBRIDEN.)

Neveu, Weingut Freiherr von Baden
Estate of some 12ha (30 acres), acquired by the von Neveu family in 1832, planted 41% in Riesling, 22% Müller-Thurgau, 15% Spätburgunder, etc. The full-bodied, firm wines are made on the estate but bottled by the huge Zentralkellerei (ZBW) at Breisach. Annual production is 4,500-7,500 cases. 10% is exported. Address: 7601 Durbach.

Nicolay'sche Weinguts-Verwaltung C. H. Berres Erben M-S-R
Mittelmosel estate dating in its present form from the 19th century, with an old vaulted cask cellar. 15ha (37 acres) of holdings in ÜRZIG (WÜRZGARTEN, and sole ownership of Goldwingert), ERDEN (TREPPCHEN and PRÄLAT), ZELTINGEN-RACHTIG (HIMMELREICH), WEHLEN

and KINHEIM (HUBERTUSLAY). Vines are 92% Riesling, 8% Müller-Thurgau. Approx. annual production is 16,600 cases of individually cask-matured wines that reflect the sometimes subtle variations between one site and another. Sales are in Germany and abroad. A cellar selling wines from other estates is attached to the Weingut. Address: Würzgartenstr. 41, 5564 Ürzig/Mosel.

Niederhausen Nahe w. ★★★
Small village surrounded by steep, game-filled woods and top-quality v'yds producing some of the most elegant Riesling wines of the region. Unusually for the Nahe there is a small plantation of Traminer. Home of the State Wine Cellars (see next entry). Grosslage: BURGWEG.

Niederhausen-Schlossböckelheim, Verwaltung der Staatlichen Weinbaudomäne Nahe
The Nahe State Wine Cellars are one of the great wine estates of the world, est. in 1902, with 45ha (111 acres) in SCHLOSSBÖCKELHEIM (KUPFERGRUBE, FELSENBERG), NIEDERHAUSEN (HERMANNSHÖHLE, sole owners of Hermannsberg, etc.), TRAISEN (BASTEI), ALTENBAMBERG, MÜNSTER-SARMSHEIM and DORSHEIM, etc. Vines are 85% Riesling (the estate, in its role as vine-breeder, has five registered clones of Riesling on sale and in use in Germany). Cool fermentation, skilled vinification and maturation in wood, guided by an outstanding cellar-master, results in Riesling wines of incredible delicacy and

complexity. Approx. annual production is 23,300 cases. Sales are in Germany and abroad. Address: 6551 Oberhausen.

Nierstein Rhh. Pop. 6,000 w. ★★★
Small town dedicated to wine-making, 20km (12 miles) from MAINZ in the heart of the RHEINFRONT. with many old vaulted cellars and a wine festival each August. The 150 or so growers incl. some of the best-known wine names in Germany. Grosslagen: SPIEGELBERG. AUFLANGEN and REHBACH (and GUTES DOMTAL for one site, the Pfaffenkappe).

Nierstein, Bereich Rhh. w. (r.)
Best-known Bereich of the Rheinland in export markets, covering the fine v'yds of the RHEINFRONT n. and s. of the small town of NIERSTEIN. as well as those in much of the rolling hinterland away from the river. A wine sold as Bereich Nierstein will not be of great quality but it will be soft, light, pleasantly fruity and likely to contain a high proportion of Müller-Thurgau. It will also be cheap. If it is very cheap, then that is how it will taste.

Nies'chen M-S-R w. ★★★
Mainly steep, SSW-facing Einzellage at KASEL on the Ruwer producing spicy Riesling wines with a positive fruity, crisp style. Sometimes suffers from frost. Grosslage: RÖMERLAY. Growers: Bischöfliche Weingüter, Deinhard Bernkastel, Kesselstatt, Simon.

Nikolai, Weingut Heinz Rhg.
Small estate, owned by the Nikolai family for four generations, with holdings in ERBACH (MICHELMARK. etc), KIEDRICH (SANDGRUB) and HALLGARTEN. Vines are 85% Riesling, 10% Scheurebe, 5% Ruländer. The Riesling wines reflect the classic Rheingau virtues of good acidity and spiciness, but the Scheurebe is the most popular with the estate's customers. Approx. annual production is 5,000 cases. No exports. Address: Ringstr. 14, 6229 Erbach/Rheingau.

Nobling
White grape variety, a crossing of Silvaner × Gutedel from the state viticultural institute at FREIBURG. planted in 165ha (408 acres), mainly in Baden. It can be harvested at the same time as Silvaner, is often heavier by some 10° Oechsle and has greater acidity. Given the right conditions it will produce SPÄTLESE and AUSLESE wines with a positive flavour and fine bouquet.

Nordheim Franken w. ★★
Village nr. VOLKACH. e. of WÜRZBURG. with the largest area under vine in Franken, incl. the massive 250ha (618 acre) Vögelein site. Powerful, soft, long-flavoured Silvaner and Müller-Thurgau wines, many sold direct by the producers. Grosslage: Kirchberg.

Nordrhein-Westfalen
Federal State, within whose s. border lie 19ha (47 acres) of Mittelrhein v'yd nr. Bonn. The capital is Düsseldorf.

Norheim Nahe w. ★★★
Village with small Einzellagen producing wines with good acidity and flavour. Riesling from the DELLCHEN site can produce great wine in good years. Grosslage: BURGWEG.

Nussbrunnen Rhg. w. ★★★
Small Einzellage at HATTENHEIM making full-bodied Riesling wines. Grosslage: DEUTELSBERG. Growers: Reinhartshausen, Ress, Schloss Schönborn, Simmern'sches Rentamt.

Nussdorf Rhpf. w. ★
Village in the Bereich SÜDLICHE WEINSTRASSE nr. LANDAU IN DER PFALZ. producing sound, inexpensive wines.

Oberemmel M-S-R w. ★★★
Village set in pleasant country nr. WILTINGEN in the Saar valley, making finely tuned, racy Riesling wine. Grosslage: SCHARZBERG. ·

Obermosel, Bereich M-S-R w.
Upper-Mosel Bereich, facing the v'yds of Luxembourg across the river. Produces simple, agreeable and refreshing quality wine from Elbling, much of it converted into sparkling wine.

Oberwesel Mrh. w. ★★
Ancient wine village in the s. Mittelrhein, 40km (25 miles) from KOBLENZ in the Rhein gorge. All its v'yds are extremely steep,

planted almost 100% Riesling and produce racy, firm wines. Gross-lage: Schloss Schönburg.

Ockfen M-S-R w. ★★★
Saar village well known for centuries for its BOCKSTEIN and HERREN-BERG sites. Top-quality, flowery, racy Riesling wine. Grosslage: SCHARZBERG.

Oechsle, Oechsle scale
Christian Ferdinand Oechsle (1774-1852), a prolific inventor and musician, was born, lived and died in Württemberg. He developed the Oechsle scale, which compares the weight of a MUST with that of water. The Oechsle figure is the specific gravity of the must with the decimal point moved three places to give a whole number. Thus 90° Oechsle is equivalent to a specific gravity of 1.090, i.e. 1 litre of the must in question would be 90 grams heavier than 1 litre of water at 20°C.

Oesterreicher
Synonym for Silvaner, a grape variety believed by some to have come to Germany from Austria (Oesterreich).

Oestrich Rhg. w. ★★★
Small Rhein town halfway between RÜDESHEIM and the outskirts of WIESBADEN, making firm, full-bodied Riesling wines that rise to greatness in fine years. Grosslagen: GOTTESTHAL, MEHRHÖLZCHEN.

Oetinger'sches Weingut, Robert von Rhg.
Estate est. in the 1820s with 6ha (15 acres) of vines, 70% Riesling, at ERBACH (MICHELMARK, SIEGELSBERG, MARCOBRUNN, etc.) and KIED-RICH (SANDGRUB). Annual production is approx. 4,500 cases of wines with powerful acidity. Dry wines, in particular, are popular with the German retail customers and in the estate's wine bar. Address: Rheinallee 1–3, 6228 Eltville-Erbach.

Offenburg, Weingut der Stadt Baden
Ancient charitable estate, founded in 1301, taken over by the town of Offenburg in 1936. Its 30ha (74 acres) of vines are 35% Müller-Thurgau, 17% Riesling, 16% Spätburgunder, plus a range of other varieties. Approx. annual production is 23,800 cases of fresh wines with good acidity, typical of the Bereich ORTENAU. No exports. Address: St Andreas Hospital Fonds, Steingrube 7, 7601 Orten-berg.

Offene Weine
See Ausschankwein

Ökonomierat
Agricultural Counsellor. Honorary title awarded for services to agriculture in its broadest sense. Appears in the title of a number of estates, e.g. Weingut Ökonomierat August E. Anheuser, Weingut Ökonomierat Max-G. Piedmont.

Ölberg Rhh. w. ★★★
S-facing Einzellage at NIERSTEIN producing full-bodied, stylish wines. Grosslage: AUFLANGEN. Growers: Balbach, Guntrum, Heyl zu Herrnsheim, Kurfürstenhof, Hermann Franz Schmitt, Georg Schneider, Schuch, Sittmann, Strub.

Oppenheim Rhh. Pop. 4,700 w. ★★★
Small wine-producing town on the RHEINFRONT, headquarters of a number of important estates and exporting houses and with a well-known viticultural institute (see next entry). Its attractions incl. the much-photographed St Katharinen-Kirche and the Deutsches Weinbaumuseum (German Viticultural Museum). Grosslagen: GÜLDENMORGEN, KRÖTENBRUNNEN.

Oppenheim, Staatsweingut der Landes- Lehr- und Versuchsanstalt Rhh.
Research and training institute, founded in 1885 and owned by the state of Rheinland-Pfalz. The institute owns 20ha (49 acres) of v'yds at OPPENHEIM (SACKTRÄGER, KREUZ, Herrenberg, Zucker-berg), Dienheim and NIERSTEIN (PATERBERG, PETTENTHAL, ÖLBERG). Vines are 36% Riesling. Because of the estate's experimental role there are also many new crossings. The v'yds are maintained to an exemplary standard and emphasis is laid on retaining the indi-vidual grape variety character in the wines. Approx. annual pro-duction of 8,300 cases is low. 20% of the wines are dry or medium-dry and many awards have been won at regional and national com-

petitions. Sales are mainly in Germany. Address: Zuckerberg 19, 6504 Oppenheim.

Optima

White grape variety, a crossing of (Silvaner × Riesling) × Müller-Thurgau, planted in 507ha (1,253 acres), mainly in the n. regions of the M-S-R, Rheinhessen and Rheinpfalz. The yield is similar to that of Riesling (about 70hl/ha) and late picking can produce fine AUSLESE quality wine, provided the acidity is not too low.

Orbel Rhh. w. ★★★

One of the many excellent Einzellagen on the slopes at NIERSTEIN, making full-flavoured, weighty wines. Grosslage: AUFLANGEN. Growers: Guntrum, Georg Schneider, Sittmann, Strub, Wehrheim.

Ordensgut Rhpf. w. (r.) ★

Grosslage at the n. end of the Bereich SÜDLICHE WEINSTRASSE. Many vine varieties and sound, quality wines.

Originalabfüllung

Estate bottling. A term used until 1971 to describe unsugared (NATURREIN) wines that had been produced and bottled by the grower. Cooperative cellars could also sell their wines as Original-abfüllungen. The term ERZEUGERABFÜLLUNG has in part superseded Originalabfüllung, although it can be applied equally to a sugared or unsugared wine.

Originalabzug

Identical in meaning to ORIGINALABFÜLLUNG.

Ortega

Early-ripening white grape variety, a crossing of Müller-Thurgau × Siegerrebe from WÜRZBERG in Franken, planted in 1,169ha (2,889 acres), mainly in the Rheinpfalz, Rheinhessen and M-S-R. It produces good, powerfully scented wine up to KABINETT quality. Insufficient acidity makes it unsuitable for late-picking. Benefits from early bottling followed by a period of maturation.

Ortenau, Bereich Baden w. (r.)

Bereich that stretches s. from Baden-Baden at the foot of the Black Forest. It produces wines of very good quality, esp. from Riesling (known locally as Klingelberger), that are beginning to be found on the export market.

Ortenaukreises, Weinbauversuchsgut des Baden

Estate founded in 1950 as a training and experimental institute. Its 7.5ha (19 acres) of v'yds lie exclusively in the Ortenberger Schloss-berg. Vines are 23% Müller-Thurgau, 19% Riesling, etc. The estate's wine list emphasizes the vine variety and quality category of each wine, and incl. an impressive range of AUSLESEN and BEERENAUSLESEN (no DTW or QbA) and two TROCKENBEERENAUS-LESEN, all of which have won prizes at regional and national competitions. Sales are mainly in Germany. Address: Schloss Ortenberg, Burgweg 19a, 7601 Ortenberg/Baden.

Ortenberg, Schloss

See previous entry.

Ortsteil

Part of a larger community, e.g. the village of ERBACH in the Rheingau is an Ortsteil of the town of ELTVILLE.

Osthofen Rhh. w. (r.) ★★

Small town with many rustic wine bars and cellars, 10km (6 miles) n. of WORMS in the Bereich WONNEGAU. Very good wines are produced, probably missing the style of those from further n. in the Bereich NIERSTEIN. Well known in Germany but less so on the export market. Grosslagen: Pilgerpfad, Gotteshilfe.

Othegraven, Maximilian v.

See Kanzemer Berg, Weingut

Palatinate

See Rheinpfalz

Pallhuber Weingut & Weinkellerei GmbH, Maximilian Nahe

Estate owners and wine merchants with 10ha (25 acres) nr. LANGENLONSHEIM, between BAD KREUZNACH and BINGEN, planted 40% Silvaner, 30% Müller-Thurgau, 10% Riesling, etc. Approx. annual production of the estate's own wine is 9,200 cases. As wine merchants, the company sells 166,600 cases of wine originating elsewhere. All sales are direct to private customers in Germany. Address: An den Nahewiesen, 6536 Langenlonsheim.

Parzelle

Plot. For administrative purposes Einzellagen are subdivided into smaller parcels of land which are named and numbered. However the Einzellage remains the smallest geographical unit that can be mentioned on a wine label.

Paterberg Rhh. w. ★★★

Largest Einzellage, 148ha (366 acres), at NIERSTEIN, producing stylish, good-quality wine. Grosslage: SPIEGELBERG. Growers: Guntrum, Georg Schneider, Sittmann, Strub, Wehrheim.

Pauly KG, Weingut Otto M-S-R

Estate of some 3ha (7 acres) dating back more than 300 years, owned by Dr Otto-Ulrich Pauly. The steep holdings are at GRAACH (DOMPROBST, HIMMELREICH), WEHLEN (SONNENUHR) and BERNKASTEL (BRATENHÖFCHEN, etc.). Vines are 95% Riesling. Approx. annual production is 4,100 cases of typical, top-quality, fresh Mosel wines, sold in Germany and abroad. Address: Bernkastelerstr. 5–7, 5550 Graach/Mosel.

Pauly, Otto Ulrich

See "Abteihof", Weingut

Pauly-Bergweiler, Weingut Dr

See Bergweiler-Prüm Erben, Zach.

Pechstein Rhpf. w. ★★★

Mainly level Einzellage at FORST making full-bodied Riesling wines. Grosslage: MARIENGARTEN. Growers: Bassermann-Jordan, Bürklin-Wolf, Forster Winzerverein, Hahnhof, Mosbacher, Spindler, J. L. Wolf.

Perle

White grape variety, a crossing of Gewürztraminer × Müller-Thurgau, with rosé-coloured grapes that produce a light, gentle white wine. It is planted in 276ha (682 acres), mainly in the Rheinhessen and in Franken where much work has been carried out improving the vine at the state viticultural institute at WÜRZBURG.

Perll, August Mrh.

Small, 100-year-old estate with 3.6ha (9 acres) of holdings in the very steep v'yds of the Bopparder Hamm, overlooking the Rhein upstream from KOBLENZ. The slate-grown, racy, lively Riesling wines enjoy remarkable success at national competitions. Production is low, approx. 1,200 cases a year, sold directly to the German consumer. Address: Oberstr. 81, 5407 Boppard.

Perlwein

Semi-sparkling wine, the result of a second fermentation in a pressurized tank or simply of impregnation with carbon dioxide. The bottling and labelling must be such that the wine will not be confused with a sparkling wine. At best, Perlwein is a cheap and pleasant drink but it usually lacks the style and the ability to retain its sparkle once opened that is characteristic of good-quality sparkling wine.

Pettenthal Rhh. w. ★★★

One of the best, mainly steep Einzellagen at NIERSTEIN. The wine is full of flavour from the red sandstone and clay soil. Grosslage: REHBACH. Growers: Baumann, Guntrum, Heyl zu Herrnsheim, Kurfürstenhof, Hermann Franz Schmitt, Schuch, Wehrheim.

Pfeffingen, Weingut Rhpf.

Estate a few km n. of BAD DÜRKHEIM with 10ha (25 acres) of modernized v'yds in UNGSTEIN (Herrenberg and Nussriegel). Vines are 40% Riesling, 18% Müller-Thurgau, 15% Silvaner, etc. Family commitment to the estate is total – both the daughter and son-in-law are qualified "Weinbauingenieure" (vine growers and wine makers) – and the wines win many awards at regional and national competitions. Approx. annual production is 6,600 cases with a high proportion of QmP, incl. dry and medium-dry wines. Sales are almost exclusively in Germany. Address: Karl Fuhrmann, 6702 Bad Dürkheim.

Phylloxera

Known in Germany as the "Reblaus", or vine louse, Phylloxera (full title *Phylloxera vastatrix*) is an aphid that causes swellings or growths on the roots of European vines (*Vitis vinifera*), which then rot in winter and the root system is destroyed.

Piedmont, Weingut Ökonomierat Max-G. M-S-R

Fourth-generation family estate nr. the confluence of the Saar and Mosel with 6ha (15 acres) of v'yds, all in Filzen. Vines are 95% Riesling, producing excellent spicy wines in good years. Approx. annual production is 4,500 cases of QmP, cask-matured and light in alcohol. Sales are mainly in Germany. Address: Saartalstr. 1, 5503 Konz-Filzen/Saar.

Pieroth Weingut Weinkellerei GmbH, Ferdinand

An organization that has had remarkable success in selling directly to the consumer in Germany and abroad, with an annual turnover of some DM 600m. The concentration is on QmP, but wines from outside Germany are also sold, many through subsidiary companies. (Pieroth also owns Barnsgate Manor, Sussex, and is one of the largest producers of English wines.) Address: 6531 Burg Layen.

Piesport M-S-R W. ★★→★★★

One of the best-known village names on the Mosel, particularly when linked to its Grosslage MICHELSBERG or its Einzellage GOLD-TRÖPFCHEN. While the high quality of the best Piesporter Rieslings cannot be disputed, equally good wines at lesser prices can often be found elsewhere on the Mosel. Unfortunately, some of the non-Riesling wines that appear on the market with Piesport in their name, originating from the wider boundaries of the Grosslage Michelsberg, do the excellent and ancient wine-producing village little credit.

Pittersberg Nahe W. ★★

Sloping Einzellage at MÜNSTER-SARMSHEIM producing fruity wines with good body but usually less finesse than those made up-river at SCHLOSSBÖCKELHEIM. Grosslage: SCHLOSSKAPELLE. Grower: Niederhausen-Schlossböckelheim Staatl. Weinbaudomäne.

Plettenberg'sche Verwaltung, Reichsgräflich von Nahe

48ha (119 acre) estate with 18th-century origins. Holdings are at BAD KREUZNACH (BRÜCKES, NARRENKAPPE. etc.), SCHLOSSBÖCKELHEIM (KUPFERGRUBE and FELSENBERG), Bretzenheim, Winzenheim, ROX-HEIM and NORHEIM, planted 65% Riesling, 20% Müller-Thurgau, etc. Approx. annual production is 25,000 cases of seriously made wine, with care being given to retain individuality and the grape characteristics. Sales are international. Address: Winzenheimer-strasse, 6550 Bad Kreuznach/Nahe.

Plump

Describes a wine with high extract, possibly an excessive alcohol content and certainly too little acid. With modern wine-making methods, in which acidity and freshness are retained, plump wines are not so common as they were 20 years ago. The Rheinpfalz, Rheinhessen, Franken and Baden are more likely to produce wines that are plump than regions further north.

Pokal

Large glass with a content of 200 or 250ml in which "open wine" (AUSSCHANKWEIN) is served.

Portugieser, Blauer

After Spätburgunder, the most widely planted red vine variety in Germany, covering 3,095ha (7,648 acres) of which more than half lie in the Rheinpfalz. The yield is large, the MUST weight is low and the acidity high. It is suggested that the Portugieser is often picked too early in the season, and that if it were gathered after the Müller-Thurgau a more satisfactory wine would result. As red wine, the colour seems light to the non-German, but the Portugieser makes an attractive WEISSHERBST in the Rheinpfalz.

Prädikat

A quality distinction. See Qualitätswein mit Prädikat (QmP).

Prädikatsweingüter, Verband Deutscher

An association of QmP-producing estates, with origins going back to the last century. The aim of the association, which has approx. 160 members, is to promote the sale of estate-bottled QmP. Some members (e.g. Schloss Vollrads, Weingut Rappenhof) use the association's emblem, a bunch of grapes forming the body of an eagle with outspread wings, on their labels.

Prälat M-S-R w. ★★★→★★★★

Very small, 2.2ha (5.44 acre), top-quality Einzellage at ERDEN, planted exclusively in Riesling. Great wines in the best years. Grosslage: SCHWARZLAY. Growers: Loosen-Erben, Nicolay'sche Weinguts-Verwaltung, St Johannishof.

Prämierung

See Bundesweinprämierung

Probe

Tasting. For details of wine tastings in Germany, see page 20.

Prüfungsnummer

See Amtliche Prüfung

Prüm, Weingut Joh. Jos. M-S-R

One of the most prestigious estates on the Mosel, best known for the 4.5ha (11 acre) holding in the Wehlener SONNENUHR, which the estate has done so much to make famous. A further 9.5ha (23 acres) are in other sites at WEHLEN and at GRAACH (HIMMELREICH and DOMPROBST), ZELTINGEN-RACHTIG (SONNENUHR) and BERNKAS-TEL, incl. part of BRATENHÖFCHEN. The grapes (95% Riesling) are usually gathered as late as possible. The wines are made with immense care and attention to detail to ensure they reach their full potential. Although the KABINETT wines in off-vintages can surprise by their style and positive SPRITZIG flavour, the estate is best known for its incredibly luscious AUSLESEN. Sales are worldwide. Address: 5554 Wehlen.

Prüm Erben, Weingut S.A. M-S-R

Estate of 5ha (12 acres) est. in 1911 when the original Prüm family property was divided among the heirs (Erben). Today the S.A. Prüm estate owns holdings at WEHLEN (SONNENUHR, etc.), BERNKAS-TEL, GRAACH (HIMMELREICH, DOMPROBST) and ZELTINGEN-RACHTIG (SCHLOSSBERG). Most are 100% Riesling. The aim is to make racy wines, matured in cask, with and without much residual sugar. Approx. annual production is 5,800 cases, 60-80% exported. Address: Uferallee 25-26, 5550 Bernkastel-Wehlen.

Pünderich M-S-R w. ★★

Small, picturesque wine village, just inside the boundaries of the Bereich BERNKASTEL nr. ZELL. Much good, sound wine is sold under the Grosslage name, vom HEISSEN STEIN. Elegant, fruity Riesling wines appear under the various Einzellage names.

Qualitätsschaumwein

Quality sparkling wine. A sparkling wine may only be described as Qualitätsschaumwein in the EEC if it has fulfilled the conditions of production laid down in its country of origin. In Germany most quality sparkling wine (more widely known as SEKT) is sold under a brand name (MARKENSEKT). Sales are increasing of sekt bearing a vintage, a regional name and sometimes a site name, made from a single vine (usually Riesling – RIESLINGSEKT), but as yet they are a small fraction of total Sekt production. The best Qualitäts-schaumwein is stylish, crisp, clean and fruity. Its flavour does not cloy and it seems to reflect, in sparkling form, many of the qualities found in a good Nahe or Rheingau still wine.

Qualitätswein eines bestimmten Anbaugebietes (QbA)

Quality wine from a specified region (bestimmtes Anbaugebiet). In the eyes of the law, the category of a quality wine is only estab-lished once it has passed the official examination (AMTLICHE PRÜ-FUNG). To qualify for consideration it will have been made from legally recommended or authorized vine varieties and its MUST weight will have reached certain minimum levels, depending on the vine variety and region of origin. It will not have been blended with wine from another region. Some 95% of German wine is classified as quality wine. In contrast, 87% of Italian and 64% of French wines are table wines.

Qualitätswein mit Prädikat (QmP)

"Quality wine with distinction": wine made from grapes with suffi-cient natural sugar to need no sugar added during vinification. The six levels of Prädikat are KABINETT, SPÄTLESE, AUSLESE, BEERENAUS-

LESE. EISWEIN and TROCKENBEERENAUSLESE. Any of these distinctions may be won by a wine from MUST of a certain minimum weight, provided it achieves the necessary "marks" at an official control (AMTLICHE PRÜFUNG) centre. The grapes will also have been harvested according to a procedure, established in law, appropriate to the particular Prädikat.

The minimum must weights – and therefore potential alcohol level – for each Prädikat vary depending on the region and the wine variety. Those for Riesling in the M-S-R, for example, are:

M-S-R Riesling	Minimum must weight in degrees Oechsle	Potential alcohol content by volume
Kabinett	67	8.6
Spätlese	76	10.0
Auslese	83	11.1
Beerenauslese	110	15.3
Eiswein	110	15.3
Trockenbeerenauslese	150	21.5

A Beerenauslese, Eiswein or Trockenbeerenauslese from the M-S-R is always a sweet wine, but the acidity prevents it from becoming cloying. Normally, an Auslese from the Mosel is also sweet, but the amount of residual sugar in a Spätlese or Kabinett wine can vary from very little (perhaps 4 g/l) to more than 30 g/l. In top-quality estates the sweetness in wines below Auslese level may not be very noticeable because it is usually just sufficient to balance the acidity and enhance the delicacy of the wine.

Randersacker Franken w. ★★→★★★
Village a few km from WÜRZBURG. with buildings that date back to the 14th century. Its steep sites produce fine, powerfully flavoured Silvaner wine and elegant Rieslings. Like all Franken wine, relatively expensive. Grosslagen: EWIG LEBEN. Teufelstor.

Randersacker eG, Winzergenossenschaft Franken
Cooperative cellar with 260 members supplying grapes from 145ha (358 acres) of v'yds in RANDERSACKER (TEUFELSKELLER. etc.), SOMMERHAUSEN and WÜRZBURG. Vines are 45% Müller-Thurgau, 35% Silvaner, etc. Approx. annual production is 100,000 cases of good-quality, earthy Franken wine, 90% sold locally. No exports. Address: Maingasse 33, 8701 Randersacker/Main.

Rappenhof, Weingut Rhh.
Estate dating from the 17th century, now owned by Dr Reinhard Muth. 30ha (74 acres) of white and red vine varieties, incl. Riesling (35%), Müller-Thurgau (10%) and Silvaner (10%). A fascinating list of wines from ALSHEIM (FRÜHMESSE. etc.), GUNTERSBLUM, Dien-

heim and NIERSTEIN in various quality categories, incl. attractive dry wines, esp. those from Weissburgunder (Pinot Blanc). In Germany, the red wines produced by the estate from Portugieser and Spätburgunder are very successful. Dr Muth is President of the German Vine Growers' Association. Address: Bachstr. 47-49, 6526 Alsheim.

Rassig

Racy. Describes a wine with pronounced but pleasant acidity and style, as is often found in the M-S-R region.

Rauenthal Rhg. w. ★★★

Important wine village on the slopes above ELTVILLE, not far from WIESBADEN. Its best-known Einzellage is BAIKEN. Typical Rauenthaler wines have excellent acidity and need bottle age to show their best. Grosslage: STEINMÄCHER.

Rebe

Vine, e.g. Huxelrebe, Müllerrebe.

Rebholz, Weingut Ökonomierat Rhpf.

9ha (22 acre) estate owned by a family involved in vine-growing for some 300 years. Holdings, 25% terraced, are at SIEBELDINGEN and Birkweiler. Vines are 30% Riesling, 30% Müller-Thurgau, 15% Spätburgunder, etc. The estate was the first to produce a TROCKEN-BEERENAUSLESE from Müller-Thurgau (in 1949) and is noted for individual wines with real quality in an area where this is not usual. SÜSSRESERVE is not used and much dry wine is made. QbA wines are enriched only if absolutely necessary and then sold as DEUTSCHER TAFELWEIN. Approx. annual production is 6,000 cases. Address: Weinstrasse 54, 6741 Siebeldingen/Pfalz.

Refractometer

Small hand-held instrument, widely used during the harvest, which measures refraction of light through a sample of grape juice, giving a quick measurement of MUST weight.

Regner

White grape variety, a crossing of Luglienca bianca (a table grape) × Gamay früh (a red grape), planted in 128ha (316 acres), mainly in the Rheinhessen. The main harvest is usually shortly before that of Müller-Thurgau but the grapes can be left on the vine to produce SPÄTLESE wine. Acidity is low but the quality is good. The wine is described as "traditional" (i.e. no extreme flavours) with a gentle Muskat bouquet.

Reh & Sohn GmbH & Co. KG, Franz M-S-R

Family business of wine merchants, exporters and (dating from the 17th century) estate owners, with an overall output of 1m. cases a year. The family owns the Weingut Josefinengrund with holdings at LEIWEN and TRITTENHEIM (APOTHEKE, ALTÄRCHEN) and the Weingut Marienhof at PIESPORT (GOLDTRÖPFCHEN, TREPPCHEN, GÜNTERSLAY and all of the steep little 100% Riesling Gärtchen site), DHRON and KLÜSSERATH (BRÜDERSCHAFT). Approx. annual production of the two estates is 11,200 cases, much sold abroad. Address: Römerstr. 27, 5559 Leiwen/Mosel.

Rehbach Rhh. w. ★★

Small Grosslage of some 65ha (160 acres) overlooking the Rhein above NIERSTEIN. Its Einzellagen incl. the distinguished HIPPING and PETTENTHAL and also one of the smallest individual sites in Germany, the 0.6ha (1.5 acre) Goldene Luft.

Reichensteiner

White grape variety, a crossing of Müller-Thurgau × (Madeleine Angevine × Calabreser-Fröhlich) from the state viticultural institute at GEISENHEIM. Planting increased from 5ha (12 acres) in 1970 to 336ha (830 acres) in 1982 and is now spread throughout the n. German vine-growing regions. The yield is similar to that of Müller-Thurgau, the MUST weight heavier by 5-10° Oechsle and acidity is also greater. The flavour of the wine is neutral and pleasant. Given the right weather conditions, a late harvest is possible.

Reichsfreiherr

Title received from the Kaiser, appears in the name of various estates, e.g. Weingut des Reichsfreiherrn von Ritter zu Groenesteyn.

Reichsgraf

Count, appointed by the Kaiser. The inheritor of the title would be a Graf but not a Reichsgraf.

Reichsrat

A state representative, at national level, in the formation of national law. Found in the title of, for example, the Rheinpfalz wine grower Weingut Reichsrat von Buhl.

Reif
Ripe. Describes a wine that is full, mature. See also FLASCHENREIF (bottle ripeness).

Reil M-S-R w. ★★
One of the best-known Mosel villages, downstream from TRABEN-TRABACH, making very good Riesling wine. The original home of the exporting house and estate owner Rudolf MÜLLER. Grosslage: VOM HEISSEN STEIN.

Reinhartshausen
See Schloss Reinhartshausen

Reintonig
Describes a wine that smells and tastes absolutely clean.

Reiterpfad Rhpf. w. ★★
Sloping Einzellage at RUPPERTSBERG producing good-quality, elegant Riesling and Silvaner wines. Grosslage: HOFSTÜCK. Growers: Bassermann-Jordan, Biffar, Buhl, Bürklin-Wolf, Dr Deinhard, Kern, Ruppertsberg Winzerverein, Spindler.

Rentamt
Originally the local authority for financial administration within a state, later used to describe a similar office on a large country estate. Appears, for example, in the title of Fürst von Metternich-Winneburg'sches Domäne Rentamt at Schloss Johannisberg.

Repperndorf Franken w. ★★
Wine village nr. KITZINGEN. Its v'yds are alleged to have been planted by Charlemagne. Now known mainly as the site of the large regional cooperative cellar that handles a third of the Franken grape harvest. Grosslage: Hofrat.

Ress KG, Balthasar Rhg.
Family estate and wine merchants, founded more than 100 years ago. Leaseholders since 1978 of SCHLOSS REICHHARTSHAUSEN, plus holdings in many well-known sites incl. BERG ROTTLAND, BERG SCHLOSSBERG, etc., at RÜDESHEIM; KLÄUSERWEG at GEISENHEIM; HASENSPRUNG at WINKEL; DOOSBERG at OESTRICH; SCHÖNHELL at HALLGARTEN; NUSSBRUNNEN and WISSELBRUNNEN at HATTENHEIM; SANDGRUB at KIEDRICH; and at HOCHHEIM and ERBACH. Vines are 83% Riesling, 5% Spätburgunder, etc. Estate-bottled wines total some 16,600 cases a year, sold in Germany and abroad. Address: Rheinallee 7–11, Hattenheim/Rheingau.

Restsüsse
Residual sugar in a wine, the result of an incomplete fermentation or the addition of SÜSSRESERVE. A certain amount of unfermented, or residual, sugar is characteristic of German wines. It is the fine balance of acid, alcohol and restrained sweetness that gives them charm and delicacy.

Restzucker
Unfermented sugar in a wine which provides the residual sweetness (RESTSÜSSE) for which it is, in practice, a synonym.

Reverchon, Weingut Edmund M-S-R
Estate dating from the 17th century with 18ha (44 acres) at Filzen (sole owner of Herrenberg) and OCKFEN (BOCKSTEIN, etc.), 80% Riesling. Fine, fruity Saar wines, sold mainly in Germany. Address: Saartalstr. 3, 5503 Konz-Filzen.

Rhein
The great river that rises in the Swiss Alps, flows through the heart of the German wine-growing regions and on to the North Sea, some 1,300km (800 miles) from its source. Along the way it is fed by the Neckar, Main, Nahe, Mosel and Ahr. For centuries the river served as the best route for moving wine from the regions where it was produced to customers in Germany and, via Rotterdam, abroad. In the last 25 years the uncertainties of river transport have put this traffic into the motorway system, but the Rhein remains important to wine for climatic reasons, as a tourist attraction and as a factor, directly or indirectly, linking many of the v'yds of Germany.

Rheinart Erben, Weingut Adolf M-S-R
Saar estate owned by Herr Heinzgünter Schmitt of H. Schmitt Söhne, with holdings at OCKFEN (BOCKSTEIN, HERRENBERG), AYL

(KUPP) and WILTINGEN (SCHLANGENGRABEN). Vines are 80% Riesling. Approx. annual production is 23,000 cases, sold in Germany and abroad. A bottle-fermented sparkling wine is also produced from the estate's Riesling base wine. Address: Weinstrasse 25, 5559 Longuich.

Rheinberg Kellerei GmbH
Wine exporters, est. in 1960, owned by Edeka, the largest trading group in W. Germany. Mainly QbA under well-known names but also more than 100 QmP, many from the Rheinhessen and Rheinpfalz. Annual turnover 4m. cases. Address: Mainzerstr. 164-170, 6530 Bingen/Rhein.

Rheinblick Rhh. w. ★★
Grosslage incl. within its boundaries the Alsheimer FRÜHMESSE. Many of the v'yds are on steep or sloping sites and the quality of wine is often higher than that sold under other Grosslage names from the region.

Rheinfront Rhh. w.
Name given to the v'yds alongside the Rhein from the village of BODENHEIM in the n. to Mettenheim in the s. With the possible exception of those at BINGEN, all the best Rheinhessen sites are on the slopes of the Rheinfront, with its two particularly famous small towns of OPPENHEIM and NIERSTEIN. The proportion of Riesling and Silvaner planted is greater than elsewhere in the region, and the wines can have much weight and depth of flavour. The name is being superseded by Rheinterrasse (Rhine Terrace).

Rheinfront eG, Bezirks-Winzergenossenschaft Rhh.
Cooperative cellar with 410 members holding 228ha (563 acres) in many of the best sites in NIERSTEIN and the surrounding district. Vines are 34% Müller-Thurgau, 33% Silvaner, 7% Scheurebe, etc. Much is sold in bulk to the wine trade, the balance to the consumer in Germany. Address: Karolingerstr. 6, 6505 Nierstein.

Rheingau w. (r.)
Compact region of 2,939ha (7,263 acres), incl. some of the best v'yds in West Germany. 79% of the vines are Riesling. There are some 2,250 growers, 84% of whom have v'yd holdings of less than 1ha. About 400 bottle their own wine, and it is among these that the greatest and well-known estates are found. It is from their presence and wine-making over the centuries that the reputation of Rheingau Riesling derives. The Rheingau climate and soil produce Rieslings that have the elegance of a Mosel or a fine Nahe wine but with more body and depth of flavour. They can vary from

straightforward, simple quality wines to complex Auslesen and yet remain successful throughout. Rheingauer wines are not the cheapest in Germany but they are often less expensive than wines of similar standing from Baden, Württemberg or Franken, and are seldom overpriced.

The circuitous Rheingauer Riesling Route that runs the length of the region makes it easy to visit the widely known wine villages by road, and for those with more time and an inclination to walk there is a well-signposted path through the v'yds.

Rheingau eG, Gebietswinzergenossenschaft Rhg.

Cooperative of 310 members, in a region where the cooperative system is not at its strongest. Members own 130ha (321 acres) in KIEDRICH (SANDGRUB), OESTRICH (LENCHEN) and GEISENHEIM (MÄUERCHEN), as well as ELTVILLE, ERBACH, WINKEL, LORCHHAUSEN, MARTINSTHAL and HOCHHEIM. Vines incl. Riesling (70%), Müller-Thurgau (20%) and Spätburgunder (3%). Approx. annual production is 119,000 cases of good wines, typical of the region. 10% is exported. There is storage for 297,600 cases, which shows the spare capacity that a cooperative cellar can provide. Address: 6228 Eltville a. Rhein.

Rheingräfenberg eG, Winzergenossenschaft & Weinkellerei Nahe

Relatively small cooperative cellar with 128 members supplying grapes from 153ha (378 acres), with a high proportion of Riesling (60%) and (for the Nahe valley) a low proportion of Silvaner (5%). Approx. annual production is 100,000 cases, sold mainly in Germany. Address: Naheweinstr. 63, 6553 Meddersheim/Nahe.

Rheinhell Rhg. w. ★★

Einzellage on an island in the Rhein called the MARIANNENAU after Princess Marianne of Prussia who bought the nearby SCHLOSS REINHARTSHAUSEN in 1855, now solely owned by her descendants. The site benefits from a mild microclimate and is planted with Riesling, Weissburgunder and Kerner. Grosslage: DEUTELSBERG.

Rheinhessen w. (r.)

Largest of the wine regions with 24,551ha (60,668 acres) of vines, incl. many new crossings – Scheurebe, Faber, Huxelrebe, etc. – from the viticultural institute at ALZEY in the heart of the region. For consistently the best Rheinhessen Riesling or Silvaner wines one must look to the RHEINFRONT nr. NIERSTEIN, with its fine sites overlooking

the river, or possibly to the v'yds at BINGEN where the Rhein meets the Nahe. Away from the Rheinfront the v'yds often occupy slightly sloping ground overlooking farmland. The wines from such sites tend to be softer than those from the Nahe or the M-S-R but have a useful ability to combine the flavour from the soil with that of the new vine varieties. Most Rheinhessen wine is sold under a Grosslage or Einzellage name and some 70% is sold in bulk by the growers to the wine trade for bottling. Approx. 3,000 growers bottle their own wine, and among these will be found some of the best estates in Germany. At the other extreme, Rheinhessen also produces very cheap wine, which should be agreeable as a light drink but will probably have very little character.

Rheinland-Pfalz

Federal State with 67% of the planted viticultural area of West Germany. The capital is MAINZ.

Rheinpfalz w. (r.)

Region of 22,359ha (55,251 acres), also known as the Palatinate, that stretches from the frontier with France to the Rheinhessen border. The n. part, the Bereich MITTELHAARDT/DEUTSCHE WEINSTRASSE, has a dry, warm climate, and the success and reputation of its wine, judged by the prosperity of the region's villages, has been noted by writers over the centuries. There are a number of leading estates, situated mainly between KALLSTADT and RUPPERTSBERG, with a high proportion of Riesling in their v'yds, making wine to the very highest standard. In a great year magnificent meaty wines are produced, often deep in colour and with great flavour, that only begin to be at their best eight years or so after the vintage. "Off" years produce slimmer wines, with attractive acidity and fruit, that show well the characteristics of the vine variety. The wines from the s. Rheinpfalz, the Bereich SÜDLICHE WEINSTRASSE, are of lesser calibre than those from further n. but are good value for money. The countryside is essentially rural and vine-growing is clearly the most important type of farming. The v'yds lie mainly

RHEIN·PFALZ

Karl Suhrmann   vorm Frih Schnell

Weingut   Pfeffingen

bei Ungstein   16   22   Post Bad Dürkheim

1980er UNGSTEINER HONIGSÄCKEL
RIESLING EISWEIN AUSLESE
QUALITÄTSWEIN MIT PRÄDIKAT   A.P. Nr. 5 141 045 15 81
ERZEUGERABFÜLLUNG   e 0.375 l

on the level land or on gentle slopes, overlooked by wooded hills rising to 600m (1,968 feet) or more. Visitors to the Pfalz will find living inexpensive, comfortable but unsophisticated.

Rheinterrasse
See Rheinfront

Rhodt unter Rietburg Rhpf. w. ★
Picturesque wine village nr. EDENKOBEN, below Schloss Ludwigshöhe, summer residence of Ludwig I of Bavaria. Produces interesting, good-value-for-money wines from many vine varieties – outstanding quality would be most unusual. A number of long-established growers and a large cooperative cellar. Grosslage: ORDENSGUT.

Richter, Weingut Max Ferd. M-S-R
Family-owned estate dating from 1680 with 15ha (37 acres) at TRABEN-TRABACH, WEHLEN (SONNENUHR), GRAACH (HIMMELREICH), BERNKASTEL, MÜHLHEIM (sole owners of Helenenkloster), VELDENZ, BRAUNEBERG (JUFFER), etc. Vines are 85% Riesling. The top-quality wines, cask-matured in the naturally cold cellars, are sold to the trade in Germany and abroad. No SÜSSRESERVE is used and EISWEIN is a speciality, even from the non-Eiswein year of 1976. The estate also sells under the Dr Dirk Richter-Wine-Selection label. Address: 5556 Mühlheim/Mosel.

Richter-Boltendahl, Weingut Rhg.
100-year-old family-owned estate with 15ha (37 acres) in WALLUF, ELTVILLE, RAUENTHAL, ERBACH (MICHELMARK, etc.), KIEDRICH and HATTENHEIM. Vines are 85% Riesling, 10% Müller-Thurgau, etc. Approx. annual production is 10,400 cases of typical, modern Rheingau wines, incl. dry and medium-dry, sold mainly in Germany but also abroad. Address: Walluferstr. 25, 6228 Eltville.

Riedel, Weingut Jakob Rhg.
Small estate with 17th-century origins. 3ha (7 acres) at HALLGARTEN (SCHÖNHELL, etc.) are 90% Riesling and 10% Ehrenfelser for SÜSSRESERVE. Dry, medium-dry and sweeter wines are bottled early to retain freshness. Sales are exclusively to private customers. Address: Taunusstr. 1, 6227 Hallgarten/Rheingau.

Rieslaner
White grape variety, a crossing of Silvaner × Riesling from WÜRZBURG grown in 44ha (109 acres), mainly in its region of origin, Franken. With a MUST weight of less than 90° Oechsle (12% alcohol) the wine tastes thin. Acidity is high, and the grapes ripen late in the season. At its best the wine is very stylish and fairly neutral in flavour (but see Weingut Hans WIRSCHING). Other vines perform more successfully and produce better wine more easily.

Riesling (Weisser)
White grape variety that produces the finest German wine. It is planted in 18,791ha (46,434 acres) – just under 20% of the total area under vine. Where the finest v'yds are to be found, in the Mittel-

haardt in the Rheinpfalz, in the Rheingau, in the middle Nahe and on the Mosel, the percentage of Riesling grown will be high, for the Riesling in Germany demands a top-quality site. Depending on location the harvest will take place in October, November or even December for certain speciality wines. One of the main characteristics of Riesling is the elegant acidity that makes the flavour of the wine last in the mouth, and gives it the ability to develop over many years in bottle. Riesling flavour is positive and yet restrained, unlike that of a full-blown Traminer. It is therefore able to transmit the taste that comes from the soil, without imposing any strong additional flavour upon it. As a result the variations between a Riesling from one region and those from another are clearly differentiated. All qualities of Riesling wine can be produced, depending on the vintage and the site, from table wine to the richest TROCKENBEERENAUSLESE.

Rieslingekt

Quality sparkling wine from the Riesling grape. Although the number of German sparkling wines that indicate a vine variety on the label is still small, interest in Rieslingsekt is increasing, because it shows well the qualities of freshness and style enjoyed in German still wine. (See also LAGENSEKT, MARKENSEKT.)

Rödelsee Franken w. ★★→★★★

Village nr. KITZINGEN producing top-quality wines that are spicy, powerful and long-flavoured. In recent years many of the v'yds, known to have been in production in the 13th century, have been reconstructed, modernized and replanted, mainly in Silvaner and Müller-Thurgau. Grosslage: Schlossberg.

Römer

Wine glass or rummer. In the n. regions the standard Römer used for the sale of wine by the glass contains 200ml; in Franken, Württemberg and Baden a 250ml Römer is used. The stem is usually green or amber and the bowl is clear but sometimes engraved. The liquid content is, by law, always marked. Finer Römer of varying sizes are produced for private use.

Römerlay M-S-R w. ★★

Grosslage covering the v'yds on the Mosel around TRIER and those of the little Ruwer valley, incl. EITELSBACH and KASEL. Very high proportion of Riesling.

Ronde, Weingut Sanitätsrat Dr M-S-R

Old-established estate with 8ha (20 acres) at NEUMAGEN, DHRON and TRITTENHEIM (APOTHEKE, ALTÄRCHEN). Vines are 92% Riesling, 4% Müller-Thurgau and – unusually – 4% Ruländer, of which the M-S-R has only 8ha (20 acres) in total. The wines from steep, slaty sites are matured exclusively in wood and frequently win prizes at regional competitions. Approx. annual production is 9,100 cases, sold in Germany and abroad. Address: Römerstr. 9, 5559 Neumagen/Mosel.

Rosengarten Nahe w. ★

Best-known Grosslage in the Nahe valley, covering more than 600ha (1,483 acres). None of the individual sites is among the best in the region and much use is made of the Grosslage name, combined with that of the village of RÜDESHEIM – not to be confused with the town of the same name in the Rheingau. A Rüdesheimer Rosengarten will usually be a blend of Silvaner and Müller-Thurgau, similar to a wine from the Bereich BINGEN in the Rheinhessen across the R. Nahe but with more acidity.

Roséwein

Pale pink wine made from red grapes, closer in style to white wine than to red. See WEISSHERBST.

Rotberger

White grape variety, a crossing of Riesling × Trollinger. See DIEL AUF BURG LAYEN.

Rotenfels Nahe w. ★★★

Steep Einzellage at TRAISEN that takes its name from the nearby rock face, the Rotenfels (the highest cliff in Europe n. of the Alps). Produces steely Riesling wines of great character. Grosslage: BURG-WEG. Growers incl. Crusius.

Rothenberg Rhg. w. ★★★
Sloping, modernized Einzellage at GEISENHEIM that produces big, balanced Riesling wines with a slight, attractive taste of the soil. Grosslage: BURGWEG. Growers: Holschier, Vollmer, Wegeler/Deinhard, Zwierlein.

Rotling
A rosé wine produced by blending red and white grapes or their pulp – not a blend of wine or MUSTS.

Rotwein
Red wine.

Roxheim Nahe w. ★★
Village a few km n.w. of BAD KREUZNACH producing Riesling and Silvaner wines well regarded in the region for their style. Cannot be compared to the best from the Nahe. Usually appropriately priced. Grosslage: ROSENGARTEN.

Rüdesheim Nahe w. ★
Village nr. BAD KREUZNACH. often linked with the Grosslage ROSENGARTEN. a Nahe answer to Niersteiner GUTES DOMTAL. The sites at Rüdesheim itself are planted in Müller-Thurgau and Silvaner, producing sound wines. Not to be confused with Rüdesheim in the Rheingau.

Rüdesheim a. Rhein Rhg. Pop. 10,300 ★★★
Town 25km (15 miles) s.w. of WIESBADEN. a major target for tourists and widely known for its street of wine bars, the Drosselgasse – tolerable only to the most gregarious. Its v'yds, protected from the north by the Niederwald (wood) and facing s. across the Rhein to BINGEN. enjoy a good microclimate but can suffer in drought years. Full-flavoured, splendid, positive wines, ultimately possibly lacking a little in delicacy.

Ruländer
Vine variety planted in 3,339ha (8,251 acres), produces good, full-bodied, soft white wines from blue grapes. Known in France as the Pinot Gris. In Baden and the Rheinpfalz, where the style of wine is softer than that made further north, the Ruländer seems to reflect the regional character particularly well. It should be planted in a good site where MUST levels can reach a least 80° Oechsle to avoid being thin and uninteresting. Ruländers, with their somewhat "barnyard" bouquet, do not have the elegance of the paler-coloured Riesling, but as a SPÄTLESE or AUSLESE they can impress by their power and fullness.

Ruppertsberg Rhpf. w. (r.) ★★
Village nr. DEIDESHEIM producing attractive Riesling and Silvaner wines and very stylish Scheurebe. Probably not among the very finest in the Bereich MITTELHAARDT/DEUTSCHE WEINSTRASSE – they often lack the depth and intensity of the best of FORST or DEIDESHEIM – but are usually cheaper. Grosslage: HOFSTÜCK.

Ruppertsberger Winzerverein "Hoheburg"eG Rhpf.
Cooperative cellar with 195 members supplying grapes from 185ha (457 acres), mainly at RUPPERTSBERG (REITERPFAD. LINSENBUSCH. etc.). Vines are 37% Riesling, 22% Silvaner, 9% Portugieser, etc. Approx. annual production is 214,000 cases, sold mainly in Germany. Efficient, modern wine-making in a top-quality part of the Rheinpfalz. Address: 6701 Ruppertsberg/Weinstrasse.

Ruwer
River that rises in the high ground of the Hunsrück and flows some 40km (25 miles) later into the Mosel nr. the village of Ruwer, close to TRIER. In good years the Ruwer v'yds can produce great Riesling wines, positive and firm in flavour, similar in weight to those of the other important river in their shared Bereich, the Saar, but the slaty character is less pronounced. The little Ruwer valley is characterized by a handful of villages of ancient origin, famous wine estates overlooked by woods and walnut trees, and some of the most interesting wines of the M-S-R region.

Saar
Tributary of the Mosel that rises in the Vosges mountains and enters the Bereich SAAR-RUWER upstream from SAARBURG. On either side of the river, beyond the v'yds, the landscape is wooded and

attractive and has been an area for relaxation for the people of TRIER since the time of the Roman occupation. The slate soil of the v'yds is harder than that of the Mosel and gives the wine a strong, steely flavour. Great wines from a number of fine estates are made in good years.

Saar-Ruwer, Bereich w.

The Bereich that covers the Saar and Ruwer regions.

Saarburg M-S-R Pop. 5,800 w. ★★→★★★

Ancient town known for its old buildings and half-timbered houses, its bell foundry and its wine. It lies on the R. Saar at the upper end of the vine-growing area. Many of the sites are owned, in part or in whole, by well-known estates. Saarburger Riesling wines in good years are among the best on the Saar. They have a positive slaty Riesling flavour, with a strong bouquet to match. Prices are comparable to those from Mosel villages such as WEHLEN, BERNKASTEL and BRAUNEBERG. Grosslage: SCHARZBERG.

Saarland

Federal State with 95ha (235 acres) of v'yds, incl. those of the Bereich MOSELTOR nr. the German–Luxembourg–French frontier. (The rest of the M-S-R is in the state of RHEINLAND-PFALZ.) The capital is Saarbrücken.

Sackträger Rhh. w. ★★★

Sloping Einzellage on the outskirts of OPPENHEIM producing refined wines, outstanding in good years. Grosslage: GÜLDENMORGEN. Growers: Baumann, Dahlem, Guntrum. Carl Koch, Oppenheim Staatsweingut, Schuch, Sittmann.

St Alban Rhh. w. ★→★★

Grosslage of just under 1,000ha (2,471 acres) between MAINZ and NACKENHEIM that takes its name from the St Alban monastery at Mainz, once a large landowner in the district. Makes sound, easy-to-drink Rheinhessen wines.

St Augustus-Weinkellerei GmbH

Export house est. in 1981, concentrating on inexpensive QbA and non-estate-bottled QmP carrying mainly Grosslagen names, sold principally in the UK. Address: Bernhardstr. 1-3, 5500 Trier.

St Johannishof, Weingut M-S-R

Small, quality estate with holdings at BERNKASTEL (GRABEN, etc.), WEHLEN (SONNENUHR, etc.), GRAACH (HIMMELREICH) and ERDEN (PRÄLAT. TREPPCHEN). Vines are 90% Riesling. The estate makes the full range of Mosel wines, which have won many prizes at national competitions. Approx. annual production is 7,000 cases; half is exported. Address: 5550 Bernkastel/Mosel.

St Michael M-S-R w. ★→★★

Large Grosslage of more than 2,200ha (5,436 acres). The best-known sites are around the villages of KLÜSSERATH and LEIWEN, where the vines are mainly Riesling. There are also significant plantations of Müller-Thurgau.

St Rochuskapelle Rhh. w. ★→★★

Grosslage of more than 2,400ha (5,931 acres) in the n.e. corner of the Rheinhessen. Some of the v'yds lie alongside the R. Nahe and the wines often have more acidity than those made further s. in the region. Best-known individual site within the Grosslage is the SCHARLACHBERG at BINGEN.

St Ursula Weingut & Weinkellerei GmbH

Wine merchants, probably best known for the excellent Goldener Oktober range of QbA. Owners of Weingut VILLA SACHSEN. Address: Mainzerstr. 184, 6530 Bingen am Rhein.

Samtrot

Red grape variety, a mutation of the Müllerrebe, planted in 41ha (101 acres), almost entirely in Württemberg.

Sandgrub Rhg. w. ★★★

Einzellage in two clearly defined and separate sections s. of KIEDRICH, planted mainly in Riesling. Produces stylish, good-quality wine that improves with bottle age. Grosslage: HEILIGENSTOCK. Growers: Groenesteyn, Hessisches Weingut, Knyphausen, Lamm-Jung, Oetinger, Reinhartshausen, Ress, Richter-Boltendahl, Sohlbach, Tillmanns, Wagner-Weritz, Weil.

Sanitätsrat

Award given to medical practitioners up to 1918 nationally, and thereafter by some individual states. Appears, for example, in the title of the Neumagen/Mosel estate Weingut Sanitätsrat Dr Ronde.

Saumagen Rhpf. w. **

Small Grosslage of about 50ha (124 acres) on the edge of the Mittelhaardt village of KALLSTADT. It covers three sites (Nill, Kirchenstück and Horn) and produces stylish wines, esp. from Riesling. AUSLESE wines can frequently be made from new crossings. Translated, Saumagen means sow's stomach – the name of a well-known local Rheinpfalz sausage dish.

Säure

Acidity. Because of the cool nights when the grapes are ripening, the acid level of German wine, at 5-9 g/l, is considerably higher than that of most wines produced in a warmer climate. As a result the wine has a unique freshness that is carefully retained during vinification and maturation. The main acids in German wine are tartaric (WEINSÄURE) and malic (ÄPFELSÄURE). The amount present depends on the ripeness and variety of grape.

Top-quality wines such as a BEERENAUSLESE or an EISWEIN often have particularly high acidity, balanced by a large amount of residual sugar. Such wines need years of maturation in bottle to reach their peak and for the acidity to soften. Wines with relatively low acidity (e.g. Müller-Thurgau) are usually best drunk young. The addition of acids to German wine is illegal, but DEACIDIFICATION is allowed.

Schaefer, Weingut Karl Rhpf.

Estate dating from 1843 with 17ha (42 acres) of holdings at DÜRK-HEIM (SPIELBERG, etc.) and WACHENHEIM (FUCHSMANTEL, GERÜMPEL). Vines are 70% Riesling, 10% Silvaner, etc. All qualities of wine are matured in cask in the old vaulted cellar and are expected to develop in bottle. In recent years the Dürkheimer wines have been particularly successful, both at national competitions and in commercial terms. Approx. annual production is 11,900 cases, sold in Germany and abroad. Address: 6702 Bad Dürkheim an der Weinstrasse.

Schales, Weingut Rhh.

200-year-old estate, run with great commitment by the sixth generation of the Schales family. Dalsheim, at the s. end of the Rheinhessen, is not well known outside Germany but the range of wines produced by the estate is wide. A number of vine varieties are grown on 33ha (82 acres) of holdings, and many wines of AUSLESE and higher quality are produced from vines such as Kanzler, Optima, Siegerrebe, Huxelrebe and Ehrenfelser. The aim is freshness and the ability to develop over years in bottle. Approx. annual production of 29,000 cases is sold to private and trade customers. Each April the estate holds a mammoth trade tasting, at which some 100 wines are on show. An impressive and progressive producer. Address: 6521 Flörsheim-Dalsheim.

Scharlachberg Rhh. w. **→***

Well-known Einzellage at BINGEN on mainly sloping ground, overlooking the R. Nahe. The wines are close in style to those of the Lower Nahe, or even the Rheingau, with attractive acidity and charm. Grosslage: ST ROCHUSKAPELLE. Grower: Villa Sachsen.

Scharzberg M-S-R w. **

Grosslage of about 1,600ha (3,954 acres) covering the whole viticultural area of the Saar, where many may feel that the archetypal German wine is produced. A light, elegant, fruity acidity is its main characteristic – more positive and less subtle than a wine from the MITTELMOSEL. Wines using the Scharzberg name are not the cheapest but are usually of much better quality than those sold at rock-bottom prices from the Grosslage Bernkasteler KURFÜRSTLAY.

Scharzhofberg M-S-R w. ***→****

27ha (67 acre) mainly steep v'yd nr. WILTINGEN on the Saar with the status of a village or community, so that its wine is sold under the single name "Scharzhofberg". Marvellously elegant Riesling wine, full of character in good years. Often one of the great wines of Germany. Growers: Bischöfliche Weingüter, Hövel, Kesselstatt, Koch, Egon Müller, Felix Müller, Bernd. van Volxem.

Schatzkammer
Literally treasure room. A part of a cellar set aside for storing the finest, and by implication the oldest, wines. Some estates list a number of rare wines from their Schatzkammer.

Schaumwein
Sparkling wine that meets certain technical standards but is basically cheap and cheerful. Approx. 10% of sparkling wine produced in Germany is classified simply as Schaumwein. The balance is QUALITÄTSSCHAUMWEIN. See also SEKT.

Schenkenböhl Rhpf. w. (r.) ★★
Grosslage of about 600ha (1,483 acres) on either side of the DEUTSCHE WEINSTRASSE between BAD DÜRKHEIM and WACHENHEIM. The individual sites are mainly flat or gently sloping with a good proportion of Riesling. They form part of the finest v'yds of the Rheinpfalz, so that a wine sold under the Grosslage name is still likely to be very stylish and full of quality.

Scheurebe
White grape variety, a very successful crossing of Silvaner × Riesling, named after its developer Dr Georg Scheu. It now covers 4,237ha (10,470 acres), spread throughout all the vine-growing regions. Planted in a good site, suitable for Silvaner, the Scheurebe can produce SPÄTLESE wine of absolute top quality. Lesser wines have a pronounced flowering-currant bouquet, but this is not so marked in fine AUSLESE wines for which Scheurebe also has a considerable reputation. The acidity in unripe Scheurebe grapes is so pronounced that the resulting wine is best used for blending with NEUTRAL, soft wines.

Schillerwein
ROTLING QbA produced in Württemberg may be called Schillerwein. The name has nothing to do with the poet Friedrich Schiller, a Württemberger by birth, but arises from the wine's varying shades of rosé colour. ("Schillern" means to change colour.) In the past, red and white vine varieties were intermingled in the v'yds and both were harvested and vinified together.

Schlangengraben M-S-R w. ★★
Einzellage at WILTINGEN planted in Riesling and Müller-Thurgau, producing fruity, stylish wines. Well known, but not the best site on the Saar. Grosslage: SCHARZBERG. Growers: Rheinart, Schlangengraben/Schorlemer, Bernd. van Volxem.

Schlangengraben, Weingut M-S-R
Estate owned by Hermann Freiherr v. SCHORLEMER GmbH.

Schleinitz'sche Weingutsverwaltung, Freiherr von M-S-R
Family-owned estate of 4.5ha (11 acres) at the underrated wine-producing end of the Mosel nr. KOBLENZ. Holdings are all at KOBERN, on one of the prettiest parts of the river. Vines are 100% Riesling, producing an impressive list of wines incl. seven AUSLESEN and three BEERENAUSLESEN. Styles range from wines with pronounced steely acidity to softer wines with more body and fruit. Many have won awards at national competitions. Approx. annual production is 4,100 cases, sold mainly to private customers. Address: Kirchstr. 17, 5401 Kobern-Gondorf/Mosel.

Schlink-Herf-Gutleuthof, Vereinigte Weingüter Nahe
Combination of three estates that were founded in 1952, 1830 and 1807 respectively, with 65ha (161 acres) mainly at KREUZNACH (NARRENKAPPE, BRÜCKES) but also at SCHLOSSBÖCKELHEIM (KUP-FERGRUBE), Winzenheim and ROXHEIM. Wines are made and stored in the cellars of Weingut Gutleuthof and follow the pattern of good-quality Nahe wine production from dry QbA to rich BEERENAUSLESE. Approx. annual yield is 58,300 cases, sold in Germany and abroad.

The estates are also members of an ERZEUGERGEMEINSCHAFT (producers' association) with a further 35 members, whose wines are made in the cellars of Firma Günther Schlink KG. Address: Planigerstr. 154, 6550 Bad Kreuznach.

Schloss

    Castle or palace. Wine that bears the name of a Schloss (e.g. Schloss Johannisberg, Schloss Vollrads) must have been made entirely from grapes grown in the castle's v'yds. It may then be called a Schlossabfüllung (castle-bottling) as opposed to the usual ERZEUGERABFÜLLUNG (estate or producer bottled). The word Schloss also often forms part of an Einzellage name (Serriger Schloss Saarfelser Schlossberg) or a district name (Bereich Schloss Böckelheim), so "Schloss" on a label does not necessarily mean that the wine comes from an individual castle or estate.

Schloss Böckelheim, Bereich Nahe w. ★→★★

    District covering the Nahe region upstream from BAD KREUZNACH, incl. the well-known sites at NIEDERHAUSEN and the village of SCHLOSSBÖCKELHEIM. Many of the v'yds are widely separated. The quality of wine is generally good and will not be as cheap as a Bereich NIERSTEIN, esp. when made from Riesling.

Schloss Deidesheim an der Weinstrasse

    See Kern, Weingut Dr

Schloss Groenesteyn, Weingut des Reichsfreiherrn von Ritter zu Groenesteyn Rhg

    Important estate dating from the 14th century and owned by the Groenesteyn family since 1640. 35ha (86 acres), 90% Riesling, 10% Müller-Thurgau, concentrated in RÜDESHEIM (BERG ROTTLAND, BERG ROSENECK, BERG SCHLOSSBERG, etc.) and Kiedrich (GRÄFENBERG, Wasserros, SANDGRUB), producing approx. 25,000 cases annually. Wines are matured in wood and are among the best in the region. Much is exported. All are offered as Schloss Groenesteyn followed by the wine name. Address: 6229 Kiedrich-Rheingau.

Schloss Johannisberg, Fürst von Metternich-Winneburg'sches Domäne Rentamt Rhg

    Great estate of 35ha (86 acres), planted 100% in Riesling, with an approx. annual production of 23,300 cases. The estate was recorded as the first (in 1716) to plant Riesling on its own, unmixed with other vine varieties. Maturation in wood in the cool cellars helps to produce the fine, weighty wines for which the Schloss is famous. Different coloured capsules are used for the various quality categories. In recent years many of the QbA and KABINETT

    wines have been medium-dry. SPÄTLESE wines are made only in outstanding years and, in common with other Rheingau estates, an AUSLESE is a rarity. Most of the buildings, restored after serious damage in World War II, date from the 17th century. Schloss Johannisberg is legally an ORTSTEIL and the wine is sold without any individual site names. Sales are mainly on the export market. Address: 6222 Geisenheim-Johannisberg.

Schloss Kosakenberg

    See Zwierlein, Weingut Freiherr von

Schloss Lieser, Weingut M-S-R

    Estate owned by Hermann Freiherr v. SCHORLEMER GmbH.

Schloss Ortenberg

    See Ortenaukreises, Weinbauversuchsgut des

Schloss Reichhartshausen Rhg. w. ★★

A much-restored castle, originating in the 12th century, now regarded as an ORTSTEIL, with 3ha (7 acres) of v'yd owned entirely by Balthasar RESS.

Schloss Reinhartshausen, Administration Prinz Friedrich von Preussen Rhg.

67ha (166 acre) estate with origins believed to date back to Charlemagne. Present owners are the great-grandchildren of Kaiser Wilhelm II. Holdings are at ERBACH (incl. MARCOBRUNN. MICHELMARK. SIEGELSBERG and sole ownership of Schlossberg), on MARIANNENAU island in the Rhein incl. sole ownership of Erbacher RHEINHELL, and at HATTENHEIM (WISSELBRUNNEN. NUSSBRUNNEN, etc.), KIEDRICH. RAUENTHAL and RÜDESHEIM. Vines are 80% Riesling plus Weissburgunder, Spätburgunder, etc. Apart from the fine traditional wines expected of a great Rheingau estate, the Schloss also makes an interesting Weissburgunder and Chardonnay TROCKEN. Approx. annual production is 75,000 cases, sold in Germany and abroad. Address: 6228 Erbach/Rheingau.

Schloss Saaleck

See Hammelburg, Stadt. Weingut

Schloss Saarfelser Schlossberg M-S-R w. ★★→★★★

Mainly steep Einzellage at SERRIG nr. the upper end of the Saar vine-growing area. Sole owner is the VEREINIGTE HOSPITIEN at TRIER. Produces scented, positive, light, stylish Riesling wines that can be superb in good years. Grosslage: SCHARZBERG.

Schloss Schönborn, Domänenweingut Rhg.

65ha (161 acre) estate owned by the distinguished church and political von Schönborn family, which acquired its first Rheingau v'yds in 1349. The Weingut's present holdings, based on HATTENHEIM, are at OESTRICH (DOOSBERG), RÜDESHEIM (BERG SCHLOSSBERG),

GEISENHEIM (MÄUERCHEN), WINKEL (HASENSPRUNG), HOCHHEIM (HÖLLE. DOMDECHANEY, etc.), JOHANNISBERG. ERBACH (MARCOBRUNN) and Hattenheim itself (NUSSBRUNNEN, and sole ownership of Pfaffenberg). Vines are 91% Riesling. Maturation is in wood, producing full, big-scale Riesling wines, and a small amount of Spätburgunder with good varietal characteristics and no residual sugar. Approx. annual production is 43,000 cases, sold worldwide. Address: Hauptstr. 53, Hattenheim, 6228 Eltville.

Schloss Staufenberg, Markgräflich Badis'ches Weingut Baden

The Margrave of Baden (the title corresponds in rank to an English Marquess) owns four wine estates, one of which, based on the 11th-century Schloss Staufenberg, is set in splendid hilly wooded country overlooking the village of DURBACH. The 28ha (69 acres) of steep v'yds are planted mainly in Riesling (35%), Müller-Thurgau (22%), Traminer (13% – a high proportion for this vine) and Spätburgunder. The Riesling wines are firm but rounded. Two-thirds of the red wines are dry or medium-dry. Approx. annual production is 12,000 cases, 7% sold abroad. The estate's wine bar has distant but spectacular views of the Vosges mountains. Address: 7601 Durbach, Ortenau.

Schloss Vollrads, Graf Matuschka-Greiffenclau'sche
Güterverwaltung Rhg.

Remarkable and possibly most famous private estate in Germany, its 47ha (116 acres) protected by the woods that shelter the Rheingau above WINKEL. The Greiffenclau family is known to have been selling wine in the 12th century, and built Schloss Vollrads at the start of the 14th century. Today, Schloss Vollrads is an ORTSTEIL, regarded in law as a "community", and sells its wine, like SCHARZHOFBERG and STEINBERG, with no additional village or v'yd name. Planted 99% in Riesling, the Schloss, with its v'yds somewhat higher than many in the Rheingau, produces wines with pronounced acidity and fine fruit but with restrained sweetness. The

estate uses different coloured CAPSULES to indicate variations in the style and quality of its wines. The current preference in Germany for drier wines is strongly encouraged by the present owner, Erwein Graf Matuschka-Greiffenclau.

As well as its own Weingut, Schloss Vollrads also owns the Graues Haus restaurant in Winkel, where a range of wines from many different Rheingau growers is served. In 1979 Graf Matuschka-Greiffenclau bought the Weingut Fürst Löwenstein in Hallgarten. 50% of the bottled wines from this estate and from Schloss Vollrads are exported. Wines that do not reach the high standard of the Graf are sold in bulk to the wine trade and are not allowed to bear the Löwenstein or Vollrads name. Address: 6227 Oestrich-Winkel.

Schlossabfüllung

Castle bottled. See SCHLOSS.

Schlossberg M-S-R w. ★★

Schlossberg is a common site name in Germany. The Einzellage at BERNKASTEL on the Mosel, half steep, half sloping, is not in the Bernkastel first division but produces stylish wines, mainly from Riesling. Grosslage: KURFÜRSTLAY. Growers: Deinhard Bernkastel, Bergweiler-Prüm, Meyerhof/Schorlemer, Selbach-Oster.

Schlossberg M-S-R w. ★★★

Steep Einzellage at ZELTINGEN-RACHTIG, next to the SONNENUHR, producing elegant Riesling wines. Grosslage: MÜNZLAY. Growers: Ehses-Berres, Ehses-Geller, Kesselstatt, S. A. Prüm, Schorlemer.

Schlossböckelheim Nahe w. ★★→★★★★

Small but important wine-making community producing elegant, fresh Riesling wines to the highest standards. Set in rural surroundings, upstream from BAD MÜNSTER AM STEIN-EBERNBURG, it is still largely undiscovered by tourists. The Schloss (castle) is now a ruin. Grosslage: BURGWEG.

Schlosskapelle Nahe w. ★★

Grosslage on the left bank of the R. Nahe s. of BINGEN. Best-known sites are at MÜNSTER-SARMSHEIM and DORSHEIM, where full-bodied, meaty Riesling wines with much style are made.

Schlotter, Weingut Valentin Rhg.

120-year-old estate with cellars tunnelling 80m (262 feet) into the steep v'yd slopes at ASSMANNSHAUSEN. Holdings are 4ha (10 acres) at Assmannshausen (HÖLLENBERG, etc.) and 5.5ha (14 acres) at RÜDESHEIM (BERG ROTTLAND, BERG SCHLOSSBERG, BERG ROSENECK, etc.). The aim is to make lively, elegant, spicy Riesling wines at Rüdesheim and red wines, mainly from Spätburgunder, at Assmannshausen, with little tannin but good, fruity acidity. The estate favours maturation in wood and some of the casks are more than 100 years old. Approx. annual production is 5,800 cases, sold to private customers and also abroad via the exporting house KENDERMANN in Bingen. Address: Lorcherstr. 13, 6220 Rüdesheim.

Schmitt, Weingut Hermann Franz Rhh.
30ha (74 acre) estate established in 1549 by the direct ancestors of the present owners. Among the well-situated holdings at NIERSTEIN are parts of ÖLBERG, HIPPING, PETTENTHAL, ORBEL and sole ownership of the 2.5ha (6 acre) Zehnmorgen site. Vines are 65% Riesling, 20% Silvaner, 7% Müller-Thurgau, etc. Style, body and good acidity are the hallmarks of the estate wines, of which the most famous is probably the 1953 Niersteiner Fläschenhahl Riesling Trockenbeerenauslese. Address: Hermannshof, Kalliansweg 2, 6505 Nierstein.

Schmitt Söhne Weinkellerei, H.
Large firm of wine merchants, taking in grapes from about 1,000 growers, concentrating on M-S-R wines but also listing EEC blended table wine and wine from other regions of Germany. Owners of Weingut Adolf Rheinart Erben in the Bereich Saar-Ruwer and other less well-known estates. Approx. annual production is 2.5m. cases of 500 different "lines". Many of the wines are very cheap but all are bottled by the best cold-sterile process, helping to retain freshness, and develop well in bottle. Sales are worldwide. Address: Weinstrasse 8, 5559 Longuich.

Schmitt-Dr Ohnacker, Weingut Rhh.
150-year-old, family-owned estate of 12.5ha (31 acres), all at GUNTERSBLUM. Vines are 26% Müller-Thurgau, 20% Riesling, 20% Silvaner, etc. The character of the wines is very much influenced by the very varied soil. Most wines spend 3-8 months in casks, some of which are 100 years old. Fermentation is controlled and special efforts are made to retain the individuality of each wine. Approx. annual production is 10,000 cases, sold in Germany and abroad – mainly through H. SICHEL SÖHNE GMBH of Alzey. Address: Alsheimerstr. 41, 6524 Guntersblum/Rhein.

Schmitt'sches Weingut, Gustav Adolf Rhh.
Estate owners, est. in 1618, wholesale wine merchants and, since the 1930s, an exporting house. 100ha (247 acres) of holdings in NIERSTEIN (PETTENTHAL, ÖLBERG, HIPPING, KRANZBERG, etc.), OPPENHEIM, Dienheim, DEXHEIM, GUNTERSBLUM and Gau-Bischofsheim, planted 75% in traditional vines (Riesling, Silvaner, etc.) and 25% in new crossings. Approx. annual production is 50,000 cases (a low yield) of estate-bottled wines, 66% exported to more than 60 countries. Address: Wilhelmstr. 2-4, 6505 Nierstein.

Schneider, Weingut Georg Albrecht Rhh.
Family-owned estate with origins reaching back over seven generations. 15ha (37 acres) of holdings at NIERSTEIN, incl. PATERBERG, BILDSTOCK, FINDLING, ORBEL, ÖLBERG, PETTENTHAL and HIPPING – all top-quality sites. Vines are 35% Riesling, 25% Silvaner, 25% Müller-Thurgau, etc. Approx. annual production is 9,200 cases. Only the better-quality wines are bottled; the rest is sold in bulk. The reputation of the estate is for fine, "nervig", fruity wines, sold mainly in Germany and the USA. Address: Oberdorfstr. 11, 6505 Nierstein.

Schneider, Weingut Jacob Nahe
Estate owned by the Schneider family – who are livestock farmers as well as vine growers – for more than 400 years. 30ha (74 acres) in fine sites at NIEDERHAUSEN (HERMANNSHÖHLE, etc.) and NORHEIM are planted 90% in Riesling. Organic manuring, late picking and individual cask maturation after a temperature-controlled fermentation produce wines of character; spicy, elegant, softer or firmer depending on the soil. Sales are mainly to private customers. Address: Winzerstr. 15, 6551 Niederhausen.

Schneider Nachf., Michel M-S-R
Estate founded in 1869 with holdings now covering 60ha (148 acres) at WEHLEN (sole ownership of Abtei, Klosterhofgut and Hofberg) and at ZELL and Merl. Vines are 75% Riesling, 10% Müller-Thurgau and 15% new crossings. Most of the wines are relatively sweet and fruity but an increasing proportion of medium-dry and dry wines is made. Approx. annual production is 55,800 cases and sales on the export market are large. The estate also owns the former Cistercian abbey of Machern nr. BERNKASTEL. Address: Merlerstr. 28, 5583 Zell/Mosel.

Schneider GmbH, Weingut Weinkellerei Rhpf.
Family-owned estate and wine merchant business, with a fine old half-timbered, heavily beamed inn. Estate holdings, all at St Martin s. of NEUSTADT, are planted with the wide range of vine varieties usual in the s. Rheinpfalz and produce light, lively, attractive wines with pronounced bouquet. Sold only in Germany. Address: Maikammererstr. 7, 6731 St Martin (Weinstrasse).

Schnepfenflug an der Weinstrasse Rhpf. w. (r.) ★★
Grosslage of more than 500ha (1,236 acres) on level land nr. the well-known wine villages WACHENHEIM and FORST, growing many different vine varieties. Not to be confused with Schnepfenflug vom Zellertal in the n. Rheinpfalz.

Scholl & Hillebrand GmbH
Exporting house dealing in 120,000 cases annually of estate- and non-estate-bottled wines. Co-owners are Weingut G. BREUER. Address: Geisenheimerstr. 9, 6220 Rüdesheim am Rhein.

Schönburger
Grape variety, a crossing of Spätburgunder × an Italian table grape, grown at present on 68ha (168 acres), mainly in the Rheinhessen and Rheinpfalz. The grapes, luscious to taste and a marvellously delicate pink in colour, produce a white wine with a bouquet reminiscent of Traminer, a high MUST weight (15° Oechsle more than Riesling) and a dangerously low acidity. AUSLESE wine can be made from grapes infected with EDELFÄULE (noble rot).

Schönhell Rhg. w. ★★★
Einzellage at HALLGARTEN making full-bodied, balanced Riesling wines. Grosslage: MEHRHÖLZCHEN. Growers: Engelmann, Eser, Hallgarten/Rhg. eG, Ress, Riedel, Vereinigte Weingutsbesitzer, Wegeler/Deinhard.

Schoppenwein
Synonym for AUSSCHANKWEIN.

Schorlemer, Clemens Freiherr von M-S-R
See Schorlemer GmbH

Schorlemer GmbH, Hermann Freiherr v. M-S-R
Combination of five estates covering 40ha (99 acres), bought from the von Schorlemer family in 1969 by Herr Peter Meyer of the Weinkellerei and exporting house Peter Meyer-Horne KG in Bernkastel. The estates are Weingut Meyerhof, Weingut Schloss Lieser, Weingut Schlangengraben, Weingut Franz Duhr Nachf., Weingut Clemens Freiherr von Schorlemer. Holdings are at BERNKASTEL (SCHLOSSBERG, etc.), GRAACH (HIMMELREICH, DOMPROBST, ABTSBERG) WEHLEN (SONNENUHR, etc.), ZELTINGEN-RACHTIG (SCHLOSSBERG, SONNENUHR), OCKFEN (BOCKSTEIN) and sole ownership of Sandberg at WILTINGEN. Vines are 90% Riesling and 10% new crossings on an experimental basis. As well as typical, racy Riesling wines the estates also produce sparkling wine from some of their individual site holdings. Approx. annual production is 34,700 cases, sold worldwide with the help of Meyer-Horne. Address: Cusanusstr. 14, 5550 Bernkastel-Kues.

Schubert'sche Gutsverwaltung, C. v. M-S-R
Fine estate of 32ha (79 acres) with origins dating back to 966, bought by the von Schubert family in 1882. The holdings are three solely owned Einzellagen at MAXIMIN-GRÜNHAUS – Bruderberg, Herrenberg and Abtsberg – nr. the confluence of the Ruwer and the Mosel. As well as the modernized v'yds there is land for cattle raising, fruit farming and hunting. Very distinguished, racy wines are made in the estate's cellar – which dates partly from the time of

the Roman occupation. Approx. annual production 16,600 cases, sold in Germany and abroad. Address: 5501 Grünhaus/Trier.

Schuch, Weingut Geschwister Rhh.
Well-known family-owned estate of 16ha (40 acres), dating from 1817. Holdings are at NIERSTEIN (ÖLBERG, PETTENTHAL, FINDLING, etc.), OPPENHEIM (SACKTRÄGER) and Dienheim, planted 50% in

Riesling, 20% Silvaner, plus a typical Rheinhessen range of new crossings. The wines, incl, some dry and medium-dry, show the grape characteristics well. Approx. annual production is 10,700 cases, sold mainly in Germany. Address: 6505 Nierstein/Rhein.

Schultz-Werner, Weingut Oberst Rhh.
Family-owned estate dating from 1833, with holdings at Gaubischofsheim nr. MAINZ. Vines are 37% Riesling, 19% Müller-Thurgau, 14% Silvaner, etc. Grapes are hand-picked (no harvesting machines are used). The wines receive individual attention, appropriate to the vine variety; all are fairly full-bodied and retain a lively acidity. Approx. annual production is 9,100 cases. Sales are in Germany and also in the UK where the family has long-established connections, reinforced since the late 1970s by a subsidiary company. Address: Bahnhofstr. 10, 6501 Gaubischofsheim über Mainz.

Schumann-Nägler, Weingut Rhg.
Family-owned estate dating from 1438, with 18ha (44 acres) at GEISENHEIM (MÄUERCHEN, KLÄUSERWEG, etc.) and WINKEL. The vines, 95% Riesling, are organically grown. Some 41,600 cases can be stored in the new cellars. The typical, well-balanced Riesling wines, and Riesling sparkling wine made from the estate's base wine, are sold in Germany and abroad. Address: 6222 Geisenheim/Rhein.

Schuster, Weingut Eduard Rhpf.
19ha (47 acre) estate founded by the Schuster family in 1840. Holdings are at KALLSTADT (STEINACKER, and elsewhere in the KOBNERT and SAUMAGEN Grosslagen), planted 31% in Riesling, 23% Silvaner, 7% Müller-Thurgau, etc. The aim is to maintain the wine's individuality and grape and vintage characteristics. Silvaners are particularly flowery and powerful. Approx. annual production is 17,800 cases, sold in Germany and abroad. Address: Neugasse 21, 6701 Kallstadt.

Schwarze Katz M-S-R w. ★→★★
Best-known Grosslage of the lower Mosel, nr. ZELL, covering some 630ha (1,557 acres). A very high proportion of Riesling is grown on the steep slopes, except in the NNE-facing Kaimter Marienburger site. Here, in less favourable growing conditions, more new crossings than Riesling are found. None of the individual sites is so well known as the Grosslage name Schwarze Katz (black cat). The wine is usually sound and often sold with a label showing a large black cat, arching its back, making Schwarze Katz almost a brand name.

Schwarzerde Rhpf. w. ★→★★
Grosslage of more than 1,100ha (2,718 acres) in the n. Rheinpfalz, with no widely known vine-growing villages. The wines will be very

pleasant, agreeable and easy to drink but will lack the distinction of those produced in the central section of the Mittelhaardt a few km further s.

Schwarzlay M-S-R w. ★★

Grosslage of more than 1,200ha (2,965 acres) in the MITTELMOSEL, incl. the wine villages ÜRZIG. ERDEN. KINHEIM. TRABEN-TRABACH and ENKIRCH. Many of the sites are planted 100% in Riesling. A good-quality Mosel Grosslage.

Schwarzriesling

See Müllerrebe

Schwarzwald

Probably the best-known forest in Europe. It protects many of the Baden v'yds, esp. those of the Bereich ORTENAU. The sites reach up to the edge of the forest, sharing the steep slopes with orchards. Wonderfully rural and pretty.

Schweich M-S-R w. ★★

Village nr. TRIER, at the start of the steep-sided Mosel gorge that follows an almost uninterrupted but erratic course down to KOBLENZ. Produces fresh and fruity wines. Grosslage: PROBSTBERG.

Schweinhardt Nachf., Weingut Bürgermeister Willi Nahe

Estate trading under the Schweinhardt name since 1859, with holdings at LANGENLONSHEIM, between BAD KREUZNACH and BINGEN. Vines are 50% Riesling plus a range of other varieties incl. Kerner, Müller-Thurgau, Scheurebe. Approx. annual production is 14,500 cases of light, fruity wines that are very successful in regional and national competitions. 40% of sales are in West Berlin. No exports. Address: 6536 Langenlonsheim.

Seal

See Siegel

Sekt

Short German word for QUALITÄTSSCHAUMWEIN, originating in the early 19th century. Since 1975 the word Sekt has no longer been reserved for quality sparkling wine produced in Germany. In German-speaking countries one therefore finds Französischer (French) Sekt, Italienischer (Italian) Sekt, etc. Sparkling-wine production in Germany amounts to 23m. cases a year.

Selbach-Oster, Weingut Geschwister M-S-R

Small, 3ha (7 acre) estate, owned by the Selbach family – involved in vine-growing since 1661. The 100% Riesling holdings are at ZELTINGEN-RACHTIG (HIMMELREICH. SCHLOSSBERG and SONNENUHR), WEHLEN. GRAACH (DOMPROBST) and BERNKASTEL (SCHLOSSBERG). Wines are matured in oak casks and are typical of the Riesling on the Mosel – crisp, racy, fruity. Many of them win awards. Approx. annual production is 3,500 cases, sold only in Germany. Address: Uferallee 23, 5553 Zeltingen.

Septimer

A crossing of Gewürztraminer × Müller-Thurgau, grown in 31ha (77 acres). The red grapes make white, full-bodied and very soft wine. Yield and acid content are low and MUST weight is high. Of some interest to estate bottlers who wish to extend the range of wine they can offer, but not generally popular.

Serrig M-S-R w. ★★→★★★

Village, almost at the furthest extremity of the v'yds, upstream on the Saar. Steely Riesling wines are made on a number of top-quality estates. Often a source of excellent base wine for sparkling-wine production. Grosslage: SCHARZBERG.

Sichel Söhne GmbH, H.

Important exporter of good-quality German wine to 81 countries. Founded in 1857, Sichel is best known for the leading and long-established brand Blue Nun Liebfraumilch but also has connections with a number of important estates. 75% of total annual sales of 2.2m. cases is to the USA and UK. Address: Werner von Siemensstr. 14-18, 6508 Alzey/Rheinhessen.

Siebeldingen Rhpf. w. ★→★★

Village tucked below the foothills of the Haardt range w. of LANDAU IN DER PFALZ. Quite well known; the wines should be good, without the weight and intensity of those of the Bereich MITTEL-

HAARDT/DEUTSCHE WEINSTRASSE. Vines are mainly Müller-Thurgau, Silvaner, Morio-Muskat. Grosslage: Königsgarten.

Siegel
> Seal. Now used to indicate the awards, sometimes in the form of a seal but also through strip labels, granted by the DEUTSCHE LAND-WIRTSCHAFT GESELLSCHAFT and other organizations.

Siegelsberg Rhg. w. ★★★
> Einzellage nr. the Rhein at ERBACH producing racy Riesling wines. Grosslage: DEUTELSBERG. Growers: Eltville Staatsweingut, Knyphausen, Oetinger, Reinhartshausen, Wagner-Weritz.

Siegerrebe
> White grape variety, a crossing of Madeleine Angevine × Gewürztraminer from ALZEY in the Rheinhessen, planted in 273ha (675 acres). Bees and wasps often totally destroy the crop, but if the grapes escape attack they can produce a MUST of considerable weight, some 15–20° Oechsle greater than that of Müller-Thurgau. The acidity is low and the wine has an extremely strong bouquet. Siegerrebe is sometimes bottled as a single-vine wine of great quality but is more often used to add interest to commercial blends.

Silvaner (Grüner)
> Once the most widely grown vine in Germany, now found in 8,861ha (21,896 acres), being steadily replaced by Müller-Thurgau and other new crossings. The wine is NEUTRAL in flavour and does not hide the character that comes from the soil and site. In a good year it can make top-quality SPÄTLESE wine, esp. on the RHEINFRONT around NIERSTEIN and in Franken. Simple Silvaner wine is often blended with Riesling, Morio-Muskat and Scheurebe. Silvaner has many synonyms. Usually spelt Sylvaner outside Germany.

Simmern'sches Rentamt, Freiherrlich Langwerth von Rhg.
> Important, 40ha (99 acre) estate, owned by the von Simmern family since 1464, with fine old cellars and administrative buildings. Holdings are at ERBACH (MARCOBRUNN), HATTENHEIM (NUSSBRUNNEN, etc.), RAUENTHAL (BAIKEN, etc.) and ELTVILLE, planted 98% in Riesling. Serious Rheingau wine-making produces topquality, long-lived wines. Approx. annual production is 29,200 cases (a low yield), sold in Germany and abroad. Address: 6228 Eltville.

Simon, Bert M-S-R
> Estate of 32.6ha (81 acres), formed in 1968 from v'yds previously owned by Freiherr von SCHORLEMER and incl. more holdings added since. Today the estate is sole owner of the Herrenberg, Würtzberg and König Johann Berg sites at SERRIG and of the Staadter Antoniusberg at the upstream edge of the Saar vine-growing region. Further holdings are at Niedermennig, EITELSBACH (Marienholz), MERTESDORF and KASEL (KEHRNAGEL, NIES'CHEN and Herrenberg). Vines are 85% Riesling, 8% Müller-Thurgau and, unusually for the M-S-R, Weissburgunder (7%) which, in particular, produces interesting KABINETT wine. Dry QbAs are also successful, as well as the more traditional styles of Saar-Ruwer wine. Yield is approx. 20,800 cases a year from the 27ha (67 acres) that are actually in production at present. Sales are in Germany and abroad. Address: Weingut Herrenberg, Römerstr., 5512 Serrig/Saar.

Sittmann, Weingut Carl Rhh.
> Largest privately owned estate in the Rheinhessen, est. in 1879, with some 100ha (247 acres) at OPPENHEIM (SACKTRÄGER, etc.), Dienheim, ALSHEIM (incl. FRÜHMESSE) and NIERSTEIN (FINDLING, HIPPING, ÖLBERG, ORBEL, PATERBERG, etc.) – all fine sites. Vines are 20% Müller-Thurgau, 15% Silvaner, 14% Kerner, 11% Riesling, etc. The estate produces a full range of typically regional wines, plus a rosé, Alsheimer Rheinblick Weissherbst QbA, that is an unlikely speciality for the Rheinhessen. The Sittmanns are now wine merchants and exporters as well as v'yd owners and sales of the approx. annual production of 104,000 cases are worldwide. Address: Wormserstr. 61, 6504 Oppenheim.

Slaty
> The soil of the M-S-R, Ahr and Mittelrhein is varied, but many of their v'yds contain slate. Its pervading greyness, both in the soil and on the house roofs, combined with the similarly coloured

basalt from the nearby Eifel hills, can make the Mosel a sombre place when the sun does not shine. However, Riesling wines from slate sites have elegance and finesse, and a particular flavour that by association has become known as slaty.

Sobernheim Nahe w. ★→★★
Village upstream from SCHLOSSBÖCKELHEIM making good, lively Riesling and flowery Müller-Thurgau wines. Grosslage: Paradiesgarten.

Sohlbach, Weingut Georg Rhg.
4.5ha (11 acre) estate, est. in 1860 but with a 300-year-old cask cellar. Holdings are all at KIEDRICH and produce a high proportion of dry and medium-dry QbA. Riesling normally contributes 71% of the harvest but Spätburgunder WEISSHERBST has a loyal following among the estate's private customers. A small amount of the aprox. annual production of 2,600 cases is exported to the UK. Address: Oberstr. 15, 6229 Kiedrich.

Söhnlein Rheingold KG, Kellereien
Sparkling-wine producers, est. in 1864. Their "Söhnlein Rheingold" was launched personally in 1876 by Richard Wagner, a friend of the Söhnlein family. The company's main brand today, in terms of volume, is "Söhnlein Brilliant", which sells at approx. DM 5.00 per bottle in Germany. See also Fürst von METTERNICH SEKTKELLEREI GmbH. Address: Söhnleinstr. 1-8, 6200 Wiesbaden-Schierstein.

Solemacher, Weingut Freiherr von M-S-R
5.5ha (14 acre) Saar estate owned by the family of Max Freiherr Raitz v. Frentz for more than 100 years, rebuilt after total destruction in World War II. Holdings are at SAARBURG and in the well-known village of OCKFEN (BOCKSTEIN, HERRENBERG), planted 80% in Riesling, 20% Müller-Thurgau. Approx. annual production is 4,600 cases, although this can vary greatly from vintage to vintage. Sales are in Germany and abroad. Address: 5510 Saarburg, Bez. Trier.

Sommerach Franken w. ★★
Village downstream from VOLKACH, with some 250ha (618 acres) of v'yds and the oldest cooperative cellar in Franken, founded in 1901. Known for its asparagus and its strongly flavoured Müller-Thurgau and Silvaner wine. Grosslage: Kirchberg.

Sommerhausen Franken w. ★★
Small village upstream from WÜRZBURG, with sweeping, modernized v'yds reaching down to the Main. Produces good-quality Müller-Thurgau and Silvaner wines. Grosslage: ÖLSPIEL.

Sonnenhof, Weingut Würt.
20ha (49 acre) family-owned estate n.w. of STUTTGART. Although the estate is only 10 years old, vine-growing has been in the Fischer family since 1522. 66% of production is in powerful, soft red wine from Trollinger, Spätburgunder and Limberger. White wines are mainly from Riesling, Kerner and Müller-Thurgau. Grapes are also bought in at harvest time, producing an annual output for the cellars of some 35,700 cases. 40% of the wine is dry. Sales are mainly in Germany, with a start being made abroad. Address: Bezner & Fischer, 7143 Vaihingen-Gündelbach.

Sonnenuhr M-S-R w. ★★★→★★★★
Two Einzellagen of this name lie side by side above the Mosel. One forms part of the v'yds of ZELTINGEN-RACHTIG, the other comes within the boundaries of WEHLEN. Both are well situated, 100% steep, 100% Riesling and make top-quality wine. The Wehlener Sonnenuhr in particular has a reputation for wines of great finesse and fruit, more gentle than those from neighbouring BERNKASTEL sites but with a wonderfully luscious flavour, that can reach the peak of wine-making on the river. Grosslage: MÜNZLAY. Growers in Zeltingen-Rachtig: Ehses-Berres, Ehses-Geller, Friedrich-Wilhelm-Gymnasium, Kesselstatt, Schorlemer, Selbach-Oster. Growers in Wehlen: "Abteihof", Bergweiler-Prüm, Jos. Christoffel, Deinhard Bernkastel, Kesselstatt, Lauerburg, Licht-Bergweiler, Otto Pauly, J. J. Prüm, S. A. Prüm, Richter, Schorlemer/Meyerhof, Studert-Prüm.

Sorte

Variety, species. (See next entry.)

Sortencharakter

Character of the vine variety. The style of a wine from any one v'yd will change each year to a greater or lesser extent, depending on the vintage. Within these variations those qualities that originate in the soil and the variety of grape will normally remain more or less constant. If the character of the vine variety is pronounced, this is usually considered a good thing. With the richest wines of AUSLESE quality and upwards, the vine character is often replaced by that of noble rot (EDELFÄULE).

Sparkling Hock

Sparkling wine from the Rhein. In the 1840s, as the German sparkling-wine industry was expanding, both KUPFERBERG and DEINHARD sold sparkling wines with names the British could easily understand, among which were "Sparkling Hock" and "Sparkling Moselle". Although Sparkling Moselle is still common today, and a number of Sparkling wines are made from Rhein wine, Sparkling Hock as a description has become rare.

Sparkling wine

See Qualitätsschaumwein, Schaumwein, Sekt

Spätburgunder, Blauer

Red grape variety, more commonly known elsewhere as Pinot Noir. In Germany it needs a good site to produce 90 hl/ha or more from its best clones, with MUST weights of at least 80° Oechsle (10% alcohol). A German Blauer Spätburgunder usually has less tannin than a French Pinot Noir and is sometimes offered on the German market with a certain amount of sweetness. As a QbA, the alcohol content will be increased by the addition of sugar. Prepared in this way it can more closely resemble a Pinot Noir from Burgundy. As a BEERENAUSLESE, with a great amount of residual sugar, it is a unique and fascinating wine. Of the 3,896ha (9,627 acres) planted in Germany in Blauer Spätburgunder, 74% are in Baden where the vine benefits from the warm southerly climate.

Spätlese

Late-picked. Grapes intended for a Spätlese wine cannot be picked earlier than seven days after the start of the main harvest of the vine variety in question. Often the Spätlese harvest of an early-ripening vine, such as Müller-Thurgau, will have been gathered before the main harvest of the late-ripening Riesling or Trollinger has begun. By delaying picking, the grapes develop more sugar. The difference in MUST weight between a Spätlese and a QbA varies depending on vine variety and region, but it can be as much as the equivalent of 4.4% alcohol (the figure in Württemberg). No enrichment (ANREICHERUNG) is allowed. Of all the QmP categories, Spätlesen are probably the most profitable for the producer and the most in demand from the consumer.

Spiegelberg Rhh. w. ★★

Grosslage of more than 600ha (1,483 acres) covering some excellent individual sites on the RHEINFRONT at NIERSTEIN, incl. FINDLING, BILDSTOCK and PATERBERG. A few top-quality growers have done a great deal to build up the reputation of the v'yds and thus of the Rheinhessen as a whole.

Spielberg Rhpf. w. ★★★

Excellent Einzellage on the outskirts of BAD DÜRKHEIM making stylish, fruity Riesling wines. Grosslage: HOCHMESS. Growers: Bassermann-Jordan, Fitz-Ritter, Karst, Schaefer.

Spindler, Weingut Eugen Rhpf.

Widely respected family-owned estate of 13.5ha (33 acres), with cellars and administrative buildings on the s. edge of FORST. Holdings are at DEIDESHEIM (GRAINHÜBEL, LEINHÖHLE, KIESELBERG, HERRGOTTSACKER), RUPPERTSBERG (incl. REITERPFAD and LINSENBUSCH) and Forst itself (PECHSTEIN, UNGEHEUER and notably JESUITENGARTEN). Vines are 65% Riesling, 15% Müller-Thurgau, etc. The estate is known for its Riesling wines with restrained residual sugar, for which maturation in bottle over a number of years is important. Sales are mainly in Germany. Address: Weinstrasse 55, 6701 Forst.

Spritzig

Slightly sparkling. Term used to describe a wine that gives a slight prickling sensation on the tongue produced by carbon dioxide. It can be found in M-S-R wine of all qualities up to and incl. AUS-LESEN and adds to their freshness and charm. If an ordinary wine from elsewhere is *spritzig* it may well be the result of carbon dioxide being used as a part of cellar technique, rather than through the natural gas formed in fermentation. In Germany, whereas white and rosé wines are sometimes expected to be *spritzig*, red wine should have no noticeable carbon dioxide.

Stahlig

Steely. Describes a wine in which the acidity is high and the flavour is very direct and clean. It is unlikely to be subtle and certainly not delicate. Wonderfully steely Riesling wines, esp. at top-quality QbA and KABINETT level from a good estate, come from the Saar and from the R. Nahe nr. TRAISEN.

Stauch, Alfred & Hartmut Rhpf.

6.5ha (16 acre) estate with all its holdings at KALLSTADT, incl. part of STEINACKER, planted with a high proportion of Riesling (80%) and 10% Traminer – once a vine widely grown in the region. Unusually, none of the wines is enriched, and elegance and fruit is aimed for in the vinification. Sales of the approximate annual production of 4,500 cases are to private customers and also through the estate's own wine bar. Address: Weinstrasse 130, 6701 Kallstadt.

Steeg Mrh. w. ★★

If Mittelrhein wines received the recognition the best of them deserve, Steeg, in a side valley of the Rhein gorge nr. BACHARACH, would be well known. The steep Riesling sites produce steely wines, with great possibilities for HALBTROCKEN (medium-dry) wines, and cheaper than an equivalent wine from the Rheingau by approx. DM 1.00 per bottle. Also excellent for sparkling wine in all but the best (i.e. warmest) years. Grosslage: Schloss Stahleck.

Steffensberg M-S-R w. ★★

Einzellage in a steep side valley of the Mosel at ENKIRCH producing firm, stylish Riesling wines. Grosslage: SCHWARZLAY.

Steil Rhg. r. w. ★★

Grosslage of about 140ha (346 acres) at ASSMANNSHAUSEN, between RÜDESHEIM and LORCH, planted in Spätburgunder and Riesling. The true-to-type red Spätburgunder wines are much respected locally. Expensive when drunk abroad.

Steillagenwein

"Steep-site wine." The cost of growing vines on steep sites is two or three times greater than it is on level sites and the yield is always smaller. Therefore it is proposed that wine from steep sites, which are usually potentially better than those from level terrain, should be able to bear the word "Steillagenwein" on their label to indicate their superiority. As yet, however, exactly what is meant by a steep site has not been finally defined.

Stein Franken w. ★★★

Most famous Einzellage in Franken, at WÜRZBURG. The steep slopes produce outstanding Riesling wines, powerful and with lasting flavour, as well as more gentle wines from Silvaner (see also STEINWEIN). Not in a Grosslage. Growers: Bürgerspital, Julius-spital, Würzburg Staatl. Hofkeller.

Steinacker Rhpf. w. (r.) ★★

Large, mainly sloping Einzellage at KALLSTADT, producing very good quality white wines from a variety of grapes and some less distinguished red wine from Portugieser. Grosslage: KOBNERT. Growers: Koehler-Ruprecht, Schuster, Stauch.

Steinberg Rhg. w. ★★★

Single v'yd, its 32.1ha (79 acres) enclosed by a stone wall, nr. KLOS-TER EBERBACH – Cistercian monks from Kloster Eberbach planted the first vines in the Steinberg in the 12th century. Today the v'yd is owned by the ELTVILLE STAATSWEINGUT. Vines are 95% Riesling and the wines have "size", breeding and finesse. They are sold simply under the name Steinberger – no village name.

Steinmächer Rhg. w. ★★

Grosslage of some 600ha (1,483 acres) almost in the suburbs of WIESBADEN. The best-known wine village in the Grosslage is RAUEN-THAL. Standard, good-quality wines that benefit from bottle age (esp. those made from Riesling) are sold under the Steinmächer name.

Steinwein

For at least 250 years, wine in BOCKSBEUTEL from WÜRZBURG in Franken was often sold simply as Steinwein. In this century the definition has become more precise, and since 1971 only wine from the STEIN Einzellage on the outskirts of Würzburg can bear the old name "Stein".

Stift

Religious foundation. A Stift must have religious connections whereas a STIFTUNG need not. Appears, for example, in the title Maximiner Stifts-Kellerei (Studert-Prüm) at Bernkastel.

Stiftung

An endowed institution. Some of the finest wine-producing estates are endowed institutions, often with religious origins (e.g. the Stiftung Staatliches Friedrich-Wilhelm-Gymnasium in Trier). Many land owners hoped that by leaving their good farming land and their best v'yds to the church while in this world they would have an easier time in the next.

Stillwein

All wine with little or no carbon dioxide, in contrast to PERLWEIN or SCHAUMWEIN, is classified as Stillwein.

Strausswirtschaft

"Bush Inn." Those for whom vine-growing is their principal occupation are allowed for a period totalling not more than four months each year to sell their wine, accompanied by simple food, on their own premises. This ancient practice is advertised by a bush (Strauss) hung outside wherever the wine is being offered. Theoretically a good wine will sell without this publicity, for "a good wine needs no bush". Also known as BESENWIRTSCHAFT, where a "Besen" (broom) replaces the "Strauss", and as "Heckenwirtschaft" ("Hecke" = hedge) in parts of Franken.

Strohwein

"Straw wine," made for centuries from grapes that had been dried on straw to concentrate their juice and increase the sugar content. Its production has been illegal in Germany since 1971. In style Strohwein was similar to a BEERENAUSLESE but even more of a rarity. Strohwein is still made outside Germany, and in particular in the Jura in France where it is known as *Vin de Paille*.

Strub, Weingut J. & H. A. Rhh.

Family-owned estate dating from the 17th century, with 17ha (42 acres) of holdings at Dienheim and NIERSTEIN (HIPPING, ÖLBERG,

ORBEL, PATERBERG and FINDLING). Vines are mainly Riesling, Silvaner and Müller-Thurgau (each 30%). A serious estate producing top-quality RHEINFRONT wine, traditional in style but now incl. some that are dry and medium-dry. Approx. annual production is

14,900 cases, sold in Germany and abroad. Address: Rheinstr. 42, 6505 Nierstein/Rhein.

Stück

Wooden cask, twice as large as the more common HALBSTÜCK, used mainly for storage.

Studert-Prüm, Stephan M-S-R

Estate of 5.1ha (13 acres), in the present family ownership since 1581, with holdings at WEHLEN (incl. SONNENUHR), GRAACH (HIMMEL-REICH, DOMPROBST) and BERNKASTEL (GRABEN) – all top-quality sites. Vines are 90% Riesling. The estate awards stars to its bottlings to differentiate between what it feels are the various qualities of AUSLESE wines: two stars equals fine Auslese, three stars equals finest Auslese. Approx. annual production is 6,000 cases, sold in Germany and abroad. Address: Maximiner Stifts-Kellerei, 5550 Bernkastel-Wehlen.

Stumpf

Blunt or dull. Describes a wine that has aged too quickly and has lost its character and life.

Stumpf-Fitz'sches Weingut

See Annaberg Stumpf-Fitz'sches Weingut

Sturm & Sohn, Weingut Rhg.

3.5ha (9 acre) estate, family-owned since 1653, with holdings at RAUENTHAL (incl. BAIKEN). Vines are 90% Riesling. Successes at regional and national competitions speak for the seriousness of the wine-making. Approx. annual production is 4,200 cases of long-lived, powerful wines, sold to private customers. Address: Hauptstr. 31, 6229 Rauenthal.

Stuttgart Würt. Pop. 590,000 r. w. ★→★★

Large industrial city and capital of the state of Baden-Württemberg, heavily damaged in World War II. Wooded hills and v'yds reach almost to the centre of the city, and Trollinger and sound Riesling wine is made. The Rotenberg Einzellage to the east of the city is a fine example of a modernized, reconstructed v'yd. Stuttgart is the site of the Intervitis viticultural and wine-related exhibition.

Südliche Weinstrasse, Bereich Rhpf. w. (r.)

District covering the whole of the Rheinpfalz, known in the past for a high yield of undistinguished wine. The quality today is much better, although it cannot rival the best from the n. Bereich MITTEL-HAARDT/DEUTSCHE WEINSTRASSE.

Süffig

Tasty. Describes a light wine, probably of not very high quality, with balanced sweetness, pleasant to drink in large quantities. Just what a good glass of "HOCK" should be.

Sugaring

See Anreicherung

Süssreserve

Sweet reserve: unfermented grape juice that is added to wine shortly before bottling to arrive at the required level of sweetness. It is widely used in most wines up to SPÄTLESE, to which a restrained addition of Süssreserve brings balance and charm. Complicated regulations govern the quality and geographical origin of a Süssreserve, but in principle both must be similar to that of the wine to which the Süssreserve is added. The use of Süssreserve has simplified the problems of bulk storage and has enabled sulphur-dioxide levels to be reduced. It has also made it possible to supply medium-sweet wines at the low price for which the consumer asks.

Sylvaner

See Silvaner

Tafelwein

Table wine. This term has been precisely defined by EEC regulations to describe the category below quality wine. It can only be produced from prescribed vines, growing within the EEC, and must reach certain analytical standards. DEUTSCHER TAFELWEIN is subject to additional national legislation. Strictly speaking, it is now incorrect to use the description table wine as a synonym for "dinner wine", or wine to accompany a meal.

Tafelwein, Deutscher (DTW)
   See Deutscher Tafelwein
Tartaric acid
   See Weinsäure
Tasting
   "Probe." For details of wine tasting in Germany, see page 20.
Taunus
   Mountain range, rising at its highest point to 880m (2,887 feet),
   defining the n. limits of the Rheingau and protecting the region
   from the worst extremes of the weather.
TBA, TbA
   See Trockenbeerenauslese
Tesch, Weingut Erbhof   Nahe
   Family-owned estate est. in 1723, totally committed to quality-
   wine production in a somewhat unfashionable part of the Nahe
   valley between BAD KREUZNACH and BINGEN. 40ha (99 acres) in

   LAUBENHEIM and LANGENLONSHEIM are planted 60% in Riesling.
   The vine-growing and wine-making is highly professional and
   many prizes are won at regional and national competitions.
   Approx. annual production is 28,000 cases, sold in Germany
   through the family's wine firm, Weinkellerei Marienburg GmbH.
   Address: Naheweinstr. 99, 6536 Langenlonsheim.
Teufelskeller Franken w. ★★→★★★
   Well-known Einzellage on the slopes at RANDERSACKER overlook-
   ing the Main, planted mainly in Silvaner and Müller-Thurgau.
   Broad-flavoured wines, typical of the region. Grosslage: EWIG
   LEBEN. Growers: Bürgerspital, Gebhardt, Juliusspital, Rander-
   sacker eG, Würzburg Staatl. Hofkeller.
Thanisch, Weingut Wwe. Dr H. M-S-R
   Old-established estate – the Thanisch family has been associated

   with vine-growing in BERNKASTEL for many generations. The 13ha
   (32 acres) of holdings incl. part of the famous Bernkasteler
   DOCTOR. Other sites are at BRAUNEBERG and in the HIMMELREICH at

GRAACH. The estate house, like that of the other major owner of the Doctor, Deinhard, is on the opposite side of the Mosel in the Kues portion of Berkastel-Kues. Approx. annual production is 5,800 cases of top-quality wine, matured in wood. The 1921 Bernkasteler Doctor TROCKENBEERENAUSLESE, a great rarity, became a sensation when one bottle reached an auction price in 1978 of DM 7,500. Sales of less exalted wine are in Germany and abroad. Address: Saarallee 31, 5550 Bernkastel-Kues.

Thiergarten, Weingut
See Nell, Georg-Fritz von

Thüngersheim eG, Winzergenossenschaft Franken
Highly successful cooperative cellar that produces award-winning wines. The 235 members own 245ha (605 acres) of v'yds on the R. Main downstream from WÜRZBURG, planted 54% in Müller-Thurgau. Vat capacity of the cooperative is the equivalent of 500,000 cases. Exports account for 10% of sales. Address: Retzbacherstr. 272a, 8702 Thüngersheim.

Tillmanns Erben Weingutsverwaltung, H. Rhg.
Estate with 12.05ha (30 acres) of holdings at ERBACH (incl. MICHELMARK), KIEDRICH (SANDGRUB) and HATTENHEIM (WISSELBRUNNEN). The estate takes protection of the environment seriously: no herbicides are used in the v'yds and the wines are left to their own devices as far as the facts of wine-making and maturation will permit. The 500-year-old cask cellar provides a marvellous atmosphere for tastings. 91% of the wines are dry or medium-dry Rieslings. Approx. annual production is 7,700 cases, sold only in Germany. Address: 6229 Erbach.

Tischwein
Literally, table wine. Not a legal definition but vulgarly used to describe a wine, probably not of high quality, that would accompany food well. See TAFELWEIN.

Ton
Has two quite separate meanings: it is a type of clay and also a characteristic style or accent. Thus wines from cellars that always follow one individual type of cellar procedure may be said to have a Betriebston, a sort of signature tune associated with the Betrieb or "works". A Kellerton usually indicates a slightly dirty "cellar flavour" in a wine.

Traben-Trarbach M-S-R Pop. 6,300 w. ★★
Health resort and tourist attraction divided by the R. Mosel, surrounded by the game-filled woods of the Hunsrück and the Eifel, and since the 16th century a centre for the wine trade. A number of wine export houses that incl. the name Languth in their title are based in the town. Their names are better known internationally than the wines from the local v'yds, many of which, nevertheless, are very steep and planted 100% in Riesling. Among the best sites is the Trabener Würzgarten, producing full-bodied, fruity wines, somewhat lower priced than those from the nearby villages of ERDEN or ÜRZIG. Grosslage: SCHWARZLAY.

Traisen Nahe w. ★★★
Village close to BAD MÜNSTER AM STEIN-EBERNBURG with top-quality Riesling sites, incl. the BASTEI, by the Rotenfels cliff. The rhyolite rock is held to give the wine its particular background flavour, which combined with a firm, lively Riesling acidity is most attractive and positive. Grosslage: BURGWEG.

Traminer (Roter)
Grape variety with red grapes that produce stylish, spicy white wine. Yield is low and the vine requires a first-class site. It is planted in 919ha (2,271 acres), mainly in the Rheinpfalz and Baden. Given the right weather conditions, estate bottlers will produce small quantities of single-vine wine from Traminer, regarded very much as a "speciality" by their customers. The Traminer seems to show unusually pronounced variations in character from one v'yd to another, making controlled improvement of the vine difficult on a national scale. Certainly, a German Traminer wine does not have quite the pungency of a Traminer from Alsace. See also Gewürztraminer.

Trappenberg Rhpf. w. ★
Grosslage of more than 1,600ha (3,954 acres) in the s. Rheinpfalz. A high proportion of Müller-Thurgau is grown on the level sites, as well as Silvaner, Morio-Muskat and a variety of other new crossings. Some Riesling is grown in v'yds nr. the old cathedral city of Speyer. Wines sold under the Grosslage name Trappenberg are unlikely to be more than sound and agreeable.

Traube
Grape. Most German grapes are white, some are red and others, such as Ruländer and Traminer, lie in between. They are grown mainly for wine-making although varieties such as Gutedel, Portugieser, Müller-Thurgau, Huxelrebe, Bacchus and Ortega also serve as table grapes.

Treppchen M-S-R w. ★★★
Very much a steep Riesling Einzellage at ERDEN, recognized as one of the best Mosel sites. Produces top-quality, stylish wines. Grosslage: SCHWARZLAY. Growers: Bischöfliche Weingüter, Jos. Christoffel, Kesselstatt, Loosen-Erben, Nicolay'sche Weinguts., St Johannishof.

Treppchen M-S-R w. ★★
Large, 250ha (618 acre) Einzellage at PIESPORT, on the right-hand bank of the Mosel, looking across the river and up to the famous GOLDTRÖPFCHEN site. Vines are mainly Müller-Thurgau and Riesling producing sound, good-quality wines, normally of no very great distinction. Grosslage: MICHELSBERG. Growers: Haag, Kesselstatt, Matheus-Lehnert, Marienhof.

Tresterwein
A rather unhealthy wine made by adding water to the pulp left behind when the grapes have been pressed. It cannot be sold commercially and is used mainly as HAUSTRUNK.

Trier M-S-R Pop. 99,000 w. ★★
Oldest city in West Germany, est. before the birth of Christ. In spite of considerable damage in World War II there are many old buildings, incl. the 2nd-century Roman gateway, the Porta Nigra, and the cathedral, part of which dates back to the 4th century. Trier has been involved with viticulture for centuries and there are more than 370ha (914 acres) of v'yds within the city boundaries. The Einzellage names are not widely known outside Germany but the city is the base for a number of important wine estates (Bischöfliche Weingüter, Friedrich-Wilhelm Gymnasium, Vereinigte Hospitien, etc.) with holdings in most of the best sites of the M-S-R. Trier is also the home of many wine-related institutions, and the birthplace of Karl Marx.

Trier, Verwaltung der Staatlichen Weinbaudomänen M-S-R
Fine 86ha (212 acre) estate, est. in 1896, owned by the state of RHEINLAND-PFALZ. Like many state cellars it operates as a testing station for new vine varieties and viticultural methods. The fully modernized v'yds are controlled from four DOMÄNE with holdings at OCKFEN (incl. BOCKSTEIN and HERRENBERG), Avelsbach between Trier and the R. Ruwer, SERRIG on the Saar and at TRIER itself. The mainly Riesling wines are light in alcohol, wonderfully refreshing and often slightly SPRITZIG. Approx. annual production is 62,500 cases, incl. the estate's own Riesling sparkling wine. Much is sold directly to the consumer in Germany but exports are also important. Address: Deworastr. 1, 5500 Trier.

Trittenheim M-S-R w. ★★→★★★
Small village nr. PIESPORT, set in a great half-circle of v'yds, already known for its wine in the 9th century. Said to be the site of the first planting of Riesling on the Mosel, in the 16th century. Today the v'yds lie on both banks of the river. Best known are APOTHEKE and ALTÄRCHEN. Grosslage: MICHELSBERG.

Trocken
Dry. A wine may be called Trocken if the residual sugar content is not greater than 4 g/l, or 9 g/l if the total acidity is less than the residual sugar content by no more than 2 g/l (e.g. residual sugar 8 g/l, total acidity not less than 6 g/l). A 10-year swing to production of dry wines in Germany seems to have slowed down in

1984. Today, about 11% of quality (QbA and QmP) wines produced in Rheinland-Pfalz are dry, 22% in Hessen and 25% in Baden. The export market, however, shows little general enthusiasm for dry German wines. The low alcohol content (approx. 8-11%) can make them seem sour to the international palate when compared with Alsace wines with 12% or more.

German wines dressed with just enough sweetness to balance their flavour are unique. Partially clothed, they can show their angular bone structure only too clearly.

Trockenbeerenauslese
An immensely rich wine with a minimum potential alcohol content of 21.5% (22.1% in certain districts of Baden), made from overripe grapes, usually heavily infected with *Botrytis cinerea* (EDELFÄULE). The most shrivelled and therefore the sweetest grapes are selected either at the moment of picking in the v'yd or in the press house. The MUST will not ferment easily and therefore, by law, the actual alcohol content need not be more than 5.5%, leaving the wine enormously sweet.

A Trockenbeerenauslese can only be harvested in fine vintages with good autumn weather. It is the ultimate in German wine-making and a high price has to be paid for it, often eight times greater than that for a "simple" AUSLESE. Production costs are also high and the yield is usually minute. It is not a commercial proposition but an act of faith.

Trollinger, Blauer
Red grape variety, usually known simply as Trollinger, planted in 2,079ha (5,137 acres) – all but 10ha of which are in Württemberg, where its popularity as a symbol of regional identity seems well established. Trollinger ripens late, even later than Riesling, producing a light wine with much acidity, often vinified as SCHILLERWEIN. Yield is high (100-150 hl/ha) and the wine is pleasant but undistinguished.

Uelversheim Rhh. w. ★★→★★★
Small village a few km. s. of OPPENHEIM. Its distinguished wines would be better known abroad if its name was more easily spoken. Grosslagen: KRÖTENBRUNNEN and GÜLDENMORGEN.

Ungeheuer Rhpf. w. ★★★
Einzellage at FORST, a few km. s. of BAD DÜRKHEIM. All the v'yds at Forst are capable of producing excellent Riesling wines. Those from the Ungeheuer are powerful, full-flavoured and show earthy regional characteristics. The whole of the site is at present being rebuilt, returning to production in 1987. Grosslage: MARIEN-GARTEN. Growers: Bassermann-Jordan, Buhl, Bürklin-Wolf, Deinhard Koblenz, Forster Winzerverein, Hanhof, Kern, Mosbacher, Spindler, J. L. Wolf.

Ungstein Rhpf. w. ★★→★★★
Village adjacent to BAD DÜRKHEIM producing excellent rich and fruity wine, possibly without the intensity of flavour of that from the finest Rheinpfalz villages. Grosslagen: HÖNIGSÄCKEL, HOCHMESS and KOBNERT.

Untergebiet
Sub-district. DEUTSCHER TAFELWEIN (DTW) may take its name from the four WEINBAUGEBIETE or their eight sub-districts (see pages 8-9). In some instances the Untergebiet name is better known than that of the Weinbaugebiet, so that whereas Deutscher Tafelwein Rhein-Mosel is not often met, DTW Rhein, DTW Mosel and DTW Saar are relatively common.

Ürzig M-S-R w. ★★→★★★
Village of half-timbered houses and old wine cellars. It lies at the foot of a sweep of steep v'yd on the opposite bank of the Mosel to ERDEN, a few km. upstream from TRABEN-TRABACH. The Ürziger WÜRZGARTEN is one of the best-known Einzellagen of the Bereich BERNKASTEL. Grosslage: SCHWARZLAY.

Veldenz M-S-R w. ★★
Village in a pretty side valley of the Mosel nr. BERNKASTEL, looking across the river to the BRAUNEBERG v'yds. Produces pleasant, stylish Riesling wines. Grosslage: KURFÜRSTLAY.

Vereinigte Hospitien, Güterverwaltung M-S-R

Ancient charitable organization in TRIER, endowed over the centuries with v'yds, forestry and farming land. 45ha (111 acres) of v'yds incl. sole ownership of four sites: SCHLOSS SAARFELSER SCHLOSSBERG at SERRIG and Hölle at WILTINGEN on the Saar, Schubertslay at PIESPORT and Augenscheiner at Trier on the Mosel. The estate also has holdings at other sites at SERRIG, WILTINGEN (incl. BRAUNFELS), KANZEM (ALTENBERG), Trier, PIESPORT (GOLDTRÖPF-CHEN) and in the SCHARZHOFBERG. Vines are 84% Riesling, 8%

VERBAND DEUTSCHER PRÄDIKATSWEINGÜTER E.V.

Unsere Mitglieder besitzen Lagen von Weltruf!

V
D&P

Dieses Zeichen verbürgt Qualitätswein mit Prädikat

GROSSER RING DER PRÄDIKATSWEIN-VERSTEIGERER VON MOSEL, SAAR U. RUWER E.V., TRIER

A. P. Nr. 3 561 104-8-83

sanctus   Jacobus

MOSEL-SAAR-RUWER   750 ml e

1982er Serriger Schloß
Saarfelser Schloßberg Auslese
(Alleinbesitz)
Riesling — Qualitätswein mit Prädikat
Erzeugerabfüllung Vereinigte Hospitien, Trier

Müller-Thurgau, 6% Kerner, etc. In the cellars under Trier, among the oldest in Germany, maturation is in oak and care is given to allow the wines to show the character of the vine variety and site. Annual production is approx. 33,300 cases and sales are international. The Vereinigte Hospitien maintains a friendly contact with its opposite number in Beaune, the "Hôtel Dieu". Address: Krahnenufer 19, 5500 Trier.

Vereinigte Weingutsbesitzer Hallgarten eG Rhg.

Cooperative cellar dating from 1902. Its members own 60ha (148 acres) of holdings at HALLGARTEN (incl SCHÖNHELL), OESTRICH (LEN-CHEN and DOOSBERG), HATTENHEIM and MITTELHEIM, producing approx. 58,300 cases annually. The wines are full-bodied, positive in character, with good fruity acidity. Originally, only growers with more than 0.75ha (about 2 acres) of vines could join the cooperative, thus excluding the poorest growers. As the English were considered the richest of nations at the time, the members of the newly established cooperative became known as "Die Engländer" – the Englishmen. Address: "Die Engländer", 6227 Hallgarten/Rheingau.

Verschnitt

A blend of two or more wines or MUST, which should normally be better in quality than the individual parts from which the blend has been made. At its simplest, a soft Müller-Thurgau, for example, may be blended with a Riesling high in acidity to produce a better balanced wine with an enhanced commercial value. The laws that govern blending are complex and incl. geographical origin, vine variety, vintage and quality category.

Blending plays a vital role in the making of Champagne, Sherry, Port and often in red-wine production. In Germany its main purpose is to provide adequate quantities of one style of wine to meet the expectations of the consumer.

Versteigerung

Auction. A number of wine auctions are held in spring and autumn every year in different parts of the vine-growing area. It is usual for a group of growers to put up for sale parcels of wine in lots of not more than about 600 bottles, for which all bidding must be made through brokers. Before each lot is auctioned a tasting sample is poured for all those attending the auction. Among the most famous groups who auction their wines are the GROSSER RING, based at TRIER, and the Messe & Versteigerungsring of KLOSTER EBERBACH. ·

Versuchsanstalt
 Experimental institute. The various Federal States own a number of viticultural institutes carrying out research and experimental work, e.g. the Staatsweingut der Landes-Lehr-und Versuchsanstalt Oppenheim, owned by the Federal State of Rheinland-Pfalz. See also LEHRANSTALT.

Verwalter, Verwaltung
 Verwaltung, meaning administration, appears in titles of certain estates, e.g. the Verwaltung der Staatsweingüter Eltville. (The Schloss Reinhartshausen estate, on the other hand, actually uses the word "Administration" in its title.) The manager of an estate is often known as the Verwalter.

Vier Jahreszeiten-Kloster Limburg, Winzergenossenschaft Rhpf.
 Cooperative cellar founded in 1900. Its members own 206.3ha (510 acres) of holdings in the immediate vicinity of BAD DÜRKHEIM. Vines are mainly Riesling (39%), Müller-Thurgau (23%) and Portugieser (21%), producing all qualities of QmP up to a Huxelrebe TROCKENBEERENAUSLESE in 1983. Many win prizes at national competitions. Approx. annual production is 333,300 cases, sold mainly in Germany. Address: Limburgerstr. 8, 6702 Bad Dürkheim/Weinstrasse.

Villa Sachsen, Weingut Rhh.
 27ha (67 acre) estate owned by the ST URSULA WEINGUT & WEIN-KELLEREI GmbH, producers of the Goldener Oktober range of quality wines. All the holdings are at BINGEN, incl. 12ha (30 acres)

 in the well-known SCHARLACHBERG site. Vines are 50% Riesling, 15% Müller-Thurgau, 10% Silvaner, 10% Kerner, etc. Approx. 20,000 cases of carefully vinified, cask-matured, true-to-type wines are produced annually, sold in Germany and abroad. Address: Mainzerstr. 184, 6530 Bingen.

Vintage
 In German, JAHRGANG. For details of recent vintages in Germany, see pages 17-19.

Visiting vineyards and cellars
 In German, Kellerbesichtigung. See pages 20-21.

Volkach Franken w. ★★
 Romantic small town 25km (16 miles) e. of WÜRZBURG, making wine from one large, 150ha (371 acre) Einzellage, the Ratsherr. Principal vine varieties: Silvaner and Müller-Thurgau. Grosslage: Kirchberg.

Vollmer, Weingut Adam Rhg.
 Long-established, family-owned estate with 5ha (12 acres) of holdings in GEISENHEIM (incl. ROTHENBERG. KLÄUSERWEG and MÄUER-CHEN), planted 95% in Riesling. Approx. annual production is 4,500 cases of typically spicy, elegant Rheingau wine, sold almost exclusively in Germany. Address: Winkelerstr. 93, 6222 Geisenheim.

Volxem, Weingut Bernd van M-S-R
 Family-owned Saar estate dating from 1876 with holdings at WILT-INGEN (incl. BRAUNFELS, SCHLANGENGRABEN and Schlossberg),

OBEREMMEL (Rosenberg) and part of the famous SCHARZHOFBERG. Vines are Riesling (70%), Müller-Thurgau (15%), Kerner and, unusually for the M-S-R, Weissburgunder and Ruländer. The style of the wines stresses acidity and fruitiness, many are SPRITZIG and every wine is identified on the price list by its A.P. number. Address: 5511 Wiltingen.

Volxem, Weingut Staatsminister a.d. Otto van M-S-R
2.8ha (7 acre) estate owned by Herr Günther REH with holdings at SCHARZHOFBERG and elsewhere at WILTINGEN, planted 100% in Riesling. Approx. annual production is 2,500 cases, sold in Germany and abroad by Weingut Reichsgraf von KESSELSTATT. Address: Oberemmel/Saar.

Vorlese
The picking of grapes in advance of the main harvest may be allowed as a result of poor weather conditions. The aim will be to rescue a damaged crop or to eliminate unsound grapes and thereby improve the general standard of the harvest.

Vulkanfelsen Baden r. w. ★★
Grosslage covering much of the KAISERSTUHL, the district in Baden with the warmest climate, well known for its red and white wines from Spätburgunder (alias Pinot Noir) and Ruländer (Pinot Gris). The white wines have a strong flavour that comes from the volcanic soil and are most often met as simple quality (QbA) wine.

Wachenheim Rhpf. w. (r.) ★★★
Village just s. of BAD DÜRKHEIM, with some of the best Einzellagen of the Bereich MITTELHAARDT/DEUTSCHE WEINSTRASSE. Fine, rich, fat and full-bodied are the characteristics of a top-quality Wachenheimer in a good vintage. Riesling and other vine varieties grown. Grosslagen: SCHENKENBÖHL, SCHNEPFENFLUG AN DER WEINSTRASSE, MARIENGARTEN.

Wachtenburg-Luginsland eG, Winzergenossenschaft Rhpf.
Cooperative cellar with 320 members owning 330ha (815 acres) of holdings at Gönnheim and WACHENHEIM, incl. part of GERÜMPEL. As usual in the best part of the Bereich MITTELHAARDT/DEUTSCHE WEINSTRASSE, the proportion of Riesling grown is quite high (54%) for the Rheinpfalz, with Portugieser the next most widely grown vine (14%). Approx. annual production is 446,400 cases, sold exclusively in Germany. Address: 6706 Wachenheim a.d. Weinstrasse.

Wagner, Weingut-Weinhaus Mrh.
5ha (12 acre) estate set in the idyllic and secluded Mühlental valley, five minutes' drive from the centre of KOBLENZ. The very steep v'yds are planted 50% in Riesling, 20% Müller-Thurgau plus a range of other varieties both old (incl. Ruländer, Gewürztraminer

and Spätburgunder) and new. The estate is a member of the ERZEUGERGEMEINSCHAFT Deutsches Eck and sells most of its annual production of approx. 7,500 cases through its wine bar and wine garden. The concentration is on light, medium-dry wines which win many regional and national prizes. Address: 5400 Koblenz-Ehrenbreitstein.

Wagner-Weritz, Weingut Rhg.
7.5ha (19 acre) estate, founded in 1878, with holdings in some of
the best sites in ERBACH incl. MICHELMARK. SIEGELSBERG and Stein-
morgen, which for Wagner-Weritz produces wines of great intensity of flavour. Other holdings are at HATTENHEIM and KIEDRICH
(SANDGRUB). Vines are 85% Riesling, in line with the estate's aim
to produce traditional Rheingauer wines. Much of the best wine
is sold through the wine merchants Rudolf MÜLLER in Reil and
exported throughout the world. Address: Eberbacherstr. 86-88,
6229 Erbach.

Waldrach M-S-R w. ★★
Village on the Ruwer upstream from KASEL, surrounded by hills.
Its v'yds, planted with a high proportion of Riesling, incl. no
absolutely top-flight sites but produce elegant, fresh wines that can
step right out of their class in good years. Grosslage: RÖMERLAY.

Walluf Rhg. w. ★★
Village nr. WIESBADEN, split into Oberwalluf and Niederwalluf by
the little R. Walluf. Makes Riesling wine that is typical of the
region and seldom found elsewhere. Grosslage: STEINMÄCHER.

Walporzheim Ahr. r. ★★
Small village, much visited by tourists, producing light, stylish red
wine from Spätburgunder that can usually only be sampled locally.

Wawern M-S-R w. ★★→★★★
Small Saar village overlooked by its hill, the HERRENBERG, from
which almost the whole length of the Saar v'yd area can be seen.
A high proportion of Riesling on steep sites guarantees outstanding wines in good years. If they lack the elegance and breeding of
a fine wine from the neighbouring AYL, they make up for it by their
sheer "zip" and life. Grosslage: SCHARZBERG.

Wegeler Erben, Gutsverwaltung Geheimrat J. Rhg.
Important Rheingau estate, acquired in 1882 by Geheimrat Julius
Wegeler, a partner in the Koblenz-based company of wine
merchants DEINHARD. The 55ha (136 acres) of holdings, planted
88% in Riesling, are at OESTRICH (incl. LENCHEN and DOOSBERG),
HALLGARTEN (SCHÖNHELL), WINKEL (HASENSPRUNG, JESUITENGAR-
TEN), JOHANNISBERG (HÖLLE), GEISENHEIM (ROTHENBERG, KLÄUSER-
WEG, etc.) and RÜDESHEIM (incl. BERG ROTTLAND, BERG SCHLOSSBERG,
BERG ROSENECK) – all top-quality sites. The aim of the vinification
is simply to translate the character and quality of the grape into
the best possible Rheingau wine, with emphasis on maintaining the
differences between the individual sites. EISWEIN is a speciality,
grapes sometimes being harvested in the early part of the year
following the main harvest. Approx. annual production is 35,000
cases, depending on the vintage. Sales are in Germany and abroad,
esp. in the English-speaking countries. Address: Friedensplatz 9,
6227 Oestrich-Winkel.

Wehlen M-S-R w. ★★→★★★★
Pleasant village, backed by a hillside dotted with fruit trees, facing
its most important sites across the Mosel. All are a little over-
shadowed by the worldwide reputation of the Wehlener SONNEN-
UHR site that forms part of the continuous sweep of v'yd from
BERKASTEL to ZELTINGEN-RACHTIG. Grosslage: MÜNZLAY.

Wehrheim, Weingut Eugen Rhh.
9ha (22 acre) estate owned by the Wehrheim family, involved in
vine-growing since 1693. Holdings are all at NIERSTEIN in FINDLING,
BILDSTOCK, PATERBERG, ORBEL and PETTENTHAL, planted 35% in
Riesling, 20% Silvaner, 20% Müller-Thurgau, etc. The estate
produces good wine at all levels but is esp. proud of its award-
winning 1975 Niersteiner Paterberg Ruländer and Huxelrebe
BEERENAUSLESE. Approx. annual production is 6,600 cases, sold
in Germany and abroad. Address: Mühlgasse 30, 6505 Nierstein.

Weil, Weingut Dr R. Rhg.
Probably the best-known KIEDRICH estate, est. in 1867, with
18.75ha (46 acres) of holdings planted 92% in Riesling. Part of the
estate house was built by John Sutton, the 19th-century Englishman who so marvellously restored the Kiedrich parish church. Dr
Weil's holdings in KIEDRICH incl. SANDGRUB and GRÄFENBERG, pro-

ducing approx. 16,600 cases annually of carefully made, good-quality Riesling wine. The estate usually includes a number of vin-

tages on its list, covering wines at all quality levels. 30% of sales are abroad. Address: Mühlberg 5, 6229 Kiedrich.

Weiler, Weingut Heinrich Mrh.
5ha (12 acre) estate owned by a family involved in vine-growing since 1607. Holdings are in steep, slaty sites at Oberwesel and Kaub, on either side of the Rhein, and incl. sole ownership of the 1.3ha (3 acre) Kauber Rossstein site. Vines are 80% Riesling, producing balanced, slightly earthy wine. In 1976 the estate produced its first TROCKENBEERENAUSLESE, from the Oberweseler Römerkrug site. Approx. annual production is 3,900 cases, sold in Germany and abroad, in cooperation with the ERZEUGERGEMEINSCHAFT im Tal der Loreley. Address: Mainzerstr. 2-3, 6532 Oberwesel.

Weinbau
Vine-growing. See pages 14-16.

Weinbaudomäne
See Domäne

Weinbaugebiete
The area from which a table wine is drawn. It is subdivided into UNTERGEBIETE and "Gebiete für Landwein" – areas for country wine. There are no separate areas for making table wine and quality wine, as in France, and the name chosen to describe the wine will depend mainly on its quality. (See also pages 8-9.)

Weinberg
Vineyard.

Weinbrand
Brandy made from wine. Much sound brandy is produced in Germany, usually from imported wine, fortified up to 20% alcohol. It is unfortunately often served in restaurants and cafés in small glasses more suited to a mini-cocktail. Producers such as Asbach, Dujardin and Chantré are household names in Germany.

Weinbruderschaften
Wine brotherhoods. Societies whose main aim is to develop and encourage interest in wine in a spirit of altruism. Wine brotherhoods are found all over Germany and not solely in the wine-producing regions.

Weinessig
Wine vinegar, which in Germany may contain a certain amount of vinegar of non-vinous origin.

Weingarten
Term used in Württemberg for "vineyard", which in other regions is usually described as "Weinberg". There are also two wine-producing villages, in Baden and the Rheinpfalz, called Weingarten.

Weingärtnergenossenschaft
Name used in Württemberg for a WINZERGENOSSENSCHAFT.

Weingrosskellerei
Wholesale cellar that buys wine, much of it in bulk, from all over the world and supplies the wine trade, hotels and restaurants in Germany and abroad.

Weingut
Wine-producing estate. A term that can only appear on a wine label if the wine and SÜSSRESERVE have been made exclusively from grapes grown on the estate mentioned.

Weinhex M-S-R w. ★→★★
Grosslage of about 500ha (1,236 acres) on the Mosel upstream from KOBLENZ. Many of the individual sites are immensely steep and planted 100% in Riesling. The wines are steely and somewhat earthy compared to those from the well-known sites of the MITTELMOSEL. In this respect they resemble those of the neighbouring Mittelrhein.

Weinkellerei
Commercial wine cellar that buys grapes, MUST or wine but does not necessarily own v'yds. Often found in the form Weingut-Weinkellerei, as in Weingut-Weinkellerei Schneider GmbH in the Rheinpfalz. This indicates that the company owns v'yds from which it makes its own wine and also buys from other growers or merchants. 40% of Mosel wine is sold through Weinkellereien.

Weinlehrpfad
"Instructional wine path" through the v'yds, esp. in Baden but also at Schweigen and EDENKOBEN in the Rheinpfalz, WÜRZBURG in Franken and at WINNINGEN and REIL on the Mosel, etc. Notices alongside the paths give details about the sites, vine varieties and other relevant information. Such paths make it possible to combine study with a little exercise and often include a wine bar en route, offering a range of local wines.

Weinprobe
Wine tasting. See page 20.

Weinsäure
Tartaric or "wine acid", the acid that gives wine its backbone and grip. Unfortunately it can also appear in bottled wine as one of the causes of a white crystalline deposit (WEINSTEIN) that ideally should have been discarded while the wine was still in bulk. The deposit is harmless, natural, falls quickly to the lowest part of the bottle and is not evidence of a sickness, but its appearance in white wine often worries the consumer. (In red wine it is usually accepted as a natural result of ageing.) The likelihood of the formation of a "tartrate deposit", as it is commonly called, cannot always be both satisfactorily and totally eliminated, but objections to it are misplaced.

Weinsberg Würt. w. ★★
Town 7km (4 miles) e. of HEILBRONN, home of the important state viticultural institute where the Kerner vine was developed (see next entry). Riesling and Trollinger produce wines typical of the region. Grosslagen: Staufenberg and Salzberg.

Weinsberg, Staatl. Lehr-und Versuchsanstalt für Wein & Obstbau Würt.
Oldest viticultural institute in Germany, est. by King Charles of Württemberg in 1868 to improve the economic position of viticulture. A large variety of vines is grown by the institute for experimental and also commercial purposes. (The Kerner, Heroldrebe and Helfensteiner grape varieties were developed at Weinsberg.) 54ha (133 acres) of holdings are all in the n. part of Württemberg nr. HEILBRONN. 99% of the wines are sold under the Einzellage names – which, unfortunately, are not well known outside the region. The aim is to produce fresh, stylish wines, models of what such wines should be. Approx. annual production is 20,800 cases, almost all sold in the Heilbronn-Stuttgart area.
  Although the institute is the largest Weingut in Württemberg, its major contribution lies in the skill of the students it trains and the benefits that result from its experimental work. Address: Hallerstr. 6, 7102 Weinsberg.

Weinsiegel
See Siegel

Weinstein
See Tartaric acid

Weinstrasse
Wine road, often met in France as *Route du Vin*. There are several

Weinstrassen that follow a well-signposted, if rambling, course through the v'yds. The oldest and best known is the Deutsche Weinstrasse that runs 80km (50 miles) through the Rheinpfalz and gives its name to the Bereich MITTELHAARDT/DEUTSCHE WEINSTRASSE.

Weissburgunder

White grape variety, also known as Weisser Burgunder, and more widely outside Germany as Pinot Blanc. It is said to be the result of a mutation of Ruländer. There are 872ha (2,155 acres), mainly in Baden and Rheinpfalz, producing good-quality wine with less acidity than Silvaner and a NEUTRAL flavour. Only succeeds in a good site.

Weisser Elbling

See Elbling

Weisser Gutedel

See Gutedel

Weissherbst

Rosé QbA produced, with its SÜSSRESERVE, from a single grape variety in the regions of Ahr, Baden, Franken, Rheingau, Rheinhessen, Rheinpfalz and Württemberg. Originally Weissherbst was made from red grapes that had lost colour through *Botrytis cinerea* (EDELFÄULE). In Baden, Spätburgunder Weissherbst is very popular for its full, fresh, gentle flavour and low tannin content.

Werner'sches Weingut, Domdechant Rhg.

Family estate est. in 1780, now into its seventh generation. The 13.5ha (33 acres) of holdings at HOCHHEIM, incl. DOMDECHANEY, KIRCHENSTÜCK and HÖLLE, are planted almost entirely in Riesling. Maturation in cask in the vaulted cellar reveals a traditional

approach to wine-making, balanced with sensible use of modern techniques. The result is racy, elegant, fruity wine with a touch of the soil in its flavour. Approx. annual production is 16,600 cases. Sales are worldwide. Address: Rathausstr. 30, 6203 Hochheim.

Westhofen Rhh. w. (r.) ★★

Vine-growing village in the Bereich WONNEGAU with a reputation for good-quality wines. Not widely known outside Germany. Grosslage: Bergkloster.

Wiesbaden Rhg. Pop. 272,000 w. ★→★★

Capital of the State of Hessen, at the e. end of the Rheingau; a modern business city, centre of the German film industry and the home of the sparkling-wine producers HENKELL and SÖHNLEIN. In a region of much fine wine, the Wiesbaden sites are not well known. High proportion of Riesling grown.

Wiltingen M-S-R w. ★★→★★★

Well-known Saar wine village, much damaged in the past by feuds between Luxembourg and the archbishops of nearby TRIER. A high proportion of Riesling is grown in sites on both sides of the river, producing wine of a quality and price similar to that of the best MITTELMOSEL villages such as BERNKASTEL and BRAUNEBERG. Grosslage: SCHARZBERG.

Wine Festivals

See Visiting the Vineyards, pages 20-21.

Wine Museums
See Visiting the Vineyards, pages 20-21.

Wingert
Rather a rustic word for a v'yd, found in a number of site names, e.g. Ürziger Goldwingert, Wachenheimer Königswingert, Piesporter Kreuzwingert.

Winkel Rhg. w. ★★→★★★★
Small village, close to the Rhein, known for Riesling wines of finesse, the best of which in a good vintage will develop over many years in bottle. The straight Riesling flavour is powerful, without pronounced overtones from the soil. Wines from most of the leading, and many less-known, estates can be enjoyed in the Graues Haus (the oldest stone house in Germany) restaurant, owned by SCHLOSS VOLLRADS. Grosslagen: HÖNIGBERG and ERNTEBRINGER.

Winkels-Herding, Weingut Rhpf.
Family-owned estate, dating from the 19th century, some 7km (4 miles) up the Weinstrasse n. of BAD DÜRKHEIM. Of the 25ha (62 acres) suitable for vine-growing, 16ha (40 acres) are planted at present, incl. 26% Riesling, 18% Müller-Thurgau, 16% Silvaner, 9% Kerner. Holdings are in deep lime-rich soil at Dackenheim (95% of Kapellgarten in sole ownership), Herxheim and Freinsheim. Two-thirds of the wines are matured in wood, which emphasizes their full-bodied character, and are sold as ERZEUGER-ABFÜLLUNG. The estate also buys in grapes to increase its production. Sales are mainly to the German consumer and in bulk to the wine trade. Address: 6719 Dackenheim an der Weinstrasse.

Winningen M-S-R w. ★★
Attractive riverside wine village, almost in the suburbs of KOBLENZ, much visited by tourists from Köln and the Ruhr district. Scene of Germany's oldest wine festival. The v'yds are excessively steep and planted mainly in Riesling. The wines, steely but possibly a little coarse compared to the best of the MITTELMOSEL, are well thought of in the district. Grosslage: WEINHEX.

Wintrich M-S-R w. ★★
Typical Mosel village, set back from the right-hand bank of the river, upstream from BRAUNEBERG. Some sites are planted 100% Riesling; others contain much Müller-Thurgau. Good wines, generally felt to be not quite among the finest of the river. Grosslage: KURFÜRSTLAY.

Winzergenossenschaft
Cooperative cellar. The first cooperative cellar in Germany was est. in the Ahr valley in 1868 to improve the low income of its members. Today the aim remains similar, and the contribution made by the cooperatives to the economics of vine-growing can hardly be overestimated. Three-quarters of the growers in Germany deliver their grapes, from approx. 36% of the total viticultural area, to cooperative cellars. 83% of the wine is sold in bottle; the rest is taken in bulk by the wine trade.

Although cooperatives can sell the wine from their members' grapes as estate bottled (ERZEUGERABFÜLLUNG), they are only involved in the wine-making and selling – not in the vine-growing. They have most support where growers' holdings are very small (e.g. Baden-Württemberg) but cooperatives in the M-S-R, Rheinhessen and Rheinpfalz have been the most active in the export markets.

The finest, most elegant German wines probably come from the well-known private or state-owned estates, but the well-equipped cooperatives have the reputation for producing sound, well-made wine, usually in considerable quantities. See also ZENTRALKELLEREI.

Winzerkeller Südliche Bergstrasse Baden
The 4,300 members of this large cooperative cellar have 1,600ha (3,954 acres) of holdings in 57 villages n. and s. of HEIDELBERG. Vines are 45% Müller-Thurgau, 25% Riesling, 12% Ruländer, 8% Weissburgunder, etc. Approx. annual production is the equivalent of 1.4m. cases of full-bodied, rounded wine, typical of the Bereich Badische Bergstrasse/Kraichgau. Sales are mainly in the surrounding district. Address: Bögnerweg 3, 6908 Wiesloch/Kraichgau.

Winzerverein
Alternative name for WINZERGENOSSENSCHAFT (cooperative cellar).

Wirsching, Weingut Hans Franken
Estate est. by the Wirsching family in 1630, now run by the 14th
generation, with 40ha (99 acres) of organically fed holdings at IPHOF-
EN (incl. KALB) and RÖDELSEE (part of the KÜCHENMEISTER). Vines
are 30% traditional Franken Silvaner, 30% Müller-Thurgau, 9%
Riesling, etc. The cellars date from the 17th century, but in 1970
a modern press house and machinery park were built outside
Iphofen. Half the estate's concentrated, firm, lively wines are
"FRÄNKISCH TROCKEN", but the 1979 Iphöfer Julius-Echter-Berg
Rieslaner Auslese QmP is a superb sweet but balanced wine, with
great length of flavour. Approx. annual production is 33,300 cases,
sold mainly in Germany. Address: Ludwigstr. 16, 8715 Iphofen.

Wisselbrunnen Rhg. w. ★★★
Einzelage at HATTENHEIM producing good-quality, spicy Riesling
wines. Grosslage: DEUTELSBERG. Growers: Knyphausen, Lang,
Reinhartshausen, Ress, Tillmanns.

Wolf Erben, Weingut J. L. Rhpf.
20ha (49 acre) estate, owned by the present family for more than
80 years (the estate house, with an enclosed courtyard, was built
in the Italian Renaissance style in 1840). Holdings are at WACHEN-
HEIM (incl. GERÜMPEL and GOLDBÄCHEL), FORST (UNGEHEUER.
JESUITENGARTEN and PECHSTEIN) and DEIDESHEIM (HERRGOTTSACKER
and LEINHÖHLE) – all top-quality sites and, remarkable for the
region, all planted 100% in Riesling, so the wines, not surprisingly,
are racy, elegant and range from dry to sweet. Approx. annual production is 12,500 cases, sold in Germany and abroad. Address:
Weinstrasse 1, 6706 Wachenheim.

Wonnegau, Bereich Rhh. w.
Covers the s. part of the Rheinhessen, the source of much good,
unsophisticated country wine in which the taste of the soil is sometimes present. Not a name widely known on the international
market – its appearance on a label is often simply a legal requirement rather than an aid to selling.

Worms Rhh. Pop. 73,500
Cathedral city that has suffered much from war damage in its long
history. The v'yds of the LIEBFRAUENKIRCHE (Church of Our Lady)
are known as the source of the original Liebfrau(en)milch. Many
events connected with wine are held in the city and its environs,
incl. the annual, oddly named "Backfischfest" (Fried-fish festival).

Württemberg w. r.
Wine region of 9,100ha (22,487 acres) spreading out on either side
of the R. Neckar and its tributaries and incl. the smallest Bereich
in Germany, the Bereich WÜRTTEMBERGISCHER BODENSEE. It is a

region of small v'yd holdings: more than half the growers own less
than 0.25ha (0.62 acre). For most, vine-growing is a part-time
occupation or hobby and more than 80% of the crop is delivered
to cooperative cellars for processing. Almost half the region is
planted in vines bearing red grapes, but 70% of the wine produced

is white, mainly from Riesling, Müller-Thurgau and Kerner. Within the region, where nearly all the wine is drunk, the big demand is for the red wines made from Trollinger, Müllerrebe, Limberger, Portugieser and Spätburgunder. They are normally light in colour and tannin and often have varying amounts of residual sugar. The white wines are well up to standard for s. Germany and are generally cheaper than the red wines. Probably for present international taste, better value for money can be found in the regions further north. SCHILLERWEIN (a rosé wine) is a speciality of the region.

For the visitor to the region who is interested in architecture and historic buildings, and appreciates attractive, rural countryside, there is much to see.

Württembergischer Bodensee, Bereich Würt. w. r.
Smallest Bereich in Germany, with 8.75ha (22 acres) at Kressbronn/BODENSEE and Ravensburg.

Würzburg Franken Pop. 128,000 w. ★★★
Fine university city and business centre, severely damaged in World War II. Fortunately many of the historic buildings survived or have been restored. The city contains a number of old cellars belonging to top-quality estates, incl. those of the BÜRGERSPITAL, the JULIUSSPITAL and the Staatliche Hofkeller (see next entry). The v'yds in and around the city produce Franken wine of style, grip and positive flavour. They can be superb but are, regrettably, expensive.

Würzburg Staatlicher Hofkeller Franken
Estate founded in 1128, with many outstanding features but few more impressive than the magnificent vaulted cellar, filled wih impeccably maintained casks. If objective judgement can survive this underworld, so clearly dedicated to Bacchus, it may be able to remain sober when faced wih the Baroque splendour of the Prince-Bishops' "Residenz" above, with its magnificent Tiepolo ceiling.

Fortunately the wines measure up to the explosion of architectural beauty in which they are made. The substantial holdings cover 180ha (445 acres) at WÜRZBURG (STEIN and INNERE LEISTE), RANDERSACKER (incl. TEUFELSKELLER), Hörstein, Grossheubach, Kreuzwertheim, Handthal, Abtswind and Thüngersheim. Vines incl. Riesling (20%), Müller-Thurgau (20%), Silvaner (10%), Rieslaner (10%) and many other varieties. The variations on the Franken style from so many different vines and sites are fascinating, but all the wines are true to type and few are sweet. Approx. annual production is 104,000 cases, sold in Germany and abroad. Address: Residenzplatz 3, 8700 Würzburg.

Würzgarten M-S-R w. ★★★
Steep Einzellage at ÜRZIG, 100% Riesling, producing some of the best wines on the river. The red sandstone, pushing in from the Eifel, adds spice (Würze) to the Mosel slate and flavour to the wine. Grosslage: SCHWARZLAY. Growers: Bischöfliche Weingüter, Jos. Christoffel, Loosen-Erben, Nicolay'sche Weinguts.

ZBW
See Zentralkellerei Badischer Winzergenossenschaften

Zell M-S-R w. ★★
There are 23 towns called Zell in W. Germany, but little Zell an der Mosel, stretched out along the river, is known worldwide for its Grosslage SCHWARZE KATZ (Black Cat). Zell has a high proportion of Riesling in its steep v'yds and the wines are usually described as full, elegant and fruity.

Zell, Bereich M-S-R w. ★→★★
Bereich that covers the v'yds downstream from Zell an der Mosel (see previous entry) to KOBLENZ. The proportion of Riesling grown is high, many on their original root stocks, and the wines are generally very true to type, firm and positive in flavour, although the finesse of the best wines of the MITTELMOSEL is usually missing. Nearer Koblenz and the Rhein the wine takes on some of the Mittelrhein steeliness. Most of the exported wine is sold with the simple appellation Bereich Zell or as Zeller SCHWARZE KATZ.

Zeltingen-Rachtig M-S-R w. ★★★

Important village of old wine cellars, fine patrician houses and a long promenade by the Mosel. Its elegant wines, largely Riesling, are usually slightly cheaper than those of its neighbours WEHLEN and ÜRZIG. Grosslage: MÜNZLAY.

Zentralkellerei

Central cellars: the largest form of cooperative cellar, taking in the MUST or wine from smaller cooperatives (Winzergenossenschaften), as well as grapes from its own members. Six cellars function as Zentralkellereien: in Baden at Breisach, in the Rheinhessen at Gau-Bickelheim (also supplied by the Rheingau), in the M-S-R at Bernkastel-Kues, in the Nahe at Bad Kreuznach/Bretzenheim, in Württemberg at Möglingen and in Franken at Repperndorf. The wines of the first four are widely distributed on the export market. (see the following two entries and also MOSEL-SAAR-RUWER ZENTRALKELLEREI, NAHEWINZER ZENTRALKELLEREI).

Zentralkellerei Badischer Winzergenossenschaften eG (ZBW) Baden

Vast central cooperative cellar, founded in 1952, taking the crops from 25,000 growers via 100 local cooperative cellars spread throughout Baden. Müller-Thurgau and Spätburgunder are the main grapes, with smaller quantities of Ruländer, Gutedel and Riesling. Wines of different origin are kept apart. Some 400-500 sound, good-quality wines are produced each year, sold mainly in Germany but a small amount abroad. Highly impressive large-scale wine-making. Address: 7814 Breisach.

Zentralkellerei Rheinischer Winzergenossenschaft Rhh.

Central cooperative cellar with more than 6,000 members divided among 32 smaller cooperatives covering the Rheingau as well as the Rheinhessen. Members' holdings amount to 3,000ha (7,413 acres) planted with the full range of Rheinhessen and Rheingau vine varieties. The Zentralkellerei has its own brand of LIEBFRAUMILCH ("Little Rhine Bear"), exported all over the world. Address: 6551 Gau-Bickelheim.

Zucker

Sugar.

Zuckerrest

See Restzucker

Zwierlein, Weingut Freiherr von Rhg.

Estate est. in 1794, planted 100% in Riesling, with 11ha (27 acres) of holdings at GEISENHEIM (incl. KLÄUSERWEG, MÄUERCHEN and ROTHENBERG) and in the Winkeler JESUITENGARTEN. The wines are made to last and are typical of the region and the vine. An analysis of each wine is available for customers, and the estate makes great efforts to recommend what food would best accompany its wine. Approx. annual production is 8,300 cases, sold in Germany and the USA. Address: Schloss Kosakenberg, Bahnstr. 1, 6222 Geisenheim im Rheingau.

Mosel-Saar-Ruwer

"Abteihof"
Bergweiler-Prüm
Bischöfliche Weingüter
Christoffel
Deinhard
Drathen
Ehses-Berres
Ehses-Geller
Fischer, Dr
Friedrich-Wilhelm-Gymnasium
Gallais
Geltz
Haag
Haart
Hain
Heddesdorff
Hövel
Immich-Batterieberg
Kanzemer Berg
Karp-Schreiber
Karthäuserhof
Kesselstatt
Kies-Kieren
Knebel
Koch
Lauerburg
Licht-Bergweiler
Loosen

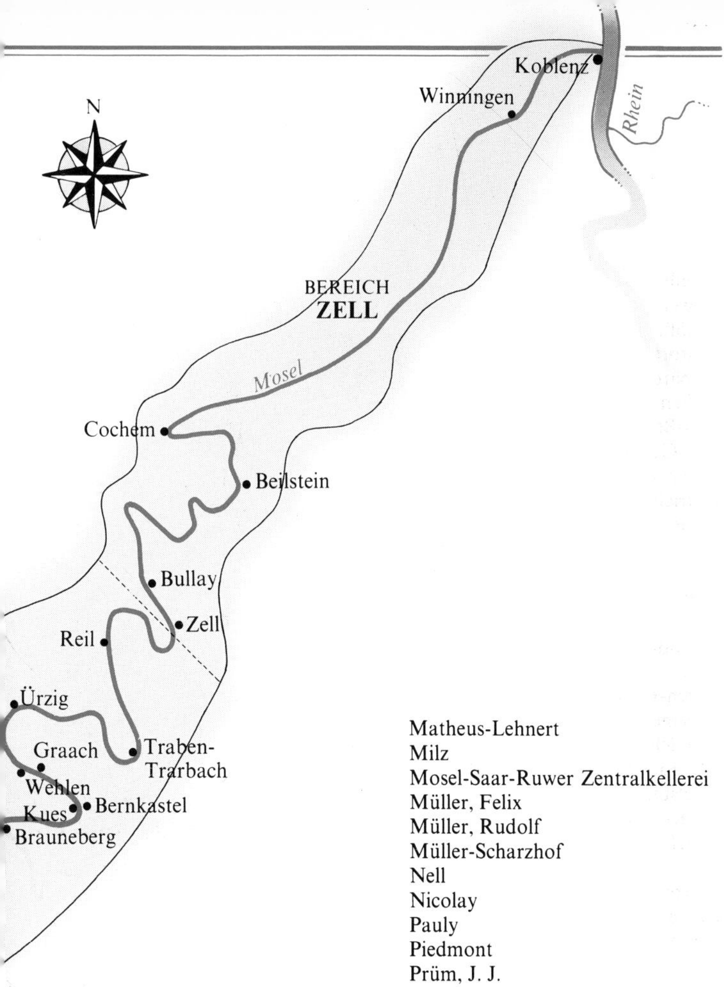

N

Koblenz

Winningen

Rhein

BEREICH
ZELL

Mosel

Cochem

Beilstein

Bullay

Zell

Reil

Ürzig

Graach

Traben-
Trarbach

Wehlen

Kues

Bernkastel

Brauneberg

Matheus-Lehnert
Milz
Mosel-Saar-Ruwer Zentralkellerei
Müller, Felix
Müller, Rudolf
Müller-Scharzhof
Nell
Nicolay
Pauly
Piedmont
Prüm, J. J.
Prüm, S A.
Reh
Reverchon
Rheinart
Richter
Ronde
St Johannishof
Schlangengraben
Schleinitz
Schneider
Schorlemer
Schubert
Selbach-Oster
Simon
Solemacher
Studert-Prüm
Thanisch
Trier Staatl. Wein.
Vereinigte Hospitien
Volxem, Bernd van
Volxem, Otto van

Rheingau, Rheinhessen

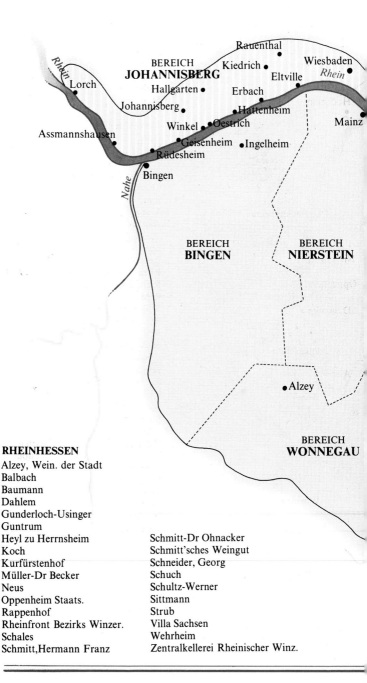

Rhein

BEREICH
JOHANNISBERG

Rauenthal

Kiedrich

Wiesbaden

Rhein

Lorch

Hallgarten

Eltville

Erbach

Johannisberg

Hattenheim

Assmannshausen

Winkel • Oestrich

Mainz

Geisenheim • Ingelheim

Rüdesheim

Nahe

Bingen

Rhein

BEREICH
BINGEN

BEREICH
NIERSTEIN

• Alzey

BEREICH
WONNEGAU

RHEINHESSEN

Alzey, Wein. der Stadt
Balbach
Baumann
Dahlem
Gunderloch-Usinger
Guntrum
Heyl zu Herrnsheim
Koch
Kurfürstenhof
Müller-Dr Becker
Neus
Oppenheim Staats.
Rappenhof
Rheinfront Bezirks Winzer.
Schales
Schmitt,Hermann Franz

Schmitt-Dr Ohnacker
Schmitt'sches Weingut
Schneider, Georg
Schuch
Schultz-Werner
Sittmann
Strub
Villa Sachsen
Wehrheim
Zentralkellerei Rheinischer Winz.

RHEINGAU

Allendorf
Altenkirch
Arnet
Aschrott
Basting-Gimbel
Becker
Brentano
Breuer

Diefenhardt
Eltville, Ver. der Staats.
Engelmann
Eser
Frankensteiner Hof
Frankfurt, Wein. der Stadt
Hallgarten Winzer.
Hessisches Weingut
"Hof Sonneck"
Holschier
Hupfeld
"Johannisberger Rosenhof"
Johannishof
Jost
Kanitz
Knyphausen
Königin Victoria Berg
Lamm-Jung
Lang
Mumm
Nägler
Nikolai
Oetinger
Ress
Rheingau Gebiets. Winzer.
Richter-Boltendahl
Riedel
Schloss Groenesteyn
Schloss Johannisberg
Schloss Reinhartshausen
Schloss Schönborn
Schloss Vollrads
Schlotter
Schumann-Nägler
Simmern
Sohlbach
Sturm
Tillmanns
Vereinigte Weinguts. Hallgarten
Vier Jahreszeiten-Kloster Limburg
Vollmer
Wagner-Weritz
Wegeler
Weil
Werner
Zwierlein

Hochheim

Main

N

Nackenheim

Nierstein
Oppenheim
Dienheim

Guntersblum

Alsheim

Rhein

Worms

3.0%

25.4%

% of total
v'yd area

RHEINGAU

RHEINHESSEN

miles 0   5   10
km 0   5   10   15

Nahe, Rheinpfalz

BEREICH KREUZNACH

Bingen

Dorsheim •

Langenlonsheim •

Rüdesheim •

Traisen • Bad
Niederhausen • • Kreuznach
Schlossböckelheim • Norheim

Meddersheim •

BEREICH SCHLOSS BÖCKELHEIM

Rhein

Nahe

Alsenz

Glan

RHEINPFALZ

Annaberg Stumpf-Fitz'sches	Kern
Bassermann-Jordan	Koehler-Ruprecht
Bergdolt	Minges, Ernst
Biffar	Minges, Rudolf
Buhl	Mosbacher
Bürklin-Wolf	Neckerauer
Deidesheim Winzer.	Pfeffingen
Deinhard, Dr	Rebholz
Deinhard Gutsverwaltung	Ruppertsberger Winz. "Hoheburg"
Deutsches Weintor	Schaefer
Fitz-Ritter	Schneider GmbH
Forster Winz.	Schuster
Friedelsheim Winzer.	Spindler
Hahnhof	Stauch
Hammel	Wachtenburg-Luginsland
Kallstadt Winzer.	Winkels-Herding
Karst	Wolf

NAHE

Anheuser, August
Anheuser, Paul
Bad Kreuznach Staats.
Crusius
Diel
Finkenauer
Höfer

Nahewinzer eG
Niederhausen-Schlossböckelheim
  Staatl. Wein.
Pallhuber
Plettenberg
Rheingräfenberg eG
Schlink-Herf-Gutleuthof
Schneider, Jacob
Schweinhardt
Tesch

Rhein

Worms ●

Bockenheim ●

Neuleiningen ●

BEREICH
**MITTELHAARDT/
DEUTSCHE
WEINSTRASSE**

N

● Kallstadt

● Bad Dürkheim
● Wachenheim
● Forst
● Deidesheim
● Ruppertsberg
● Neustadt

Speyer ●

● Maikammer
● Edenkoben
● Rhodt
Schwegenheim ●
Siebeldingen
●
● Landau in
  der Pfalz
BEREICH
**SÜDLICHE
WEINSTRASSE**

NAHE

RHEINPFALZ

4.8%

23.1%

% of total
v'yd area

● Bad Bergzabern

miles 0   10
km 0   10   20

● Schweigen

141

Hessische Bergstrasse, Franken, Württemberg, Baden

HESSISCHE BERGSTRASSE
Bensheim, Weingut der Stadt
Bergstrasse, Staatsweingut
Bergstrasser Gebiets Winzer.

FRANKEN
Bürgerspital
Castell
Franken eG, Gebiets.
Gebhardt
Hammelburg, Stadt Weingut
Hohenlohe Langenburgsche
Juliusspital
Knoll & Reinhart
Löwenstein-Wertheim-Rosenberg
Randersacker eG
Thüngersheim eG
Wirsching
Würzburg Staatl. Hofkeller

Mainz

Main

BEREICH
UMSTADT

Darmstadt

BEREICH
STARKENBURG

Seeheim
Adsbach

Bensheim
Heppenheim

Heidelberg

BEREICH
**BADISCHE BERGSTRASSE,
KRAICHGAU**

Rhein

Karlsruhe

Pforzheim

Baden-Baden

BEREICH
ORTENAU

Durbach
Offenburg

BEREICH
BREISGAU

Neckar

BEREICH
**KAISERSTUHL-
TUNIBERG**

Breisach

Freiburg

0.35%
5.0%
9.4%
14.9%
% of total
v'yd area

BEREICH
MARKGRÄFLERLAND

Basel

Rhein

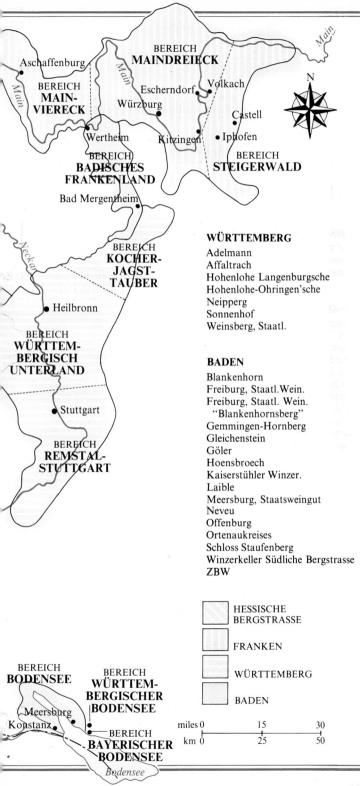

BEREICH
MAINDREIECK

Aschaffenburg

BEREICH
**MAIN-
VIERECK**

Escherndorf • Volkach

Würzburg

Castell

Wertheim

Kitzingen • Iphofen

BEREICH
**BADISCHES
FRANKENLAND**

BEREICH
STEIGERWALD

Bad Mergentheim

N

WÜRTTEMBERG

Adelmann
Affaltrach
Hohenlohe Langenburgsche
Hohenlohe-Ohringen'sche
Neipperg
Sonnenhof
Weinsberg, Staatl.

BEREICH
**KOCHER-
JAGST-
TAUBER**

• Heilbronn

BEREICH
**WÜRTTEM-
BERGISCH
UNTERLAND**

BADEN

Blankenhorn
Freiburg, Staatl.Wein.
Freiburg, Staatl. Wein.
 "Blankenhornsberg"
Gemmingen-Hornberg
Gleichenstein
Göler
Hoensbroech
Kaiserstühler Winzer.
Laible
Meersburg, Staatsweingut
Neveu
Offenburg
Ortenaukreises
Schloss Staufenberg
Winzerkeller Südliche Bergstrasse
ZBW

• Stuttgart

BEREICH
**REMSTAL-
STUTTGART**

HESSISCHE
BERGSTRASSE

FRANKEN

WÜRTTEMBERG

BADEN

BEREICH
BODENSEE

BEREICH
**WÜRTTEM-
BERGISCHER
BODENSEE**

Meersburg

Konstanz•

BEREICH
**BAYERISCHER
BODENSEE**

Bodensee

miles 0   15   30
km 0   25   50

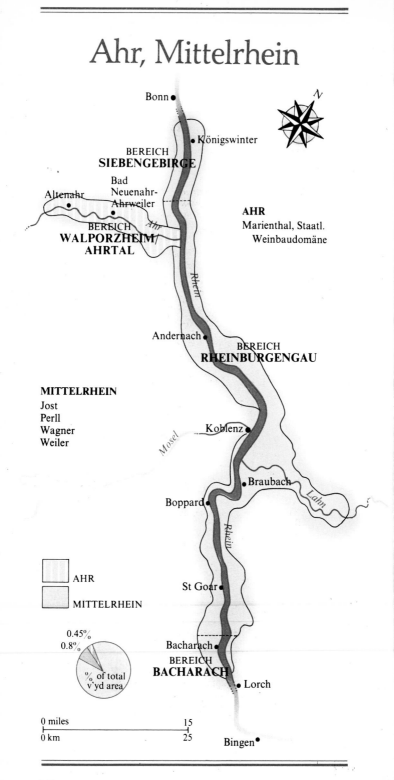

Ahr, Mittelrhein

Bonn

Königswinter

BEREICH
SIEBENGEBIRGE

Bad
Neuenahr-
Ahrweiler

Altenahr

AHR
Marienthal, Staatl.
Weinbaudomäne

BEREICH
**WALPORZHEIM/
AHRTAL**

Ahr

Rhein

Andernach

BEREICH
RHEINBURGENGAU

MITTELRHEIN
Jost
Perll
Wagner
Weiler

Koblenz

Mosel

Braubach

Lahn

Boppard

Rhein

St Goar

AHR

MITTELRHEIN

0.45%
0.8%

Bacharach

% of total
v'yd area

BEREICH
BACHARACH

Lorch

| 0 miles | 15 |
| 0 km | 25 |

Bingen